DATE DUE

DEMCO 38-296

Pleasure Island

University of Nebraska Press

Lincoln and London

Pleasure Island

Tourism and Temptation in Cuba

Rosalie Schwartz

; of America

ie minimum

l Standard for

:e of Paper for

).48-1984.

🌺

Library of Congress Cataloging-in-Publication Data
Schwartz, Rosalie, 1936–
Pleasure Island : tourism and temptation in Cuba /
Rosalie Schwartz.
p.   cm.
Includes bibliographical references and index.
ISBN 0-8032-4257-3 (alk. paper)
1. Tourist trade—Cuba—History.   I. Title.
G155.C9S38   1997
338.4′791729104—dc21   96-40476
CIP

TO LARRY

CONTENTS

ILLUSTRATIONS

Photographs

Maps

The inspirational spark for this book struck a decade ago. To reconstruct the Cuban example of tourism's transformative potential, I mined newspapers, periodicals, travel guides, and archival materials. Cuban archives yielded nuggets but no rich veins of ore. Political upheavals have played havoc with government files. Personal papers of prominent participants were unavailable, destroyed or lost in revolutions, or scattered as a consequence of the post-1960 Cuban diaspora. Interviews with acquaintances who visited Cuba in the 1950s and with Cubans who worked in the tourist industry at that time were extremely helpful for both substantive information and color.

Department of State and Department of Commerce records at the National Archives in Washington DC generally dealt with tangential topics rather than tourism per se. For example, a file labeled "narcotics traffic" contained information about U.S. mobsters who were engaged in casino gambling in Cuba. The Organization of American States' Columbus Memorial Library holds guide books and commemorative publications from Cuba. The travel sections of newspapers proved invaluable. Photographic collections in both the Cuban and U.S. archives suggested topics that needed to be investigated, such as the scene of a deserted Cuban beach that became a center of tourist activity twenty years later. Aspects of popular culture—theater, cabaret, movies, and television—suggested an imagined Cuba to the prospective travelers.

The material thus assembled provoked as well as enlightened. For one thing, both socialist and capitalist governments have found tourism's benefits compelling and the costs unpredictable. For another, many tourist industry workers are women who have adapted homemaker and craft skills or various entertainment talents to the demands of an unfamiliar market. We are just beginning to recognize and evaluate the effect of that employment on their personal and social status and on social and cultural adaptations in general. Tourism also offers a new perspective on international relations and antigovernment resistance movements, including Cuba's political struggle in the 1950s.

ACKNOWLEDGMENTS

While few historians took any interest in tourism as a scholarly pursuit at the time that I began my research, social scientists had been at work on the subject for at least a decade. The anthropologist Valene L. Smith conveyed her own enthusiasm and offered early encouragement. Since that time, a number of individuals and institutions have contributed to the effort. Lynn Stoner extended a helping hand with introductions to Raul Benavides and Luís Hartley-Campbell, Havana residents who guided my first steps into the world of Cuba's tourist industry. Staff members at the Biblioteca Nacional José Martí and the Archivo General de la Nación graciously assisted my dogged search for materials. Tomás Fernández Robaina's continued assistance and support proved essential to my research. A grant from the National Endowment for the Humanities supported a critical year of writing.

Several people afforded me an opportunity to see Cuba through their eyes. They include Alberto Ardura, Luís Barranca, Meg and Herb Copelan, Tony Gálvez, Frank and Tony García, Ina Habif, Julio Luís, Agustín Menéndez, Otto Mérida, Eddie Millán, Merrill Rudman, Valerie Stallings, Ida and Isaac Szuchman, and Percy Steinhart.

My friend and colleague Paul Vanderwood advised, prodded, encouraged, and sharpened my focus through grant proposals and manuscript revisions. His incisive and insightful questions added immeasurably to the finished work.

Always an inspiration, Larry Schwartz shared my fascination with Cuba and tourism. He traveled to Havana with me, and his witticisms and constructive criticism kept this book on target.

Introduction

The Tourist Drama

The concept of drama, or theater piece, suits the study of tourism. In the British playwright Michael Frayn's chaotic comedy *Noises Off*, the curtain opens on the comfortable home of an upper-class British family. A member of the household staff enters. It soon becomes apparent that the scene is a blundering dress rehearsal for a play within a play and that the larger plot turns on the sometimes absurd antics of theater people. In act 1 the audience watches the very ragged rehearsal. Act 2 opens with the first act's set reversed; that is, the view is backstage, and the action encompasses the confused behind-the-scenes problems and personal peccadillos of the cast. Stage entrances familiar from act 1 become exits from the action in act 2. In this second-act reversal, when someone enters, he or she has left the theatrical performance to become a "real" person, that is, the actor or actress who plays a stage character.

Similarly, most contemporary tourist scenes are staged, scripted experiences. A ship docks, or an airplane lands. The "players" make their entrances onto a set filled with local color, native artifacts, ethnic food, "typical" music, preselected aspects of culture and history, beachfront bars, gambling casinos, red-light districts, exotic or historic sites, souvenirs, folkloric entertainments, and other market-researched attractions. (The travel brochure probably reads, "On Sunday we visit the market, where the local natives trade their wares. You have an opportunity to buy their quaint crafts.") At the scheduled time, the players exit the scene and reboard the bus, ship, or plane.

Now, turn the set 180 degrees to expose the people and the activities behind the scene. The staged experiences are packaged by tourist commissions, businesspeople, and marketing experts. The residents, their lives occupied by daily chores, have expectations, ambitions, conflicts, satisfactions, risks, and rewards. They are actors in a larger play, in many cases a more interesting work than the sights and sites prepared for tourists. Reversing the scenery reveals the visionaries, workers, politicians, land speculators, culture packagers, and various manipulators who make the destination attractive. Using Frayn's device to study Cuba, the scripted scene of glamour, romance, and rumba gives way to the more haphazard backstage drama, where the action centers on intrigue, political chicanery, real estate schemes, murder, abduction, mobsters, and rebellion. Few travelers enjoy such dramatic encounters on a packaged tour.

Illusion plays a significant role in tourism; therefore, reading this book may be dangerous to your travel pleasure. Mass tourism in fact pits the illusions of pleasure seekers against reality and fascinates by its very defiance of expectations. "Round the next bend may be Eden, but Eve will have endemic syphilis and live in a tarpaper shack, while Adam will work at a construction project downriver."[1] Irony and the unexpected outcome appropriately suit the peculiarities of a business based on pleasure, where leisure creates work. The contradictions prevail whether the location is Havana or Hanoi, Lagos or Los Angeles, Milan or Manila. Because mass tourism has broadened the market, working-class travelers command the services of other workers, making the industry both democratic and hierarchical. Tourism also encourages the preservation of historic sites and folk culture (some of it imagined), even as it changes them.

This book, then, is less tourism history than tourism *as* history; that is, the idea and the actuality of tourism initiate action, alter behavior, shape attitudes, and influence culture (art, music, religious ritual, food preferences). Although the book focuses on Cuba between 1920 and 1960, I became aware of tourism's power because I live in San Diego, California, a tourist city in a tourist zone that stretches northward beyond the city's celebrated zoo and beautiful beaches through the original Disneyland to Hollywood, eastward to glittering Las Vegas and the natural beauty of Arizona's Grand Canyon, and southward to Mexico. In 1995 billboards in the downtown area proclaimed, "Tourism Is San Diego's Business." The industry also is a major contributor to the state's economy and the third largest business in the United States. In fact, the many millions of tourists who spend billions of dollars around the world have pushed the industry into the top ranks of international trade, alongside petroleum and automobiles.[2]

Tourist transactions take place daily in the largest, most sophisticated metropolitan areas and in small isolated outposts. Voluntary, pleasure-oriented travel across geographic, ethnic, and linguistic boundaries raises many intriguing and important questions. Scholars have identified and examined industrial, consumer, and technological revolutions as historical processes in which people have refocused their behavior, altered concepts of space and time, and reshaped relationships to art, history, culture, the natural and built environments, and other people. If we agree that the ways in which a society accommodates to leisure can be as revealing and significant as the nature of its production and consumption, then the magnitude of the tourist industry signals similarly profound behavioral and attitudinal changes.

Have we reconciled the often-noted tensions between work and leisure, between thrift and indulgence, that have characterized industrial society? Are we revising the criteria for the "good life"? If work conferred dignity on earlier generations and saving money indicated strength of character, what does it mean when people live for holidays and put travel expenses on credit cards? Members of societies that were once suspicious of idleness now pass vacation days relaxing on the beach, evenings indulging in gluttony, and nights satisfying sexual urges, with little social disapproval. Moreover, they probably derive as much status from the success of their vacations as they formerly did from their dedication to labor.

What cultural influences fostered a profligate use of time and money? How did people come to regard touring as a positive, even productive, way to occupy their time? When and how did hedonism (and even prurience) become a rationale for travel, along with—or superseding—education and self-improvement? And how did North Americans make the transition from family-centered sociability to a love of entertainment—that is, from barn raisings, quilting bees, picnics, inviting the minister to Sunday dinner, and celebrating marriages and births—to plays, concerts, circuses, dance halls, amusement parks, and cabarets, and then on to horse racing and jai alai in Havana?

The emergence of mass tourism depended on three elements—motivation, destination, and transportation. In other words, when a sufficient number of people viewed travel favorably, when they had enough time and money to leave home, when they could reach locations considered worth visiting comfortably and conveniently, they did so. For an increasingly mobile and relatively prosperous segment of North Americans, Cuba fulfilled the requirements for desirability and accessibility, most notably after 1920 and before relations between the United States and Cuba soured in 1960. Thus, a North American travel revolution transformed Havana into a tourist mecca. Four decades of Cuban successes and failures afford an opportunity to observe, and enhance our understanding of, this process.

The industry mushroomed in and around the capital city, cultivated by hard-dealing profit seekers who at first lured North Americans to enjoy the exotic charms of a distinctive old Spanish colonial city and, later, to experience the excitement of gambling casinos. Partners in pleasure, businessmen and tourists reshaped the city and its culture in the 1920s only to see the industry collapse upon its foundation amid the economic and political upheavals of the 1930s. First the Great Depression reduced the number of tourists dramatically; then Cuba's revolution of 1933 savaged the island's reputation as a desirable destination. Tourist promoters had barely pushed the industry back on track late in the decade when World War II derailed it once more.

The tourist roller coaster struggled laboriously upward again in the 1950s, pushed to new heights by an aggressive national government and U.S. gambling interests. When an anticrime crusade, spearheaded by the U.S. government, closed Florida's illegal gambling establishments in the early 1950s, the owners and their clients moved offshore. Cubans put out the welcome mat and optimistically counted the coins that jingled in the slot machines, the chips that slid across the gaming tables, and the dollars totted up by hotels, bars, nightclubs, restaurants, and souvenir shops. Havana became a wide-open town, a tropical alternative to glamorous Las Vegas. This is the era most people remember. However, the industry plummeted even more rapidly than it climbed. Triumphant rebels swept into Havana on 1 January 1959, ending extravagant New Year's Eve celebrations and disorienting tourists who had visited the island for the holiday season. The revolution itself attracted a few curious visitors at first and failed to deter the most intrepid revelers until internal upheaval and the increasing tension between Cuba and the United States drove them away. The hotels and casinos languished for lack of business in 1960 and finally succumbed to reality.

In the last decade (and more intensely since the collapse of the Soviet Union), Cuba has revived tourism and made the industry central to its economic viability. More tourists visit Cuba now than in the 1950s, their experience disconnected from the reality of Cuban daily existence. Housed in well-appointed—even luxurious—hotels and fed from well-stocked larders, they are conveyed from place to place in air-conditioned buses, while citizens endure the hardships of an extended economic crisis. The drama plays to a worldwide audience eager to know the fate of Cuba's socialist and tourist experiments.

A NOTABLY IDIOSYNCRATIC INDUSTRY

Tourists travel long distances to save sea turtles, seek sexual partners, shop, hike, bike, study; they hope to be awed by human achievement, moved by breathtaking scenery, titillated by oddities. They often are lured to their destination by imaginative entrepreneurs and marketing professionals. For example, Splendid China, a theme park in Kissimmee, Florida, profits from a miniaturized China (surely an oxymoron). Capitalizing on the ancient nation's centuries of historical treasure, the park has downscaled more than sixty of China's best-known scenic, historic, and cultural sites—including the intriguing Forbidden City, foreboding Imperial Palace, and a half-mile-long replica of the Great Wall.[3]

Equally imaginative civic leaders of Mauch Chunk, Pennsylvania, resurrected their languishing coal-mining town in the Appalachian mountain country. They interred the remains of a well-known Oklahoma Native American football player, erected a suitable memorial, changed the town's name to Jim Thorpe, and turned the modest little community into a tourist destination. Not far away, in a similar mining town where West Virginia's Hatfields and McCoys long ago settled their legendary family feud, a descendent, Robert W. McCoy Jr., hopes to capitalize on the oft-repeated and memorialized saga of nineteenth-century clan battles and lure tourists to the site of vengeance and recrimination. This small, struggling town survived other battles too, and someday Matewan's bloody coal workers' strikes of the 1920s might also find an audience among touring history buffs.[4]

Exploitation of natural and found resources is routine for tourism promoters, but some schemes evoke skepticism, scorn, and even righteous indignation. In an urban ghetto where gang fights add to the weekly death toll, we need to question the judgment and sensitivity of the Bronx Tourism Council members who, hoping to win a share of New York City's multibillion-dollar annual tourist revenue, catered to a taste for the macabre and led thirty-two gawking tour operators on a six-hour excursion through the poverty-ravaged borough to watch drug dealers ply their trade in burned-out houses. The council called it the "Kojak" tour, after television's popular bald-headed policeman. Even more distasteful, if not reprehensible, is "Hitler's Bunker Disco," a theme park located near the Nazis' World War II Eastern Front command post, with uniformed personnel and nightly dancing.[5]

Admittedly, most destinations attract tourists with far less bizarre offerings. Greece has ancient temples, theaters, and marketplaces; Egypt its enduring pyramids. Israel benefits from biblical sites; Rome contains the center of an ancient empire and Vatican City. London has theater and royalty; Paris its cafés and artists. The Caribbean and Mediterranean regions boast favorable climates and inviting beaches and capitalize on their proximity to population centers where residents suffer through seasons of less benign weather. Some tourist destinations develop casually. People "discover" a location, a seaside village not too far from a growing urban metropolis, perhaps. Visitors spend a weekend or two in the village, and local people provide food and shelter. Relaxed visitors enjoy the casual atmosphere and the camaraderie at the local bar. They return home and relate their experiences to friends. More people arrive; someone opens a guest house, or a restaurant, or a cold-drink stand by the beach. A foreigner stumbles across the village, is captivated, and alerts friends. Like a stone cast into a quiet pond, infusions of tourist cash and personal encounters ripple across the village. Urban—or foreign—preferences in dress, music, and food enter the cultural mix. Earnings increase and employment sources diversify. Outmigration of job seekers stops. The amount, nature, and distribution of material goods change. The seaside community remains a village, perhaps, but its economic and social life follow new paths. On the other hand, planned, structured, heavily capitalized resort developments or entertainment attractions can introduce large numbers of strangers to a location in a very short time span. Tourism can define the economy and social outlook of an entire area or be confined to specialized leisure enclaves. Its impact varies according to size and nature.

PLAYERS ON THE TOURIST STAGE

No migratory instinct prompts the human urge to travel. Men and women had searched for food before they settled down and grew crops. Once sedentary, most of them quite contentedly stayed at home. Thus we might define tourists as sedentary people who leave home for pleasure and intend to return.[6] People depart from everyday activities, take a holiday, look forward to it, daydream about it. They are seduced by imagination to secure a change of scenery, to recharge psychological and physical batteries, to display individualism or a sense of adventure, to look for romance, to gain or improve knowledge, to be entertained or amazed, to explore for themselves the places they have read about, to pursue "authentic" experiences that elude them in a mechanized modern world, or to seek the excitement of large cities if small-town life bores them.

About the same time that large numbers of people entered machine-based factories, railroads and steamships became common modes of mass transportation. Organized group travel in Europe first emerged among English workers, rather than in the ranks of the wealthy. Thomas Cook, the altruistic and moralistic secretary of Leicester's Temperance Society, wanted to take workers away from the stresses of an urban industrial society that he felt fed their penchant for vice and violence. After he convinced railroad managers that discounts might induce skeptical potential customers to overcome fears of the smoke-belching iron horses, he hired brass bands and entertainers and transported working-class audiences to healthful surroundings. Cook fed his excursionists, softened them up with cricket games, and put them in a good mood with music before temperance spokespersons harried them about the evils of drink. Combining social idealism with hard-headed business sense, he profited by printing the brochures that advertised the excursions as well as the literature that praised abstention. He also took a cut from the tour arrangements. This profitable foray in the travel business launched a lifetime mission, and "Cook's Tour" entered the lexicon, defined as a journey that touches the major features of a place or area.

Through most of history, travel had been difficult and uncomfortable. Pilgrims of various kinds had sought religious solace or cultural uplift; adventurers had explored uncharted terrain; soldiers had gone to war; merchants had established commercial links; curiosity seekers and natural scientists had ventured into exotic realms. Their travel had not been considered "fun." Cook, on the other hand, eliminated confusion, risk, and discomfort. He recommended destinations, routes, hotels, and restaurants; he promoted seaside holidays and chartered trains for group travel. Targeting the middle classes as customers, he extended his operation to the continent, encouraged women to travel apart from their husbands, made all the arrangements, and looked after them well. For the Paris Exhibition of 1855, Cook moved his clients through the maze of trains and boats and sheltered them in comfortable lodgings. His guidance and care produced the phenomenon of the Victorian lady traveler. The "ladies" remained the mainstay of his business through the end of the century, a significant departure from the time when travel largely attracted men or couples.[7] Most international tourists still opt for prearranged pleasures. They relax, transported in ease, sheltered in comfortable hotels, and fed in a style suited to their tastes. They move about and sample foreign cultures, though often isolated from the people whose countries they visit.

As railroads and steamships connected more people with more places, middle-class North Americans also vacationed, mostly in resort areas close to home—at the seashore, near a lake, or in the mountains. Only about 30,000 or so traveled outside the country in the 1850s, but with changed attitudes and the availability of safe, comfortable, and relatively inexpensive transportation, by 1928 more than 400,000 U.S. citizens went abroad. In 1954 about 1 million adventurous tourists left the United States for places other than Canada or Mexico. In 1985 more than 5 million went to the Caribbean alone, and by 1990 more than 20 million ventured beyond North America.[8] What once had been risky travel had become tourism.

Who spread the word in the United States about foreign travel? For one thing, amateur and professional photographers captured distant, exotic places on film. Some of them tried to earn money for their next

trip with illustrated slide shows held in churches, schools, and people's homes. But the popular and provocative Mark Twain had a much wider audience. The skilled storyteller published the exploits of his 1867 trip as *Innocents Abroad, or The New Pilgrim's Progress*.[9] Newspapers all over the country had hawked this trip as a "gigantic picnic" for 150 select cabin passengers aboard a first-class steamer bound for France, Italy, Greece, Turkey, Palestine, Egypt, and Malta. Many of those same newspapers rewarded their readers with Twain's accounts, recorded while aboard ship and on land: anecdotes, adventurous tales, observations, opinions, illustrations, descriptions, droll humor, analysis, and a little history thrown in. His adventures on the "great Pleasure Excursion to Europe and the Holy Land" filled more than two hundred long letters, published individually while Twain was en route and collectively in the book. Those tales probably whetted appetites for similar experiences, and as the work ethic gradually succumbed to a play ethic, tourism filled new needs and desires.

New dress styles reflected the revised attitudes toward life and leisure that eventually laid the groundwork for a twentieth-century mass-market tourist industry. Fashionable women began to exchange corsets and floor-sweeping dresses for less restrictive apparel after the turn of the century. Men abandoned their stiff collars and boiled shirtfronts. Society, by redirecting the pursuit of happiness from an emphasis on production to the exaltation of the consumer and sanctification of the shopper, opened itself to pleasure travel. Self-denial, plainness, and thrift may have represented ideal values for a struggling young society, before the ability to consume became emblematic of the nation's promise to its citizens. Even the humblest workers might save a little something from their meager salaries for an indulgent purchase or two.[10]

A shopping "culture" had invested consumerism with emotional satisfactions even before John Wanamaker purchased the huge Pennsylvania Railroad depot (constructed to handle thousands of visitors who arrived in Philadelphia to attend the 1876 American centennial celebration), gutted the spacious interior, and stunned the public with his "department" store. He creatively arranged a great variety of merchandise in showcases, and shoppers walked through aisles formed by rows of glass-enclosed temptations. He enticed strollers with goods attractively displayed in street-level windows and advertised his wares in newspapers and magazines. At Wanamaker's, shopping became a leisured activity to be shared with friends, not a housewife's chore. Purchases became rewards for work and confirmation of social status. Shoppers meandered down the aisles and gazed longingly at the infinite choices, enthralled with their potential transformation into style setters—not unlike browsers who spin dreams as they leaf through travel magazines.[11]

Scarcity may have fashioned an American character for the eighteenth and nineteenth centuries, but abundance gave birth to self-congratulatory materialists with a taste for luxury, figures more suitable to the twentieth century. Today's tourists impress peers with their ability to spend money frivolously. They go where all their friends have gone or where none have ventured. They engage in behaviors abroad that are criticized or forbidden at home. In a quest that would have horrified Thomas Cook, they also pursue vice. Pesky drunks on a week's vacation fall besotted on the streets of resort villages. Planes fly to various cities in Asia and Africa with full loads of passengers responding to advertisements that promise "guiltless" sex in some faraway venue. Both men and women search for same-sex, opposite-sex, and cross-racial partners, protected by the anonymity of the tourist milieu. And wherever they go, tourists are met by workers. Unlike industrial labor, however, tourism workers rarely enter buildings to attend to machines. Instead, they may be singers, gardeners, taxi drivers, toilet cleaners, translators, fire eaters, hotel clerks, guides, or crafts makers. Together, traveler and worker act out the tourist drama.

PARTNERS IN PLEASURE: MARKET AND MERCHANT

Long before Cuba became a playground geared to fun seekers from the United States, the island had satisfied its neighbors' appetites for other pleasures, selling sugar and tobacco to ensure its own prosperity. Cuban sugar had filled an unrelenting craving for candy and sweetened beverages, and some of the world's most aromatic tobacco smoke spiraled upward from the end of a fine Havana cigar. Like candy or sweetened coffee and tea (or even Coca-Cola), cigars became one of numerous social rituals, offerings shared in friendship. More than mere tobacco leaves twisted into a column, they signified happiness at the birth of a baby, the successful close of a business deal, or a general sense of well-being. Premium Cuban cigars symbolized good taste

for men of fashion and stature, as well as for ambitious strivers who staked their reputations and advancement on appearances. Paper rings from cigars were given to children; cigar boxes held such mementos of youthful explorations as sea shells, rocks or bottle caps.

Even before Cuba achieved its independence from Spain in 1898, a trickle of U.S. visitors had enjoyed the tropical island's warm winters and its foreign atmosphere, their interest perhaps stirred by adventure-laden tales of Christopher Columbus and Caribbean pirates. As both Cubans and North Americans began to see the revenue potential of tourism, writers of travel guides filled their pages with superlatives. Cuba became a smiling, luxuriant tropical land where romance, beautiful women, soft music-filled nights, and the enchantments of Spanish culture awaited visitors.[12]

The tourist industry sold pleasure—by definition, enjoyment, satisfaction, gratification, or delight. If one person relished a period of indolent pampering, another thrilled to the excitement of the racetrack or fell exhausted into bed after a night of rumba. Each experience could be enjoyed in Cuba, for a price, and pleasure became the island's business.

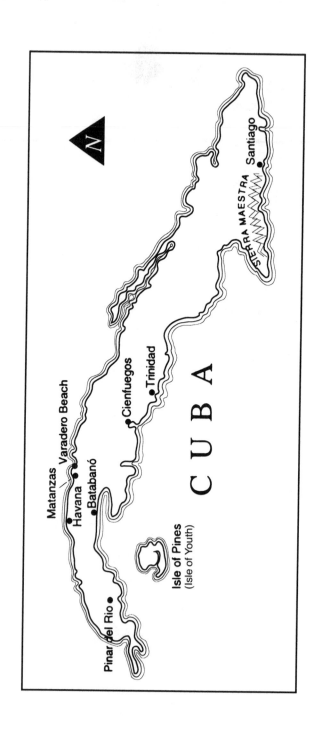

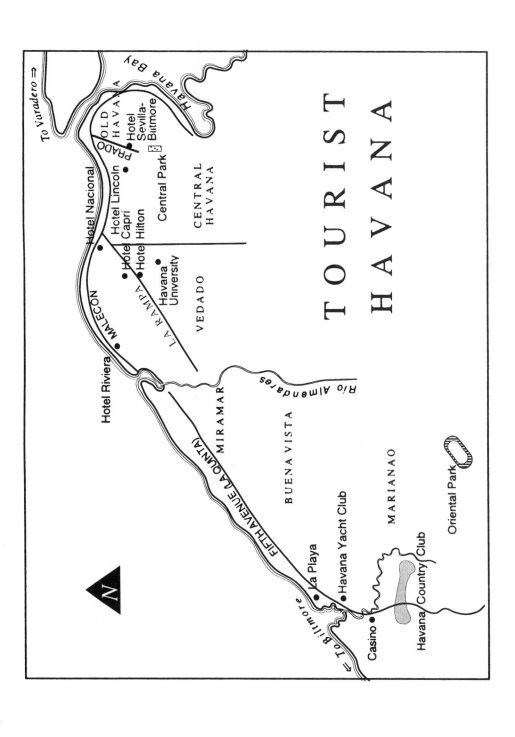

TOURIST HAVANA

N

To Varadero ⇒

Havana Bay

OLD HAVANA

PRADO

Hotel Sevilla-Biltmore

Central Park

Hotel Nacional

Hotel Lincoln

Hotel Capri

Hotel Hilton

CENTRAL HAVANA

MALECON

LA RAMPA

Havana University

VEDADO

Hotel Riviera

Rio Almendares

MIRAMAR

BUENA VISTA

FIFTH AVENUE (LA QUINTA)

To Biltmore ⇒

La Playa

Havana Yacht Club

MARIANAO

Casino

Havana Country Club

Oriental Park

Chapter 1

Act 1

The Road to Cuba

Ideal weather graced Oriental Park's 1925 grand opening day. Havana's suburban racetrack occupied the north side of a natural slope that offered an impressive panorama of surrounding villas, sugarcane fields, and distant hills. The breeze from the Gulf of Mexico teased the bending green palms that fringed the track and highlighted them against the blue sky, while it cooled the sun-washed fans who lined the rail to watch the horses cross the finish line. Some five thousand cheering Cubans and tourists filled the newly renovated grandstand seats or crowded the standing room on that balmy December Saturday afternoon. Exhilarated bettors turned the wagering area into a beehive, buzzing with hot tips and hunches as money changed hands.

Only club members and their guests gained access to the luxurious Jockey Club, located in its own building to the west of the grandstand, with salons for dining and dancing between races and banquet halls for after-hours events. Casual elegance marked the stylish foreign tourists and members of Havana's exclusive social circles who greeted, chatted, and sometimes flirted there. In groups of three and four they surrounded small tables placed on the multitiered terrace that overlooked the track, or they stood on the covered verandas that faced the road leading to the park and waved as their friends arrived.

The track's North American operators had taken particular pains to ensure a spectacular introduction to the Jockey Club's new management. Bright-colored flowers decorated the clubhouse and the verandas, complementing the purple bougainvillea and lush green tropical plants that adorned the colonnaded entrance below, where multicolored glazed tiles recreated patterns originally designed by ancient Egyptians. The stunning setting suited Havana's socially prominent race fans and horse owners, as well as their North American counterparts.

Affluent equestrian aficionados vocally encouraged the horses they owned or favored, and messengers placed their bets while they remained seated in one of the 130 private boxes. Friends, relatives, acquaintances, and business associates met and mingled familiarly in cross-generational, multinational sets. They chatted, ate, drank, cheered, and bet. In the opulent surroundings, unescorted women apparently moved comfortably among their peers, both male and female — not the traditional practice in Cuban upper-class families.

Whatever their social station and wherever they sat or stood, opening-day fans admired the refurbished racing facility. Many of the devotees caught a glimpse of Cuba's recently elected leader: Gerardo Machado occupied the flag-draped presidential box specially installed for the chief executive by Jockey Club officials. Distinguishable even at a distance by his blue business suit against the uniforms of his military escort, Machado stood at attention for Cuba's national anthem and then relaxed while the band played *danzones* and other familiar music before the first race. A horse breeder himself, Machado relished the excitement of the race and the sociability of horsemen, business colleagues, and government officials. Cubans had voted for him the previous year in anticipation of economic and political achievements outlined in his campaign speeches. Clearly, Oriental Park offered more than amusement during its hundred-day meet; it was a place to cement personal friendships and business partnerships, a place to be seen.[1]

The lighthearted, expectant mood of the crowd reflected a tangible optimism, infectious in tourist circles, as Cuba kicked off the 1925–26 winter season. More than thirty thousand tourists had visited Cuba the previous year. As the profitability of the trade permeated the conscious-

ness of Cuba's business community, entrepreneurial *habaneros* put their support behind government and private-sector efforts to draw visitors to the city. Those conversations at the race track were not simply chitchat; Cubans had a critical need to diversify Cuba's faltering, sugar-dependent economy. With Machado's backing, tourist commission officials expected to keep Havana's hotel rooms filled at least until April, when the island turned hot and the United States thawed out.

Three hundred members of the Bankers Investment Association of America attended the races on Sunday as the guests of the new management. Financiers from all over the United States were visiting Havana after their annual meeting in Saint Petersburg, Florida. They had spent Saturday night at the *frontón* learning the intricacies of jai alai, the fast-paced handball game of Basque origin. On Sunday they bet the horses, enjoyed a buffet lunch at the Jockey Club, and met various well-established Cubans—perhaps introduced by U.S. Ambassador Enoch Crowder. The bankers should have been in a good mood, with no legalistic officials to confiscate their alcoholic beverages. In contrast to Prohibition-dry Florida, Cuban rum flowed freely.[2]

SETTING THE TOURIST STAGE

As crowds of visitors flocked to Cuba and enjoyed Havana's hospitality, the more elite among them compared the island favorably to the likes of France's Deauville or Riviera resorts. "Since the tourist trade has become one of Havana's chief assets," the travel writer Frank Carpenter wrote in 1925, "the winter season finds the old Spanish cathedrals and forts of the city thronged with sight-seers from the United States." Carpenter's *Lands of the Caribbean* no doubt furrowed the brows of uneasy French resort operators. The noticeable decline of American guests on the Côte d'Azur prompted them to fight back with new attractions, such as an automobile race for international debutantes who would speed competitively along the hazardous curving roads of the Mediterranean shoreline.[3]

At least twenty steamships a week traveled between U.S. ports and Havana's commodious harbor. Encouraged by a Cuban government subsidy, Clyde Steamship Line established Miami–Havana service. The Aeromarine Airway's competing seaplane service hopped between those two cities with eleven passengers in each of its twin-motor "flying boats." A profusion of U.S. automobiles, transported by ferry from Key West in a matter of hours, crowded Havana's narrow streets. Eager for business, Havana Hotel Association representatives advertised in U.S. newspapers, opened information offices, and sent personal representatives to Florida's resort cities to promote the delights of Cuba.[4]

Cuba's Consolidated Railways inaugurated auto service between Havana and the fascinating southern seaport of Batabanó, where picturesque fishermen with long-handled hooks left the harbor everyday in small boats to harvest sponges from the bottom of the sea. A new Havana-Santiago train carried first-class passengers in comfortable cars equipped with dining car, baths, a barbershop, and observation platforms from which to view emerald green sugarcane, coffee plantations, and the thatched-roof *bohios* (huts) of farm families.[5]

By 1925 Cubans touted tourism as a potential second crop—an exaggerated comparison with sugar, of course, but hope and enthusiasm outpaced reality. Havana's newspapers encouraged public expenditures on transportation facilities, urged more attractions to lure visitors, prodded the government to clean the streets and ensure that tourists with full purses regarded Havana as a comfortable, healthy, exciting city.

Without a market, there could have been no tourist boom. Cuba succeeded in the 1920s because Cubans took advantage of a North American state of mind that had been developing for some time. In the late 1920s up to eighty thousand tourists visited Cuba each year. Workers as well as socialites left routine cares behind in search of an earthly paradise. Although most of them could not have articulated the push toward Cuba, a long series of events and social changes propelled them in the direction of pleasure seeking: new forms of recreation and entertainment, for example, as well as a downward flow of upper-class consumption patterns, an upward flow of lower-class entertainment activities, a southward shift of resort hotels in the direction of warm weather, and wartime disruption of familiar travel patterns.[6]

Elite Pastimes and Sunny Climes

The upper classes in the United States spent their money on extravagantly decorated mansions at the turn of the century. They impressed each other with stylish clothing, elaborately prepared and properly served meals, imaginatively contrived balls, and innovative entertainments. They traveled luxuriously and pursued their recreational activities at exclusive resorts. Some one thousand millionaires composed the wealth-based elite in 1875; their numbers increased to fifteen thousand in 1927, an extraordinary year for Cuban tourism.

Long before Havana moved the center of its social world to the Oriental Park racing oval, distinguished horse breeders on the east coast of the United States displayed and traded their animals and socialized at the track. Horse owners had arranged their first race and trade meeting at Saratoga, New York, for example, during the Civil War when the more familiar southern tracks became unavailable. Over the years, Saratoga had gained a reputation as a retreat for the affluent.

Horse breeding gained competition as a pastime of the wealthy with the introduction of tennis and golf. Newport Casino, Rhode Island, playland of the privileged, inaugurated its tennis court in the 1880s and hosted the first national championships in 1881. The game had originated in royal circles—played at "court"—and was popular among elites all over Europe. An American who played the game while visiting the British colony of Bermuda introduced it to friends at her Staten Island, New York, club. Before long eager players swung their stringed rackets on grass courts at all the better clubs and mansions.

Even though golf had begun as a game for rural lower and working classes on the sheep pastures of Scotland, in 1888 the Saint Andrews Club of Yonkers, New York, opened to a wealthy clientele. Avid golfers had established seventy-five exclusive clubs in the United States by 1895, and the appeal increased when Presidents Theodore Roosevelt and William Howard Taft took to the fairways and greens. Restricted country clubs barred the middle and lower classes from membership, of course, as did the yacht clubs along the shore. Nevertheless, the estimated one million golfers of 1905 grew to some three million a decade later. A procession of holiday resorts where golfers could play in the winter season marched southward down the eastern seaboard, eventually crossing the Florida keys and reaching Havana. The Havana Country Club offered memberships to wealthy North Americans in the 1920s and lured hundreds of addicted golfers with warm sunshine when snow blanketed northern links.[7]

Henry Morrison Flagler's railroad along Florida's eastern coast reached Key West in 1912. Flagler had constructed luxury hotels at stops along the way where his rich, hard-working friends could relax when Newport was cold. He named his first hotel after the legendary Spanish seeker of youth, Ponce de León. Sunshine, revitalization, youth—the images blended together beautifully. Pampered guests loved the heated swimming pools, casinos, polo grounds, golf course, and tennis courts. For those not too exhausted from the rigors of the day's activities, the hotel's orchestras played music into the late evening hours.

While Flagler built resorts, Cuba suffered through its bloody 1895–98 independence struggle. Havana was hardly a desirable vacation destination at the time. Neither was Miami before two shrewd Fort Dallas businesswomen, Julia Tuttle and Mary Brickell, offered to trade Flagler half of their land holdings near the Miami River if he would extend the railroad to their still-slumbering city. Surveys were underway by June of 1895, and the first train rolled into Fort Dallas (later renamed Miami) in 1896. Five years after Cuba's war ended, a confident, aggressive Munson Steamship Company boasted that Havana, not the Florida coast, would soon be the mecca of winter tourists.[8] Munson's enthusiasm proved somewhat premature. For most tourists, Cuba's appeal was still two decades, significant cultural changes, and one war away.

Entertainment and Leisure

At the turn of the century the United States stood on a cultural battlefield between the rifles of propriety and the cannons of revelry, grappling with the relationship between affluence, morality, and a changing social order. Guardians of respectability and morals, often religious leaders who doggedly protected standards of gentility, approved of the symphony, the classical theater, ballet, art and music lessons, lectures, and museums. Those activities imposed discipline and restraint. By contrast, they labeled as vulgar the popular leisure-time pursuits of the urban masses: saloons, dance halls, skating rinks, vaudeville, sports, movies, and burlesque. By the 1920s most North Americans wanted to be entertained. The urge to let loose and to have fun challenged a cultural inheritance that had frowned on mis-spent time and on amusements that served no socially useful ends. Consumer culture already had identified happiness with material ac-quisition, but a pleasure principle urged gratification of less tangible longings. Hedonism condoned the pursuit of some behaviors that ran contrary to traditional ideals of appropriate conduct.[9]

Indeed, entertainment in the United States had a colorful—and sometimes aggressively unrefined—history. Variety and minstrel shows, traveling circuses, mobile menageries, music and dance halls came to life or expanded in the second half of the nineteenth cen-tury. Theatrical reviews lampooned Shakespeare and grand opera, while half-naked actors treated audiences to burlesques of biblical scenes. Popular theaters gained a foothold, despite critics who labeled them devil's workshops. The quintessential entertainer and promoter Phineas T. Barnum sold an exotic slice of the world to his audiences. They bought their tickets to see trained fleas, rope dancers, ven-triloquists, giants, dwarfs, and Fiji mermaids. The Ringling Brothers brought music, dance, and skits to opera houses and concert halls in the midwest before they inaugurated their tented shows in 1884. Ringling Brothers Circus featured tightrope walking and trained ani-mals in the big top, as well as unusually strong, fat, short, or tall people, "wild men" from far-off Borneo, snake charmers, and albinos in the sideshows.[10]

Barnum and Ringling entertained the masses. So did the Coney Island amusement parks. The era of popular playlands that began in 1895 reached its heyday by World War I. Steeplechase Park, named for its elaborate mechanical racetrack, opened in 1897 at the Brook-lyn, New York, shore. Spectacular Luna Park transformed the bathing beach into a fantasyland of bright lights and action. Electric trol-leys transported a swelling population of city dwellers on excursions to beaches and parks with band pavilions, where they danced and rode the thrilling Ferris wheel.[11] Places such as Coney Island brought people together and blurred distinctions that had characterized a choice between symphony halls and saloons. Factory workers and pro-fessionals alike lined up to board the rides and buy ice cream.

The battle between cultural uplift and popular amusements accel-erated with the explosive growth of variety theaters, cabarets, vaude-ville, burlesque, and movies. Burlesque had sacrificed social satire for wriggling ladies and had captured an audience of lone males in big cities. Churches countered the appeal of commercial entertainment with socials, literary societies, and concerts, but big-city nightlife hardly suffered. People gladly paid for an evening's amusement. Empresarios fed the growing demand for excitement and entertainment, copying P. T. Barnum's showmanship and salesmanship. Vaudeville's singers, dancers, acrobats, and magicians performed in palatial theaters, not in tents or barns with backless benches. Geared to workers' dreams of success, vaudeville offered visions of luxury instead of a glorification of hard work.[12]

New Yorkers took their first steps toward the "scandalous" cabaret when Tony Pastor moved variety theater uptown to Fourteenth Street. Even "respectable" patrons paid good money to watch Pastor's chorus girls. One socially prominent family invited Manhattan showgirls to its country estate to teach the cakewalk to guests, defying critics who condemned the popular dance as "a milder edition of African orgies."[13]

Members of the elite who regularly visited Europe had had their first taste of cabaret in the Paris of the Gay Nineties. Wealthy North Americans followed in the footsteps of Europeans who traditionally gathered at the appropriate seasonal resorts as part of the social conventions to which they subscribed. They similarly paraded their wealth in London, Paris, the Riviera, and the spas of the continent. Families from the United States established themselves at Claridge's or the Savoy in London, the Maurice or the Ritz in Paris, the Carlton in Cannes, or the Riviera Palace in Monte Carlo and courted the aristocrats among whom they sat at the opera, the ballet, or the gaming tables. They bathed in and drank curative mineral waters at the spas surrounding some of Europe's natural springs. Germany's "badens" added gambling to physical therapy, and in seaside resorts such as England's Brighton and France's Trouville, "taking the waters" conferred an old-fashioned approval of health cures on what had become primarily social encounters.

When the railroads made northern Europe's elite destinations accessible to tradespersons, the upper classes headed south, and resort areas bordering the Mediterranean Sea flourished. Cannes and Nice boasted old money and even royalty among their clientele. The patronage of England's Queen Victoria in the 1890s confirmed the area's stature. When the queen's retainers—turbaned Hindus, kilted Scots, and beautiful ladies-in-waiting—descended from the royal train at

Nice, followed by the monarch herself, newspapers covering the arrival communicated to a broad audience the excitement and glamour that wrapped all wealthy tourists in the cloak of royalty. Queen Victoria's son, Edward VII, embellished the Riviera's cachet when he accidentally ignited his liquor-soaked thin pancakes one evening and named his invented dessert in honor of Suzette, his dinner companion. An occasional visit by a well-attended Russian czar or the Aga Khan contributed to the mystique of Europe's posh resort, and status-conscious North Americans mingled with royalty hoping to snare a titled gentleman or lady as a spouse.

If Cannes and Nice basked in the prestige of foreign royalty, neighboring Monaco boasted its own princes. Less elitist than other resorts perhaps, Monaco welcomed new and old money, earned through trade and industry as well as inherited. Status in its gambling casino reflected a more practical standard, that is, the ability to wager and, more importantly, to pay one's gambling debts.[14] North Americans fit right in.

Charles Garnier, renowned architect of the Paris Opera House, had redesigned Monaco's gaming room with spectacular results, and the opulent Casino Royal at Monte Carlo had opened in 1868 amid colorful flowers and lush greenery. The prince also improved access roads and persuaded the railroad company that served Cannes and Nice to extend the line to Monaco. Monte Carlo became synonymous with fashionable gambling, and Monaco's ruler became the first European leader to direct tourist revenue to the national treasury, rescuing the principality from the brink of bankruptcy. Shared profits ultimately relieved his grateful subjects of all tax burdens. From May to September, when the summer heat engulfed Monte Carlo, Deauville, on the Normandy coast, entertained the gambling set. Wrapped in luxury, awash in champagne and diamonds, Deauville earned the sobriquets City of Spectacular Sin and Lotusland of the Lavish.[15]

Parisian low life, rather than casino glitter, marked France's cabarets, where visiting Americans shared "bohemian" thrills with artists and outcasts, as well as their European peers. The famous Maxim's opened in the 1890s and helped to build the city's reputation as a place to indulge human frailties. In the popular apache dance (named after bands of lawless persons who roamed the Paris streets at night), male dancers literally flung their female partners around the cabaret's dance floor. The rather sinister athletic performance fascinated audiences in New York as it did at Maxim's and later captivated breathless tourists in Havana.

Cabaret crossed the Atlantic to New York, and while the more conservative crowd continued to fill popular hotel ballrooms and roof gardens, dancing to music that was "sweet," a craze for something "hotter" swept the nation. New dances carried names suggestive of barnyard or less domesticated animals. People gyrated in fanciful or suggestive body movements to the turkey trot, bunny hug, monkey hug, fox-trot, and lame duck. The sensuous Argentine tango, in which partners clung together as though glued, vied for popularity. Originally a dance of working-class Buenos Aires, the tango had crossed the Atlantic with merchant seamen who sailed the waters between that Argentine port and Marseilles and had become an exotic fad in Paris. When cabaret owners also yanked ragtime from the whorehouse and included its syncopated rhythms in their repertoire, they sent reformers screaming for government restrictions against public dancing.

Despite the outcries, dancers from all social levels responded to the new music, encouraged perhaps by mental health gurus who urged them to let go and reveal their inner selves. Men and women met and socialized informally at the cabaret, a dreaded circumstance for upper-class parents who preferred private gatherings where invitees were acceptable marriage partners for their children. As cabarets moved from more unsavory neighborhoods to accessible locations, high-society families lamented the permeable boundaries between the sexes. Afternoon dances called tango teas proved even more threatening to conventional female behavior. Single (and sometimes even married) women only pretended to go shopping with friends, or they combined trips to department stores with visits to cafés where they danced with partners hired by the management. Daring young women looked for excitement among overtly sensual and obviously ethnic gigolos, men whom their parents (or husbands) scorned. In other words, rich young women had a good time while young, generally poor, male immigrants earned a living.

Thus the cabaret and the café further undermined notions of gentility and self-control. In these wicked and exotic dens of iniquity, men and women met in anonymous, uncontrolled environments. Among embracing dancers, sexual attractiveness figured in partner selection. To the critics, youthful self-expression, sexuality, and frivolity produced moral degenerates who sidestepped propriety and class barriers in pursuit of excitement and glamour.[16]

Prohibition, not prudity, pulled the profits from the cabarets and sent some owners into bankruptcy. Fun-loving flappers wore short skirts and bobbed their hair; they flattened feminine curves into boyishness, drank whiskey, smoked cigarettes, danced the latest dances, and shocked their parents and the community. Their ideal male partners preferred the type of woman who flaunted convention, a girl who might travel with friends in search of pleasure. By the 1920s Cunard Lines reported that 60–65 percent of its passengers were women and girls traveling alone or in groups.[17] Mountains of magazine and newspaper complaints, Sunday sermons, and protests to public officials only fueled defiance. Scandalizing one's parents and pastors became the thing to do.

MOVIE FANTASIES AND CUBA: REEL TO REAL

While the sentinels of propriety fretted over the social implications of cabarets and tea dances and begged government authorities to protect the public morality, a more insidious influence lurked behind the drawn curtains of urban storefronts. Thomas Alva Edison's kinetoscope, invented in 1889, made people in photos appear to move. Two decades later, motion pictures outdistanced vaudeville and cabaret as a favorite form of commercial entertainment. The middle classes disdained this new form of amusement, too, but the fascination with stories recorded on film spread through the immigrant working classes like an epidemic. Prescient businessmen rented empty stores and put screens on the walls, chairs on the floors, and announcements in the windows. Convenient and cheap, the nickelodeon—a theater that only cost a nickel to enter—was within the means of most workers and well worth the opportunity to retreat from factories and crowded apartments. By 1909 New York City alone counted some 350 moviehouses. About a quarter million of the city's men and women watched films most days—twice that number on Sundays.

In time, even the disapproving middle classes succumbed to the power of moving images in dark theaters. Industry executives moved their films from spartan storefronts to padded and gilded "picture palaces," where uniformed doormen opened the portals and courteous ushers escorted patrons through ornate lobbies and down carpeted aisles to their plush seats. They also added stories involving the country club set to standard working-class melodramas. Clashes between passion and respectable restraint filled the screens, facsimiles of conflicts that raged over the dangers of the cabaret. Heros and heroines challenged their families' authority and defied social conventions.[18]

From the very first showings, movies enveloped mass audiences in make-believe. Dark rooms and bright screens swept people into fantasy worlds and transported them to foreign locations more swiftly, surely, and completely than the fastest trains or ships. Most of us have left a movie theater at one time or another barely able to speak, responding to the emotional impact of screen drama, exhilarated by powerful messages of personal triumph, or deeply touched and haunted by the character of a fictional personality. Exotic locales invite us to be someone else, somewhere else.

Early movies suggested possibilities of sexual freedom and built up a Latin mystique. Powerful stirrings filled the audience when Rudolph Valentino swaggered across the screens and through make-believe worlds where sex, romance, marriage, and money intertwined. Even if you dared not dance the tango with a swarthy gigolo at a tea dance, you could look into Valentino's smoldering eyes in a dark theater. The dark hero epitomized eroticism, and his earliest films cast him as a passionate Latin lover. In *The Four Horsemen of the Apocalypse* Valentino plays the heir to one of Argentina's wealthiest and most powerful landowners, a lovable scoundrel. The Argentine playboy, a bohemian artist in Paris, dances the tango in tight trousers and lavishes his money on the unhappy wife of a work-obsessed man. The lovers barely consummate their steamy affair before the playboy goes off to war and a heroic death.

Horseman was released in August 1922 and became the highest-grossing film of the 1920s. In November Valentino portrayed a passionate Spaniard, Juan Gallardo, in *Blood and Sand*. A bullfighter who casts aside his young bride for the attentions of an alluring and sophisticated woman of wealth, Gallardo loses his life because of the voluptuous temptress. But, then, didn't Latins risk everything for love? Valentino returned once more to South America in *The Sainted Devil*, a story filled with bandits and romance.[19]

While Victorian ladies had traveled around Europe to appreciate art and history, to nourish the part of oneself believed superior to mere animal instinct, an earthier twentieth-century female tourist might pursue her Valentino, like the defiant "vamps" who slithered across the silent screen. Theda Bara played seductresses in more than forty films between 1915 and 1919, while Marlene Dietrich personified the sexual danger of the cabaret. Pola Negri played a countess in *A Woman of the World*, at ease with her sexuality, visually contrasted with less sophisticated, inhibited midwesterners—relatives who had departed sensuous Europe for hidebound America.

Vamps acquired a Latin mystique when Hollywood turned the sensational Greta Garbo from Nordic beauty to Spanish femme fatale in her first two films. Banished to Paris after her beloved's haughty mother forbids their cross-class romance, Garbo's beautiful Spanish heroine in *The Torrent* gains fame and an independent life. Reviewers called Garbo's performance fiery, animated, and abandoned. In *The Temptress* she again turns adversity into sensational seduction. After her impoverished, titled husband (a marquis) gives her to a banker so that he can have money to live in luxury, she meets an Argentine engineer at a masked ball. Lured by lust and unencumbered by guilt, she follows the engineer to Argentina.

For moviegoers not yet ready to abandon spouses for exotic lovers, the Hollywood director Cecil B. DeMille prescribed pleasure to cure a dull marriage; he dressed up desire as domestic revitalization. If bored spouses danced all night in cabarets, listened to "primitive" music, and sometimes gave in to temptations, their mates needed to rekindle romance to save the marriage from the designs of flappers, gold diggers, and gigolos. In the work of the premier film interpreter of 1920s fads and foibles, wives could be as erotic as movie vamps. They could seduce their business-addicted husbands with revealing dresses and the latest hairstyles, while a husband willing to dance the fox-trot might save his marriage from a rival. Sex appeal signaled a willingness to take risks, to loosen social constraints, and to pluck a new personality from under the apron or the pinstriped suit.[20]

Hollywood had more than stories to sell; it peddled a lifestyle, and a lavish one. Film stars spent money as exorbitantly in their real lives as in their fictional ones, and audiences hung on every extravagance. Movie ads of the 1920s featured jazz babies, petting parties, midnight revels, champagne baths. An aura of sybaritic, impulsive self-indulgence radiated outward from the screen and engulfed audiences already primed to contemplate their inhibitions and the effects of sex starvation. Simplified versions of Sigmund Freud's complex theories had begun to proliferate in the mass media. Books and articles distorted the serious work of professional clinicians, repeating such terms as libido, sexual repression, and subconscious over and over, while advertisements offered to interpret dreams, solve sexual problems, and psychoanalyze people by mail. The power of the unconscious became a rationale for succumbing to temptation.

References to the romantic shadows cast by Havana's palm trees on secluded beaches and the abandon of the tropics played to dream lives stimulated by the cabaret and movies, images absorbed by tens of thousands of imaginative potential travelers. Cubans filled tourist ads with invitations to consumers of filmed fantasy to realize their dreams of romance and adventure on an island of pleasure. A trip to Cuba, a little rum and rumba, were movies-come-true for throngs of bankers, lawyers, industrialists, teachers, sales clerks, and housewives who boarded steamships bound for Havana.

DISASTER AND WAR

Hot, crowded, odorous holds of steamships had carried millions of European emigrants to the United States, the promised land of jobs and farms. Thousands of beneficiaries of their hard work crossed the ocean in the opposite direction, traveling in elegant style on ships of the transoceanic luxury fleet to visit Europe's historic cities, sumptuous spas, and seaside resorts. Furnished to replicate the finest hotels and provisioned with exquisite cuisine and the best wines, the ships competed vigorously in the effort to convert service and comfort into substantial profits.

Munson, Ward, Cunard, and White Star offered every extravagance, but the White Star Line's ss *Titanic* promised its passengers a unique advantage—the ship could not sink. Wealthy voyagers eagerly booked passage on the *Titanic*'s maiden voyage. More than two thousand passengers looked forward to their journey as they mounted the gangplank, headed for New York after European jaunts. Some of them were heirs to Gilded Age fortunes. As the massive ship departed Southampton, England, the suction created as it left the pier pulled its sister ship, the ss *New York*, away from the dock. The powerful force broke the *New York*'s mooring ropes and set it adrift in the direction of the *Titanic*. People along the shore and aboard ship gasped and held their breath while the *Titanic's* captain jammed the ship's engines into reverse. An audible, collective exhale signaled a disastrous collision barely avoided. But the *Titanic* hit an iceberg in the North Atlantic and carried fifteen hundred people to their deaths in dark and frigid waters.

The disaster did not end luxury travel to Europe, of course, but some cautious people may have had second thoughts about transoceanic travel in wintertime and found relatively short, relaxing voyages to warm climates preferable. Moreover, unrestricted submarine warfare undertaken by Germany against Allied ships discouraged most trans-Atlantic leisure travelers. The war itself put many European tourist destinations temporarily out of bounds, and by the 1920s North Americans left their homes not for Europe but to dip into exotic tropical waters, lured by temptation.

Cuba carved its tourist niche according to the appeals that Cuban entrepreneurs, foreign investors, and its tourist commission thought the U.S. market would buy. Few travel magazine writers and brochure scribes of the 1920s failed to link Cuba to entertainment, excitement, recreation, romance, and indulgence. Vaudeville and amusement parks, cabarets, and movie theaters had laid the groundwork for the Cuba portrayed by tourist promoters. The island possessed the potential to compete favorably with Europe for the luxury tourist trade, with California for adventurers, with Florida for golfers and boaters, with Saratoga for horsemen, and with New York for entertainment. Lush tropical foliage, climate, and location were fortunate accidents of nature, but human inventiveness, imagination, and perseverance turned Havana into a naughty Paris of the Western Hemisphere and a luxurious Riviera of the Americas for tourists. Businessmen baited the hook for a consumerist, hedonistic market, and tourists leaped at the temptation. As partners, they created a successful tourist industry.

Chapter 2

Public Works, Politics, Property
The Action behind the Scrim

A stylishly attired crowd of dignitaries clustered in eager anticipation before the carved mahogany doors of the Church of the Sacred Heart of Jesus on Havana's Reina Street. President Machado, no doubt, was the most prominent. Members of the city's distinguished families married in this house of worship, the city's newest and arguably its most elaborate. Many of them had contributed money for its construction. In spectacle and refinement, few weddings at the church had surpassed the December 1926 festivities marking the marriage of Public Works Secretary Carlos Miguel de Céspedes to Margarita Johanet. A serious-looking, round-faced gentleman—made more serious and round faced by circular, dark-rimmed spectacles, Céspedes was the Cuban official most responsible for the country's flourishing tourist industry.[1] With one hand on tourism and the other on public works, he brought jobs and profits to thousands of Cubans.

Carlos Miguel carried the family name of the patriot Carlos Manuel de Céspedes, whose call for "Cuba Libre" in 1868 began the prolonged struggle for independence that cost him his life. The younger Céspedes also had engaged in political struggles, as a supporter of President José Miguel Gómez in 1902, as an opponent of President Mario Menocal in 1917, and as a strong Machado backer in 1924. A number of influential Liberal Party leaders already had proposed Céspedes as a likely candidate in the presidential elections scheduled for 1928.

U.S. Ambassador Enoch Crowder praised Céspedes's keen business sense; on the other hand, he equivocated when asked about Céspedes's ethical standards.[2] Unquestionably, the secretary had enhanced the value of his investments—and those of business partners—through the expansion of public works in support of tourism. At the same time, Céspedes and his partners had become Havana's principal owners of tourism-related gambling concessions. Anyone familiar with the development of a contemporary theme park or similar tourist attraction understands its influence on surrounding real estate values.

CÉSPEDES, CORTINA, DE LA CRUZ, CONCESSIONS, AND CRONYISM

Cubans referred to tourism's prime movers as the "three Cs": Carlos Miguel de Céspedes and his two partners, José Manuel Cortina and Carlos Manuel de la Cruz. A fourth C—government concessions, that is, contracts or permits for the exclusive operation of private enterprises—played a crucial role as financial rewards for political cronies. The government's major source of public revenue came from the customhouse: sugar and tobacco exported, industrial and consumer goods imported. Political parties competed electorally to gain control over these funds. Success at the polls meant money in the pocket for the party faithful. The intermingling of private and public interests invited corruption in Cuba, as elsewhere.

As Havana grew, profits accompanied urban expansion. The pattern is familiar. A city council plans a new park, for example, or chooses a transportation corridor. An astute individual, most likely a political insider, goes to the area under consideration and buys property. When the city officials publish their plans and precipitate an increase in land values, the investor enjoys a profit. If speculators buy land first and then manipulate the legislative process to push a project, is that business, or corruption? Shady dealings or visionary leadership?

The three Cs worked the system, and their connections increased their wealth. Ambitious young men, they obtained positions of public trust when the Liberal Party held power. José Miguel Gómez took office in 1909, and Cortina and de la Cruz served in the Cuban Congress, while Céspedes remained in the private sector. Céspedes and Cortina were law partners. Loyalty and hard work won Cortina the coveted chair of the congressional public works committee, a powerful patronage position. De la Cruz moved up in the party ranks, and Gómez appointed Céspedes to the critical post of consulting attorney to the Department of Public Works. They traded on excellent credentials and gained the advantages that accrued to political supporters. They used political leverage to develop Cuba's infrastructure, and their political and financial activities gave a critical boost to the tourist industry.

A pleasant experience turns visitors into valuable boosters. Conversely, a collapsing bridge under a train or tourist bus, or microbe-filled water, has the opposite effect. Public officials like Céspedes and his associates worked to make Havana a safe and desirable place to visit, as well as to live, with sufficient pure water and adequate sanitation.

Havana suffered from recurring water problems. In the previous century, an ancient, uncovered aqueduct had carried water some five miles from the Río Almendares to the city's center. Covering the conveyor increased the purity of the water but not the supply. Later the Spanish authorities had captured the water from four hundred springs nine miles south of Havana, enclosed the springs in a huge tanklike building, and built an aqueduct under the river and a storage reservoir in the Havana outskirts. By 1900 the project supplied Havana with good water, distributed throughout the city by pipes that ended in storage tanks under most buildings. Hotels as well as houses tapped into this system, and guests turned faucet handles to get clean running water, just as they did at home.[3]

Although the Spaniards had resolved Havana's water supply problem, they had woefully neglected the city's sewers and drainage. Ships' passengers who neared Havana's docks in the late nineteenth century were greeted by the stomach-turning stench of Havana's sewage, wafted by the breeze from the water to the deck. Sewers served less than one-eighth of the rapidly expanding and increasingly crowded urban area, home to a population of some 250,000. Badly constructed and poorly planned, the sewers emptied directly under the docks into the harbor, spreading sickness in the part of town nearest the wharfs. In most houses, waste and refuse accumulated in a cesspool in the patio or courtyard. Workmen cleaned the cesspools at infrequent intervals and dumped the contents into the harbor, where the natural ebb and flow of the tides were insufficient to move the waste out into the gulf. It sank to the bottom and stayed there.[4]

Havana's spacious, protected harbor has been the city's center of economic life since the earliest Spanish commerce. It measures one to one and one-half miles across and about three miles long, with three smaller bays that indent the southern and eastern shores. Spaniards had built the old colonial city on land that juts out into the harbor. Fortresses on either side of the mile-long channel protected the treasure fleets as ships gathered each year to make their silver- and gold-laden return to Europe. The overwhelming portion of Cuba's trade — slaves, sugar, tobacco, and merchandise — entered and left through Havana harbor. In the twentieth century it became the docking place for thousands of pleasure seekers.

Tourist promoters dared not risk shiploads of customers falling ill because of inadequate sanitation. To provide drainage and sewers, roads and bridges — in other words, to turn Havana into a healthy, delightful tourist city — the Cuban government undertook massive public works projects. Between 1907 and 1919, when public coffers swelled with the increase in sugar exports, Cuba spent $21 million on new highways, roads, and bridges; $10 million on highway maintenance; $19 million to pave Havana's streets and to improve the sewer system; and $4.6 million to channel rivers and upgrade ports.[5] By 1919, when Cuba stood on the threshhold of the tourist boom, civic authorities had completed 187 miles of sewer lines and 79 miles of storm drains in and around Havana and had constructed a sewage tunnel under the bay. They connected sewer lines to the tunnel and installed a pumping plant to pump the refuse several miles east, to be discharged into the gulf near Cojímar. Storm drains also emptied rainwater along the shore rather than into the harbor.

In addition to physically improving the island, these projects distributed financial gains to government officials and their private-sector friends and facilitated capital development. Money earned on contracts, concessions, kickbacks, and bribes accumulated in banks as personal savings, mobilizable for investment in real estate, tourism, and other enterprises.

The Three Cs and the Ports Company Scandal

No one quarreled with the need to dredge Havana's harbor. Removal of accumulated wastes and silt was necessary for the passage of ships vital to the island's economic lifeline, as well as for sanitation purposes. President Gómez granted the contract to the Ports Company, an entity created by a multinational (British, North American, Spanish, and Cuban) investors' group specifically for that purpose. Norman H. Davis, a U.S. citizen and president of the Trust Company of Cuba, prepared the complex agreement. The company would clear and maintain various Cuban ports for thirty years, work estimated to cost some ten million dollars. In return, a percentage of customs revenues would bring the company approximately one million dollars in earnings the first year, increasing as trade expanded over the duration of the concession. The terms being quite generous, Cuban officials— from the president down—anticipated a share of the spoils.

Carlos Miguel de Céspedes joined the Ports Company as a member of the legal department, which was headed by Gómez's protégé, Orestes Ferrara, another rapid climber up the political ladder. Ferrara entered Congress in 1910 and was elected Speaker of the House of Representatives in 1911, the year of the Ports Company concession. His law partner served as a director of the company. Ports Company profits existed only on paper in 1911, but Norman Davis's generous projection encouraged investment in the company. The prospectus indicated that the company could clear indebtedness in fifteen years and that substantial income for the remaining fifteen years of the contract, less expenses, would be shared by stockholders. No actual dredging had begun when the company issued ten million dollars' worth of stock and close to one million dollars in first mortgage bonds. Davis's company loaned the Ports Company one million dollars and appraised the value of the concession at twenty-five times that amount. Davis himself traveled to London to shepherd the sale of six million dollars' worth of stock in the European market.

The company sublet the actual dredging work to T. L. Huston Contracting Company, whose principals included Norman Davis and

Tillinghast L'Hommedieu Huston, an engineer who had arrived in Cuba at the beginning of the century and had gained his share of government contracts to build roads, bridges, and buildings. Huston Contracting passed Ports Company subcontracts to its subsidiaries, Huston Concrete and Huston-Trumbo Dredging.[6]

The Ports Company became a feeding trough for political favorites. Rather large amounts of money apparently changed hands between the government and the company (as its share of customs income) in a comparatively short time. New York bankers who held Cuban government notes guaranteed by customs revenues issued ominous warnings and complained to all who would listen. The understandably fearful financiers accused Gómez and his buddies of turning Cuba's chief source of repayment for their notes—the customs revenues—to other purposes, namely, overpayments to supporters. Moreover, revenues quickly raised the value of company stock, facilitating profitable sales by early shareholders.

When Gómez lost the 1912 election, he moved to bestow more favors on the Ports Company. Before leaving office in 1913, he decreed that the government would purchase outstanding company stock at a price to be set by three "impartial" appraisers. The new Conservative Party president, Mario Menocal, had neither reason nor inclination to protect Gómez's buddies. He canceled the dredging contract on the grounds of initial illegalities and refused to negotiate the claims of stockholders. When bondholders pressed the government, the Cuban courts upheld Menocal's action. Eventually the government assumed the company's debts, thereby spreading the losses to most Cuban citizens while only a few had enjoyed the financial gains.

Because of its murky history, "Ports Company" became synonymous with scandal; the historian Carleton Beals characterized the concession as the "most exorbitant deal in the annals of Cuba." Most of the original investors, Carlos Miguel de Céspedes included, profited in the early financial wheelings and dealings. They sold their stock while the price was high and invested the profits in other moneymaking schemes.[7] The three Cs plunged into tourism concurrently with Ports Company activities, and substantial evidence ties Ports Company profits to tourism investments.

Real Estate and the Cuban Monte Carlo

By the time that the Ports Company scandal broke in 1913, a number of new hotels already had altered Havana's skyline, adding several hundred comfortable, modern rooms with plumbing designed to appeal to the steady stream of North American businessmen and a trickle of travelers. Economic expansion had created an urgent need for hotel space. The older Hotel Inglaterra, with its colorfully tiled restaurant and bar recalling Cuba's ties to Spain, had been a favorite hangout of correspondents who reported back to New York, Boston, or Washington on the battlefield successes, failures, and stalemates of the 1895–98 independence war. After the war the Inglaterra had catered to myriad salesmen, engineers, and contractors who arrived to participate in Cuba's physical reconstruction.

The Hotel Pasaje also welcomed new arrivals and old hands to its pleasant surroundings. A block-long arcade, or passageway, gave the hostelry its name. High-ceilinged rooms opened on a balcony that overlooked the social area where guests enjoyed a drink, a cigar, and conversation, as well as a commercial center that included the hotel's barbershop, cigar store, and travelers' information stand. Huge windows and multitiered chandeliers lit the public dining room and were reflected in the polished marble floors. Several smaller hotels could be found in the central commercial district and one or two in the expanding, fashionable Vedado suburb.[8]

Responsive to the demand for accommodations, Manuel López, the proprietor of the Inglaterra, and Urbano González of the Pasaje combined forces and opened the Hotel Sevilla, considered the ultimate in hotel design and elegant appointments for its time. The five-story building captured the spirit of Andalusian Spain in its ornate Moorish façade and met the needs of the most fastidious modern North Americans with private baths for each of its 250 rooms. Guests slept on beds and mattresses imported from the United States, surrounded by elegant furniture sent from France; they descended staircases fashioned from German marble—when they chose not to take the modern elevator.[9] The owners of the Herald Square Hotel in New York similarly recognized a good opportunity and began work on a hotel facing Havana's Parque Central (Central Park); another North American partnership purchased land on the Prado, the fashionable promenade that extended for more than a mile from the park to the seaside.

Unfortunately, the newest hotels had barely opened their doors for business when Cuba's fledgling political parties fought their first electoral battle. Control of the presidency and its patronage power brought out the guns as well as the ballots and brought the United States in for a second military occupation. Most potential tourists found no compelling reason to alter familiar travel habits or to trade relaxation in Europe or Florida for risk in Cuba.

With peace restored in 1906 under U.S. supervision, the Cuban Racing Association inaugurated horse races as a travel incentive to bettors and breeders. However, the military governor turned thumbs down on the sport of kings. Republican Party leaders in Washington strongly condemned horse betting in the United States and did not welcome it in U.S.-controlled Cuba. Automobile races failed to catch on as a tourist attraction, perhaps because few people in 1908 identified automobiles with the thrill of speed.[10]

While central Havana experienced most of the hotel-building activity at the time, Céspedes, Cortina, and de la Cruz focused on Marianao, a lovely community to the west of Havana and in 1910 a relatively undeveloped area. Céspedes, Cortina, and de la Cruz turned their attention to Marianao just as newly installed transportation and utilities greatly enhanced its convenience. A casino promised to raise Marianao land values even more.

An early, rather fuzzy photograph of Marianao's beach, taken around 1890, reveals a sandy shoreline, a weathered old lookout tower, one or two riders on horseback, a few small houses along the sand, and sailboats among the gentle waves. The rather primitive, frontierlike atmosphere belies the cultivated society that resided in the municipality a short distance inland. Neither does the photo offer much of a hint that, in the full bloom of Cuban tourism, playful crowds would romp through the surf or dine, dance, and gamble nearby.[11]

Affluent *habaneros*, mostly Spanish officials and sugarcane growers, had made Marianao their place of summer residence in the nineteenth century, attracted by cooling sea breezes and health-restoring hot springs. As in many of the residential pockets that surrounded central Havana, Marianao's founders had laid down its first streets on an elevated stretch of land that caught the cool winds during the hot summer and remained safe from floods in the rainy season. The shallow rise, two miles from the shore, stood some eight or nine miles from central Havana. For their own convenience the sugar barons and bureaucrats constructed a railroad out from town. Completion of both the railroad in 1863 and a good carriage road in 1864 provided convenient access. Transportation and the attractive surroundings combined to bless Marianao with a thirty-year-long golden era. While independence struggles raged elsewhere on the island, the upper strata of Havana society took their ease close to the sea.

After the Spanish rulers left the island, U.S. occupation forces also found the comfortable area much to their liking. General Fitzhugh Lee, military governor of the island's western end, located his headquarters in the Marianao *barrio* (neighborhood) of Quemados, in the abandoned mansion of a Spanish nobleman who understandably had transferred his place of residence to Madrid. Lee, who had been U.S. consul in Havana before independence, knew the area well. A revealing 1897 snapshot captured the consul surrounded by friends at the Marianao shore, taking a break while Cubans fought the war.[12] Lee's urgent requests to Washington in December of that year sent naval forces to protect U.S. interests against anti-American outbursts in Havana. The seaborne show of strength included the battleship *Maine*, and the subsequent explosion and sinking of the *Maine* in February 1898 precipitated the United States' formal entry into the independence struggle.

Marianao understandably drew the attention of tourism entrepreneurs. The breathtaking view from the second-story terrace of Lee's headquarters at Quemados swept past luxuriant gardens and stately promenades to the rolling countryside, its verdant valleys broken by gentle hills, and on one side the startling blue of the Gulf of Mexico. Just beyond the residential and commercial center of the small town, pineapple, banana, and coffee plantations alternated with vegetable farms and cow pastures in the pleasant rural landscape.[13]

General Lee chose another Marianao location as the site for Camp Columbia, military headquarters of the U.S. occupation forces. Strategic advantage as well as convenience to central Havana underlay Lee's decision to put the troops on Marianao's heights, where they could overlook both land and sea. The military base, with its contingent of salaried American soldiers, soon served the neighborhood as an unanticipated agent of prosperity and population growth. First of all, vendors capitalized on the substantial market created by the soldiers and set up shops to meet their needs. Second, and more important, base operations required the extension of water and electricity to the location. These amenities encouraged population growth, which in turn made feasible the extension of Havana's electric tramway to the area in 1903, completed after U.S. troops had withdrawn.

Population expanded rapidly. Growth in Marianao, including various barrios (Playa, Buena Vista, Columbia, Quemados, etc.), outpaced all but two other municipalities in western Cuba between the census years of 1907 and 1919. The doubling of its population, from 18,156 to 37,464, resulted from the extension of urban amenities, a considerable increase in personal wealth among Havana residents, and intense promotion by the developers of its new suburbs.

Havana's earlier residential development had extended outward from its ancient quarter near the harbor along various trails or roads that followed the topography. Houses occupied plateaus, ridges, and hills separated by valleys that flooded in the torrential tropical rains. Immigrant Chinese gardeners slowly occupied the flood-prone lowlands, dug ditches to drain them, and planted vegetables and flowers to sell to *habaneros*. As Havana's population grew, these agricultural valleys impeded efficient transportation and occupied potentially valuable urban space. As part of its public works activity, the government moved tons of earth to raise the surface level of the valleys, thus facilitating transportation and adding acreage for residential development. House lots replaced lettuce beds and rose gardens, and surveyors marked the roads that would allow crosstown automobile and truck traffic to connect Príncipe Hill directly with Vedado and the growing suburb of Cerro.[14]

Property owners in outlying areas experienced a boon once new streets shortened the journey to the central city. Nicanor del Campo, for example, converted agricultural properties in Marianao, demarcating and leveling lots for houses and grading land for streets that drained excess rainfall to the sea. He laid out his subdivision when the electric railway first reached Marianao in 1903 and sold part of the development at a considerable profit a decade later when home construction ran at a fever pitch.[15]

This period of frenzied real estate activity paralleled the Ports Company scandal and set the stage for the first significant political campaign for a tourist attraction. Speaker of the House Orestes Ferrara, a legislative colleague of Cortina and de la Cruz and Carlos Miguel de Céspedes's boss at the Ports Company, introduced the so-called Monte Carlo bill into the Cuban Congress in 1910. The proposed legislation granted an exclusive thirty-year concession to the three Cs' Compañía Fomento del Turismo en Cuba, authorizing the company to conduct all types of amusements, including gambling and sports, on land located between the Camp Columbia military base and the sea—the very heart of Marianao property development at the time. (Even before the Ports Company subcontracted their dredging work to the Huston Contracting Company, Huston had won a twenty-five-thousand-dollar contract to pave the newly laid streets of Marianao.) As company principals, Céspedes, Cortina, and de la Cruz would operate the casino to be built on the land. Clearly, the casino's 1 November to 30 May season would draw Florida's winter tourists to Havana.[16]

Unfortunately for its sponsors, the bill spurred widespread vocal criticism in the United States. U.S. occupying forces had just left Cuba for the second time. The Republicans who controlled the White House had balked at Cuban horse racing when its appointees ran the island. Their supporters objected even more strenuously to casino gambling that would attract U.S. citizens to Cuba. Furthermore, U.S. social reformers, already upset by a perceived deterioration in behavior and values at home, jumped nervously at the thought of further erosion encouraged by gambling excursions to Havana.

Letters of protest from self-assigned protectors of American morals bombarded Washington. Bishop Willard Mallalieu of the Methodist Episcopal Church called the bill a "degrading and disgraceful scheme" and lobbied President Taft in the name of the church's three million members and seventeen thousand preachers. The secretary of the Massachusetts Civic Alliance pointed out that President William McKinley had done away with disgraceful bullfights in Cuba; clearly Taft could do no less to defend the national honor.[17]

The U.S. government could not legally stop the casino bill but could bully the Cubans. So Taft pushed the State Department, whose representatives in Havana conveyed his concerns to President Gómez, adding that "passage of this bill might probably cause complications in the postal as well as other relations of the two Governments." Predictably, the casino proposal succumbed to pressure, forceful debate in the Cuban Congress and a promise to share gambling revenues with charitable organizations notwithstanding. Taft had muscled his Cuban counterpart, and despite Cuba's constitutional sovereignty, a pragmatic Gómez worked to kill the bill. On 12 November 1910 the head of the U.S. legation in Havana triumphantly confirmed the Cuban Senate's rejection of the casino legislation.[18]

A second attempt to secure gambling for Marianao proposed a thirty-year concession to the renamed Compañía Kursal de Buena Vista, which pledged to spend $1.5 million (Ports Company profits?) to construct attractions for tourists in Marianao. (*Kursal* is German for "casino"; Buena Vista is a Marianao barrio.) To sway official opinion in both capitals, proponents argued that visitors would stimulate the economy and circulate money among the industrial and working classes in the form of jobs. A number of Cubans and North Americans complained bitterly that they had lost good business opportunities owing to U.S. government meddling. They lobbied members of the U.S. legation in Havana, insisting that Cuba required sporting attractions to lure tourists. Michael Dady, a New Yorker who stood to lose lucrative contracts to build jai alai courts, a pavilion, and a grandstand, took his complaint directly to President Taft.[19]

The tourism measure failed once more, brought down by U.S. opposition fueled in part by bombastic journalists. A Cleveland newspaper headlined: "Havana Is World's Wickedest City, Press Man Finds; U.S. Must Act." Sodom and Babylon were a kindergarten compared to the Cuban capital, the exposé explained, a place where prurient exhibitions bid for the trade of decent Americans. For the twenty-cent price of admission, three hundred people per hour in each of four theaters watched the ultimate in depravity, naked women who gyrated on a stage.[20] The strident clamor for action against evil once again moved Washington to pressure Havana. The Cuban leadership advisedly weighed the uncertain benefits of tourism against good relations with its prudish and powerful neighbor. Gambling lost.

Cutthroat Real Estate Competition

The legislative disappointments did little to discourage real estate operators who anticipated tourism's profits. Several North American speculators, unfortunate rivals of ambitious Cuban citizens, felt the sting of cunning political opponents. They beat on closed doors at

Cuba's halls of justice and faced personal attacks and assaults on their possessions. The properties in question lay in areas in which the three Cs held considerable financial interests.

As astute as the most prescient of Cubans, the long-term Havana resident Joseph Barlow recognized the potential value of undeveloped land located on the outskirts of the dynamic city. Because low sales prices and negligible taxes on real property encouraged speculation, Barlow bought or arranged options on several large lots. He called his land-trading company Compañía Buena Vista, after the Marianao barrio where he began to accumulate holdings as early as 1905. Not surprisingly, Barlow backed the 1910 and 1911 Monte Carlo bills. He had registered and plotted his Buena Vista acreage, knowing that the casino and other attractions would raise their value. In the face of opposition to the legislation, Barlow harangued officials at the U.S. legation in Havana. When failure of the casino bill delayed his profit taking in the suburbs, he churned out another scheme, this one for central Havana. His instinct for real estate prospects unfortunately out-distanced his political clout—a sure formula for misfortune in a land boom manipulated by insiders.

Even without a seaside casino, Barlow reasoned, Havana could attract more visitors. Did not thousands of Americans visit Paris because of the city's beauty? Well, then, Havana would be reconstructed to rival Paris. Borrowing a page from Baron Georges Haussmann's book, the visionary investor began to plan Havana's beautification.[21] Boldly extravagant, Barlow proposed to widen several of Havana's thorough-fares leading to a magnificent boulevard that would slice across the city from the crowded center through the newer suburbs to terminate in a magnificent park (patterned after Paris's Champs-Élysées and the Bois de Boulogne). The new motorway and promenade would be a vital transportation artery and a source of civic pride. Elegant shops, well-designed theaters, and inviting open spaces with tree-shaded walkways, bordered by well-planned and landscaped foliage, would pull visitors from the ancient harborside district to the grandeur of new areas ripe for residential development.

Barlow in fact combined imagination with ambition. He had pur-chased a huge, undeveloped tract of land in central Havana, the equivalent of some thirty-two city blocks, from the heirs to an old Spanish land grant. A 1900 map of Havana depicts this area (west of the Calzada de la Infanta and east of Vedado) as vacant land between two sections already laid out in residential blocks. Barlow's boulevard, his "Gran Vía," facilitated access to his own property before it joined a proposed ten-mile southward extension to the newer suburbs and the planned park. Engineers, both Cuban and North American, prepared drawings for a three-square-mile area of parks, playgrounds, a lake for boating, sports fields, a zoo, and a hotel, all tied together with a network of new streets linked to the great central thoroughfare. He packaged the sketches and text into a prospectus and offered shares to investors.

In his enthusiasm, poor Barlow, too good a salesman by half, convinced the wrong audience. Although deeds to the land already had been registered in his name, challenges to Barlow's ownership forced him into the courts against formidable opponents. Unfortunately, the Spanish grant that he had acquired set boundaries without benefit of an accurate survey. His property simply extended as far as the barking of a dog could be heard from a central point. In the 1920s, when Havana already enjoyed considerable tourism, a son-in-law of President Machado (the son of a Machado cabinet officer, as well) opened an amusement park on the land, citing legal possession by right of a lease from the Gómez Mena Land Company. José Gómez Mena, a wealthy, politically connected owner of sugar properties and developer of urban real estate, claimed the land as part of a farm that he had purchased.

While Barlow fought for his central Havana property rights through Cuban courts, government officials fenced in his Buena Vista holdings. Clearly designed to intimidate him, the government deprived him of revenue from one property needed to fight encroachment on the other. Over the years Barlow had sold numerous lots carved from his Buena Vista property, and purchasers had never encountered difficulty in transferring legal ownership. The court even refused repeated demands that the parties who had enclosed the property show cause why they had done so. Prevented from redress through Cuban institutions, Barlow eventually appealed to the U.S. government. When Céspedes became public works secretary in 1925, he developed his own beautification project for Havana, and city maps show the disputed central Havana area fully demarcated in streets and blocks, even as Barlow continued to pursue his claim. By the time the U.S. Senate held a claims hearing in 1928, Barlow was well into his sixties. The Cubans derided him as a crazy old man and even threw him in jail for a time. Although a settlement ultimately favored Barlow, his lawyers probably gained more than he had from his Havana real estate ventures.[22]

Barlow's tortuous ordeal is significant: in a situation where tourism—actual or anticipated—contributes to inflated real estate values, profit potential makes for a game of political hardball. Charles Harrah, an outsider like Barlow, proved another losing player. Harrah found his niche in the rather pedestrian sand and gravel industry, an uninspiring enterprise compared to Joseph Barlow's grand schemes, but essential to Havana's construction industry. In 1908 Harrah bought beachfront property in Marianao and farther west along the coast in Jaimanitas and Santa Fe. He secured government permission to haul sand and gravel from the beaches and to build a seven-mile-long railroad spur along the shore to ship his materials to town by means of the Havana Railway. He operated his business profitably for several years and then returned to the United States, leaving a business agent in charge. The agent drained the profits and conspired to take possession of the railroad, bringing Harrah back in a rush to fight for property that was becoming more valuable as Marianao experienced its transformation from neglected beach to valuable suburb and potential tourist resort. He was still fighting in 1917 when workmen, acting on orders signed by the secretary of the treasury and approved by President Menocal, destroyed the railroad and burned the terminals. Like Barlow, Harrah fought the Cuban system for years until the U.S. government acted on his behalf. He finally reached a settlement in 1930, for half the amount he had claimed in damages.[23]

A Tourist Bill Passes

As World War I diverted tourists away from Europe toward Florida, Céspedes, Cortina, and de la Cruz redoubled their efforts to pull them toward Cuba. Most of Cuba's wartime tourists stayed at hotels in central Havana and visited Marianao for the thoroughbred horse races that finally made their appearance. Harry T. "Curly" Brown, later the owner of Chicago's Arlington Park track, opened Havana's Oriental Park in 1915. The track made a little money, and then a little more at the war's end, when increasing numbers of North Americans enjoyed Havana's winter sunshine, its foreign sights and smells. They sailed from New York on a Ward Line ship for as little as forty dollars, one way, first class, all meals included, or twenty dollars each way, second class. They bought souvenirs: coral and turtle shell articles; hand-embroidered scarves and tablecloths; cigars, of course; and jewelry redeemable at bargain prices from pawnshops whose high interest rates and short redemption times increased the amount of available merchandise. "Ask Mr. Foster," the travel agency that had sold information on farms and industry to prospective settlers at the turn of the century, escorted visitors on sight-seeing excursions to Morro Castle, La Punta Fortress, Cathedral Square, and the Havana countryside. Tourists could replenish Kodak supplies to record on film the most exciting moments of their adventures.[24]

The three Cs wasted none of the war years. Their Compañía Urbanizadora Playa de Marianao bought land, sold lots, and planned residential subdivisions near the seaside. The company also renewed the battle for a Marianao casino. Cuba had changed presidents since the three Cs had pushed the old Monte Carlo bill. While the opposition controlled the presidency, Cortina and de la Cruz protected the trio's interests through influential positions inside the Congress. President Mario Menocal proved neither less corrupt nor less profligate with public money than his predecessors.

In the same year that Charles Harrah's railroad fell to arson, 1917, the three Cs charged the government battlements again. First their Casino de la Playa Company approached Marianao's municipal officers with a deal they could hardly refuse: in exchange for public avenues, streets, and plazas installed on company land at company expense—to be turned over to Marianao at no cost—the city fathers would permit the company to establish and exploit "diversions" on the remainder of its private land. The proposed amusements might include theaters, movies, games, sports—and gambling. Marianao authorities, cognizant of the revenue and growth potential of the offer, quickly agreed. Since they had already permitted Oriental Park's owners to take bets on horse races, why should they object to games of chance conducted in casinos?[25]

While Marianao's leaders might not discourage casino operations, neither could they authorize them. Jurisdiction for such legislation rested with the national government. While using Casino de la Playa company funds for Marianao's public improvements, the three Cs also worked on the Cuban Congress. Their casino and tourist bill finally came up for consideration in 1919. (Given the political hostility between President Menocal and the Liberal Party in 1917, it might be presumed that enemies in the national government impeded their efforts for a time.) Speaker Ferrara moved the bill through the House, and as editor of Havana's *Heraldo de Cuba* he attempted to mobilize public opinion. Although Cortina still headed the public works committee, the legislation ran a gauntlet of angry critics and passed only after considerable lobbying and a long debate.

The legislative session opened at 3:00 P.M. on 4 August and finally closed at 7:30 the next morning. Determined opponents denounced the negative moral and social consequences of gambling and raised the familiar specter of political corruption. Unyielding antagonists also expressed fears for Cuba's national culture and sense of identity (considered still tenuous in the young republic) once substantial numbers of tourists arrived from the United States. Among the bill's most outspoken and tenacious adversaries, German Wólter del Río, representing a center-island district in Santa Clara that could expect little benefit from tourist dollars, tried to rally the opposition. He had visited Baja California, just south of the U.S. border, where legal gambling had transformed the place into a "toilet" for the United States. Gambling and fun-seeking tourists, he warned his colleagues, would despoil Cuba.

The bill finally passed, a credit to the prodigious and persistent efforts of its authors. In another measure approved during the same long night after angry debate over its propriety, members agreed to fund a bridge over the Río Almendares to connect the seaside suburbs under development in Miramar and Marianao with the affluent neighborhood of Vedado. Once completed, the bridge would afford wealthy *habaneros* more convenient access to the recreational areas to be developed in Marianao.[26]

Four months before the Congress approved the tourist bill and the Río Almendares bridge, a mob of about one hundred Cubans had seized Marianao land belonging to Walter Fletcher Smith, claiming "urgent public utility." A respected businessman, Smith operated the popular Plaza Hotel in the commercial heart of Havana. Enthusiastic about the growth of the travel business, he had purchased beachfront Marianao property and built a hotel, a bathhouse, and his personal residence. Forced from his house, Smith sued, charging that private interests, not public purpose, lay behind the property seizure. He was undoubtedly correct. Municipal authorities, using condemnation proceedings pushed through the Marianao courts, awarded the property to the Compañía Urbanizadora de Parque y Playa de Marianao, SA, owned by Céspedes, Cortina, and de la Cruz. When a higher court affirmed Smith's arguments, his determined opponents appealed the case through Cuba's legal system and delayed resolution. Seven years later, with the tourist industry well under way, Smith's claim remained unsettled, while developers, most likely the Céspedes company, constructed buildings where his house once stood and collected an estimated $175,000 in rents. The Cuban government ultimately confirmed the validity of Smith's claim and awarded damages, but the valuable property had changed hands.[27]

The 1919 tourist law clearly bore the stamp of blatant private and personal gain. First of all, the bill benefited only one company, the Casino de la Playa, owned by Céspedes, Cortina, and de la Cruz. Broadly paraphrased, it conceded permission for games of chance to seaside resorts where private persons and businesses had already obtained permission to establish shows or games, as long as it could be proven that those persons or business concerns had invested at least $1.5 million in preparation and creation of places suitable for high-class residences, amusement parks, and bathing establishments. The Casino de la Playa Company alone qualified under these provisions, based on its signed agreement with the municipality of Marianao. The $1.5 million investment figure repeats the sum referenced in the 1910 and 1911 Monte Carlo bill, which favored the three Cs' Compañía Kursal de Buena Vista.[28]

Article 6 of the bill perhaps co-opted a few high-minded opponents of gambling when it devoted a small percentage of the gaming proceeds to fund a national commission to oversee the health and welfare of indigent mothers and infants. Article 7 provided for a committee to promote tourism, with members drawn from the public and private sectors, including the president of the Senate, Speaker of the House, secretary of public works, the mayor of Havana and of any other municipality where businesses covered by the law operated, and representatives of business concerns that would operate under the new law.

To no one's surprise, a number of these officials had personal financial interests in the success of Cuban tourism. President Menocal signed the bill with little hesitation. His family gained the concession to operate jai alai games granted under its provisions. Menocal's friend and political ally, Senate president and fellow race horse owner

Ricardo Dolz, headed both the new tourist commission and a company organized to promote racing. Dolz's animals carried his stable's colors when they ran at Oriental Park against horses brought to Cuba by wealthy North Americans for the 1920 racing season. Competition against better-known horses and breeding possibilities most certainly raised the value of Dolz's animals as well as his reputation as a horseman.[29]

❧

IN REAL ESTATE, TIMING IS EVERYTHING

When President Menocal left office, and his successor, Alfredo Zayas, appointed José Manuel Cortina to the pivotal post of presidential secretary, the Compañía de la Playa appeared to have carved its initials on the trunk of a money tree. Ironically, with tourism poised to expand, Cuba's sugar-based economy stumbled. After years of steady price increases and an abrupt escalation during World War I, the sugar market collapsed just as the eager entrepreneurs of the Compañía de la Playa stood ready to shove the island in a new direction. Thousands of tourists, whose incomes did not rely on sugar, would pay to enjoy Cuba. Moreover, wealthy winter residents could work wonders for Havana's threatened real estate market.

Even when sugar had enjoyed peak prices, some Cubans had channeled earnings to alternate investments such as urban and suburban real estate, construction, and import-substitution manufacture (to replace goods unavailable in wartime). Bank deposits had increased 1,000 percent on the basis of sugar profits, and investment of the accumulated capital had helped to accelerate property values—as much as 300 percent according to some reports, 500 percent in others. (Location and degree of development accounted for some of the disparity.)[30]

Contrary to expectations, real estate continued to flourish despite the sugar market collapse. The 1920 issue of Madrid's *Guía comercial de la isla de Cuba* (published yearly since the late colonial era for the benefit of Spanish merchants and investors) listed fifteen Havana companies that bought and sold lots, as well as several firms that dealt in raw, unplotted acreage. Madrid's 1924 *Guía* added five Havana land companies to the 1920 total. Real estate in fact acted as an economic engine, though not on a scale comparable to sugar. Agents sold commercial and residential properties; developers built houses and employed workmen; bankers loaned money in exchange for mortgages; insurance agents protected owners from loss; home furnishing importers, manufacturers, and retailers applauded the type of investment that swelled their customer base. The Marianao Industrial Company, for example, an extensive complex that manufactured all types of furniture made from locally grown Cuban mahogany, responded to the demand created by newly constructed homes, offices, and hotels. Businessmen and laborers cheered the real estate profits that turned over in the economy to benefit the community at large.[31]

Idiosyncracies of Cuba's economic fluctuations during and after World War I played a part in this economic countertrend. A somewhat convoluted but logical cause-and-effect pattern of capital accumulation and material resource availability fostered the construction boom. Wartime sugar profits had generated exceptional levels of personal savings that turned over, in part, as real estate loans. Some speculators had sold their sugar before the market crashed and banked or invested the proceeds. However, war-related shortages of construction materials, particularly steel and cement, raised their prices beyond feasibility for profitable construction. Furthermore, increases in sugar output, contracted under agreements with the U.S. government, strained the available labor pool, because high wages in agriculture drained laborers who otherwise might have worked in the building trades.[32]

When the war's end released materials and labor, a building frenzy ensued based on pent-up demand. Record sugar prices funded a rush to enshrine wealth in suitable edifices. Cubans contracted to build homes and apartment houses, office and commercial buildings. An expectant atmosphere, comparable to that of a gold or oil strike, enveloped Havana. Contractors worked on new headquarters buildings for thriving banks and other businesses and on apartment houses comparable to the latest New York offerings. Modernizers warmed to the idea of transforming colonial Havana into the dynamic capital of Latin America.

Ironically, the sugar crash encouraged creative business arrangements that saved the construction industry. Contractors had stockpiled materials to meet obligations for buildings already under construction and in anticipation of increasingly intense demand. Then the disaster threw laborers on the market, temporarily depressed land values, and caught builders with an oversupply of steel, lumber, pipe, cement, and other structural materials. As a way of disposing of excess stock, building materials dealers joined forces with prospective builders; that is, they extended credit for purchases, and some even went so far as to advance cash for payrolls. Real estate bargain hunters began to build on properties that they had purchased.

Homes, hotels, office buildings, manufacturing facilities, and commercial buildings rose on empty lots that had been purchased on speculation since the war. Corner buildings two and three stories high placed cafés and stores at ground level and divided the floors above into residential spaces. Modern apartment houses and hotels replaced ancient buildings, destroyed because their ground space increased in value beyond that of the standing structure. New buildings sold at a good profit, filled with desirable tenants. Owners of older buildings remodeled or rebuilt to keep renters. At least part of the urban bourgeoisie rode out the economic storm on the basis of real estate investments and construction activity.[33] Some of them moved to the suburbs, where a formidable array of multistory, palatial residences in a variety of architectural styles—Tudor manors, French châteaus, Italian palazzi—emerged from newly planted lush green lawns dotted with Cuba's famous palm trees and fringed with flowers. José Manuel Cortina, for example, built an elaborate three-story mansion alongside the Havana University grounds, easily identified by its distinctive rooftop cupolas.

The building boom left its mark on Havana. An hour's walk from the city's inner core to the western seaside communities—possible for anyone with comfortable shoes—afforded a stunning visual history of real estate development and the population's move to the suburbs for any tourist who wanted to move beyond the arranged setting to peek behind the scenes. In typical Spanish architectural style, central city houses stood wall against wall, closed to the street, with a doorsill or carriage entry separating public walkway from private quarters. Residents carried on business and household activities unobserved by outsiders in patios or courtyards that were filled with a variety of plants in varying shades of green and dotted with the vibrant colors of tropical flowers.

In less crowded urban neighborhoods that lined the city's edge by 1910, houses with front porches dominated by the ubiquitous Cuban rocking chair opened on narrow patches of grass surrounded by iron fences. Farther on, past the church where Céspedes married and the property that Barlow fought for through the Cuban courts, the walker took in the broad sidewalks and the trees that replaced the shade-giving properties of buildings and balconies on crowded narrow streets in the colonial quarter. Open space and greenery moved from private patios to exterior areas, and neighbors greeted each other from shaded porches or front yards rather than through doorways or the traditional street-level windows, barred for security and often shuttered for privacy and protection from the tropical sun.

Havana's physical reaching out from cramped quarters to openness symbolized the optimism of a generation. Claudio G. Mendoza caught the spirit. Banker, farmer, and residential subdivision developer, father of six sons and kin to other Mendozas numbering around one hundred, he may have headed Havana's most affluent family in the 1920s. The tightly knit family, like other leaders of the active business sector, included tourist ventures and real estate development in its extensive, diversified investment portfolio. Hand in hand the Mendozas and Carlos Miguel de Céspedes developed Miramar, a neighborhood of sumptuous homes and lush gardens west of the Río Almendares. (Remember the iron bridge approved by Congress along with the 1919 tourist bill?) Mendozas developed the subdivision and financed homes; Céspedes, in his capacity as public works secretary, built streets and highways to make those homes convenient to downtown Havana—and to Marianao's country club, where an emerging Cuban elite learned to play golf with instructions from North American friends and colleagues.

In a short time Céspedes built one home in Miramar and another in the splendid new residential area of Marianao alongside the golf course. Several of Claudio Mendoza's sons, along with their wives and children, shared another huge estate in Marianao. In the social milieu that enveloped Cuba's economic and political leadership, upper-class *habaneros* worked together and played together.

By the 1920s a healthful and pleasurable city unfolded before the tourists' eyes. Electric lights illuminated parts of Havana in the evenings, and electric street railways carried the curious visitor to the city's suburbs or to the markets and shopping streets that appeared so foreign and exotic to the North American eye. In the awning-covered stalls of great market squares, the smell of mango, papaya, pineapple, cherimoya, malanga, peppers, onions, and garlic, along with the sight of heaps of cheap jewelry, glassware, shoes, caps, saddles, fish, chickens, and meat, confused the first-time viewer with its apparent chaos. Even the more familiarly arranged shopping streets of the central area—

Obispo and O'Reilly—disoriented the unfamiliar visitor with a profusion of banners and commercial signs hung from one building to the other across the confined colonial-era passageway.

The narrow streets of Old Havana, a section of the city that once had been surrounded by protective walls to guard against marauding pirates, contrasted with wide boulevards that reached out from the hotels, banks, offices, and retail stores of central Havana to fashionable new residential and recreational areas.

To sustain the upward momentum of real estate in the absence of a full recovery in the sugar sector, developers of property in the outlying areas encouraged North Americans to visit the island as tourists and to build their own homes alongside friendly Cubans. Given Cuba's beauty, its racetrack, jai alai palace, gambling casino, and other attractions, many visitors found in Havana the perfect location for a winter residence, a paradise close to home but far from snow and ice. By 1923 promoters fulfilled the promise of the 1919 legislation. They brought tourism to Cuba, wealth to themselves and other entrepreneurs, and jobs to thousands of fellow citizens. Unfortunately, tourism proved as vulnerable to market forces as sugar, and the boom lasted less than a decade.

Chapter 3

Tempests and Tourists,
Dreamers and Schemers

Natural disasters—hurricanes, earthquakes, floods, erupting volcanos—undermine carefully packaged images of vacation respite and send tourists in search of more soothing and safer terrain. In this way, a brutal hurricane laid waste to southern Florida in 1926. It only bruised Havana, however, and brought financial sunshine for Cuba behind it. While Floridians counted their losses, Cuban investors expanded their pleasure industry.

Florida was both a competitor and a market for Cuba in the early 1920s. Henry Flagler had put people on railroad trains to Florida; Henry Ford put them in automobiles. Mobile North Americans drove past Flagler's hotels to participate in southern Florida's land booms where another generation of resort builders fed their dreams. Addison Mizner developed Boca Raton, south of Palm Beach, while George Edgar Merrick drew thousands of boomers to the Miami suburb of

Coral Gables. Havana was a logical geographic extension to the pro-
gression of resort cities that marched southward along Florida's coast-
lines from the 188cs to the 1920s, promoted by capitalists no less ambitious than their Cuban counterparts.

An architect and international playboy, Addison Mizner went to
Florida for his health around 1920. While recuperating amid the social
whirl of Palm Beach, he befriended a wealthy young man named Paris
Singer, who became his mentor. Singer had invested part of his sew-
ing machine company inheritance in Palm Beach acreage. He built
a clubhouse and advertised the sale of estate-sized lots carved out of
the property. Mizner designed the million-dollar houses to be built
on those lots and then decided to strike out on his own. For the
stretch of beach at Boca Raton, Mizner envisioned a blend of Seville,
Venice, and golf. He surrounded a palatial Mediterranean-style hotel
with canals where gondolas cut through the water to carry guests from
place to place — particularly from the hotel to well-planned homesites
in a residential development. Land sales quickly climbed to two million dollars a week.[1]

In the land boom madness, pitchmen ranked alongside financiers
as critical players. Elephant parades epitomized the circuslike atmosphere. President Warren G. Harding played golf with an elephant as
an unwieldy, but admittedly amusing, caddy. Celebrities such as the
boxing champion Gene Tunney promoted land sales. Bathing beauties
scandalized the more reserved customers, but most buyers responded
favorably to public displays of young women in the one-piece beach
costumes considered "racy" at the time. They were more attractive
than elephants, by far.

George Merrick paid the handsome, charming idol of the masses,
William Jennings Bryan, one hundred thousand dollars a year to hype
his Coral Gables residential community. Was it the fee that induced
the former Democratic presidential candidate and secretary of state
to employ his famous golden-throated oratory in the cause of Florida
house lots, or did Bryan share Merrick's vision of thousands of contented citizens living peacefully in a tree-shaded community under
benevolent Florida skies?

Pine forests and citrus groves had filled Merrick's ten thousand acres
before he turned modest financial resources into a real estate fortune.
His father was a minister who had left New England to grow oranges,
grapefruit, and guava in Florida. George's childhood memories in-

spired a dream of a community where other American families could raise their children among trees and flowers. Merrick planned Coral Gables as a city with broad streets, Spanish-style squares complete with fountains, and well-spaced stucco houses. He opened a land office and advertised widely in magazines read by solid citizens with some financial resources: the *Saturday Evening Post, Vogue,* and *Forbes.* He sold 150 million dollars' worth of property in a relatively short time and reinvested two-thirds of his profit in improvements, such as the canals that wound among the residential lots, and a multimillion-dollar hotel and country club.

The Miami Biltmore Hotel featured a replica of Seville's ornate Giralda tower, in keeping with the Spanish architectural theme of the community. A promotional brochure proclaimed the hotel's purpose: to attract the right kind of people to the land, "the moneyed men of the country."[2] Those gentlemen of means played golf at the hotel while their families bathed at Merrick's private beach on Biscayne Bay. Prospective real estate customers heard Bryan declaim the merits of Coral Gables while he stood on a float anchored in the middle of a pond. Some of them bought property on speculation; others wanted to live in the land of sunshine.

Unfortunately, Florida isn't always sunny. Howling gales of up to 125 miles per hour and torrential rain toppled southern Florida's trees and houses in September 1926, flooded low-lying areas, and carried boats from moorings along the shore into houses and backyards. New residents of the area emerged when the rains stopped and stared at the remains of their houses, unaware that the calm was only the eye of the storm. Many of them drowned when the rains returned.[3]

The tempest blew Addison Mizner out of Boca Raton, where land sold at ten cents on the dollar after the storm. Many of George Merrick's partners and clients also lost their investments. His financial associate in the newly constructed Miami Biltmore Hotel fared better, however. The hotel survived the storm, and a New York hotel magnate, John McEntee Bowman, the owner of Havana's Sevilla-Biltmore Hotel and operator of the Oriental Park racetrack, expanded his power in Cuba's resort industry.

As the devastating hurricane exposed the dark and cruel underbelly of Florida's ordinarily benign and healthy climate, people turned their sights southward. Floridians offered pseudo-Spanish architecture, golf courses, bathing beaches, and residential lots. Cubans lived in authentic Spanish colonial houses, played golf, sailed yachts, and sold residential lots. The capricious winds that burst the Florida land bubble swept North Americans in Cuba's direction.

ENTREPRENEURS AT WORK

Cuba, the pearl of the Antilles, had startled Christopher Columbus with its lush tropical beauty and sweetly scented air. Four hundred years later, other visitors indulged their senses and abandoned their cares on that island. In 1920, however, the mass market still waited to be tapped. Curly Brown's Oriental Park racetrack had opened in 1915, just as people's minds turned to war. Fewer than two thousand travelers enjoyed Cuba's charm and distinctiveness in 1918, when war still raged in Europe. Not enough prominent horse breeders or tourists came to Havana to boost the track's reputation, but Charles Stoneham bought the track when the 1919 tourist law and a newly formed tourist commission raised expectations of improved attendance.

Perfumers mix chemicals in the factory, but they sell love. Automobile makers combine metal and rubber into a transportation mode but push social status. Similarly, Cuba's tourist commission transformed travel, food, and lodging into romance, adventure, and revelry. By 1925 thousands of tourists scattered dollars among Cuba's hotels, restaurants, shops, and nightclubs, filled the cash boxes at the casino and racetrack, saw the sights from Havana's electric railway or the national railroad lines, and drank the domestic rum and beer. Dozens of them also built luxurious vacation homes in new residential developments. Why should they sail for days, sometimes braving angry seas, to escape cold weather and routine cares in Mediterranean climes when Cuba offered warmth and excitement so much closer to home?

Carlos Manuel de la Cruz, the business partner of Céspedes and Cortina, served as secretary of the tourist commission for several years and then became president, just as the three Cs formed a new enterprise, Compañía de Sports y Fomento del Turismo de la Habana, and bought Oriental Park racetrack from Stoneham. Unfortunately, the trio knew more about real estate than racetracks. Oriental Park deteriorated, and the 1925 racing season was in doubt until John Bowman rescued it. When Bowman agreed to operate the racing concession, horse owners applauded and bettors cheered. He knew the most prominent East Coast horse breeders and could easily persuade many of them to race their horses in Havana. Coming so close to the start of the winter season, the news restored the enthusiasm of government officials, hotel and restaurant owners, real estate investors, taxi drivers, street vendors, and porters—in fact, everyone associated with tourism.

At age fifty, Bowman looked the very image of a romantic redeemer, with his square jaw, eyes marked by lines of frequent laughter, and dark hair turning gray at the temples. Few people could have imagined his life's journey from rural Canada to Havana's Jockey Club. His father had delivered mail by horse—or dog-pulled sled, depending on the season—in the sparsely populated northern reaches of Ontario. When railroads replaced sleds for long-distance postal hauling in the 1890s, they destroyed the family business. Bowman left school and headed for New York, working for a time in a men's clothing store in Yonkers, outside New York City. He traveled a little, worked in tourist hotels and in a riding academy, saved some money, and returned to New York. With two horses and a few dollars for feed, he opened his own riding establishment, catering to an upper-class clientele. The business did poorly, and Bowman willingly locked its doors when Gustav Baumann, the owner of New York's Holland House hotel, offered him a steady job. He worked as the hotel's purchaser of wines and cigars for several years until promoted to personal secretary, where he learned the basics of lodging and restaurant management, advertising, and finance. Baumann built the Biltmore Hotel with Bowman as construction superintendent.

The New York Biltmore opened on New Year's Eve 1913 with Bowman as its vice president. When Gustav Baumann died unexpectedly a few months later, the youthful executive assumed the presidency of one of the city's best hotels. Ambitious and energetic, he bought and sold hotels and began to build the Bowman-Biltmore chain, which eventually stretched into Cuba and across the continent. He opened New York's two-thousand-room Commodore Hotel—the world's largest at the time—in 1919. He built the Atlanta Biltmore in partnership with Coca-Cola's William Candler. For the 1923 opening of the Los Angeles Biltmore, Bowman filled eleven railroad cars with guests and took them across the country to California. He built the Miami Biltmore for George Merrick at Coral Gables and bought another Florida hotel before the bust.

The affable hotelier made friends as fast as he made deals, and he provided for the comfort and amusement of wealthy colleagues and friends in grand style. His six-million-dollar Westchester Biltmore Country Club in Rye, New York, boasted golf courses, tennis courts, polo fields, shooting traps, and a private beach on Long Island Sound. When the club opened for membership in 1922, Bowman's associates gladly enrolled. Many of the same people filled his hotel banquet halls, where they enjoyed Bowman's impeccable hospitality and a showmanship that leaned far in the direction of extravagance. He once brought a circus into the Commodore's grand ballroom, complete with elephants and clowns. He also transformed the Biltmore ballroom into a replica of the Belmont Park racetrack for a party. Twenty or so horses stamped about in facsimile stables while party guests dined and danced.

Horsemen, golfers, and yachtsmen, as well as financiers and captains of industry, might join President Woodrow Wilson or some representative of European royalty when John Bowman entertained. Civic activities had widened his circle of acquaintances to include celebrities in Washington and Europe. Wilson's food administrator, Herbert Hoover, had chosen Bowman to serve as chief of the Hotel, Restaurant, Dining Car, and Steamship Division of the U.S. Food Administration during World War I. In that capacity Bowman had traveled all over the country on a campaign to implement Hoover's slogan, "Food Will Win the War." He had earned accolades from Hoover for his effective performance and decorations from the French and Belgian governments for his altruism.[4] His wartime boss became commerce secretary under Presidents Harding and Coolidge and then president himself, while Bowman added hotels to his company and fostered tourism in Cuba.

John Bowman had launched his hotel and recreation empire in the United States about the same time that Cuba entered the tourism competition. His love of fun and profit—and a little help from the U.S. guardians of rectitude—brought the two together. Legislators passed the Eighteenth Amendment to the Constitution in December 1917. When enough states ratified the measure, Congress gave it teeth with the Volstead Act. On 1 July 1919 the United States legally prohibited the manufacture, sale, or transportation of alcoholic beverages within the country. Bowman publicly lamented the potential impact of Prohibition on his hotel interests and bought Havana's Hotel Sevilla within months of the United States' going dry.[5]

Another self-made North American with a colorful background introduced Bowman to Cuba and the Hotel Sevilla. Charles Francis Flynn came from a middle-class New England family. He had pre-ferred to learn his father's lumber and building trade rather than attend college, and he had picked bustling Florida over his native Massachu-setts to launch a business career. Bowman and Flynn shared a number of characteristics, including an interest in horses and an ability to make leisure profitable. Flynn had left Florida in 1914 and had headed for Havana, where he used his construction experience to supervise the building of Oriental Park for Curly Brown. When the track opened in 1915, Flynn managed its operations. He left that job in 1919 when Brown sold the track to Stoneham. That same year Cubans opened the way for casino gambling, the U.S. Congress closed down the saloons, and Charles Flynn introduced John Bowman to Havana.

Bowman fully appreciated a city that was short of hotel rooms and long on liquor—a perfect combination for a man with wealthy, thirsty friends who could no longer drink openly at his stateside hotels. The Hotel Sevilla, hardly more than twenty years old, its Spanish decor somewhat neglected and shabby, exhibited potential. Bowman hired Flynn to coordinate half a million dollars' worth of renovations, and they opened the Sevilla-Biltmore with great flair in 1920. A few years later Bowman added a ten-story tower to accommodate the crowds of people who had learned about Cuba. Once completed, the 352-room, modern, well-appointed hotel far surpassed any other in the region for luxurious amenities. The Havana hostelry offered such conveniences as long-distance telephone and cable service. Bilingual interpreters met the guests at the docks, took charge of their luggage, and escorted them to the hotel.

Luxury-loving North American guests delighted in the hotel's festive atmosphere. Music accompanied tastefully prepared meals served in elegantly appointed dining rooms. The elite clientele glided smoothly across the polished dance floor and around the potted palms of the rooftop garden that overlooked Havana. They danced to not one but two orchestras, which alternately played popular Cuban and North American music into the early hours of the morning. Then they went to bed in comfort.[6]

Bowman shared the optimism of Cuba's tourism boosters: Havana would be another Riviera or even Paris. Moreover, his associates easily could afford the lots and houses offered by real estate developers in

Miramar and Country Club Park. A "Winter in Cuba" campaign urged North Americans to escape the chill and enjoy Cuba's warm embrace until spring. They would have a wonderful place to stay, the Sevilla-Biltmore, while awaiting the completion of new homes. Meanwhile, the Machado administration would build the roads and pave the streets to transport them to the racetrack and home sites. Bowman's proven business success, as well as his socially prestigious and financially powerful upper-crust hotel patrons, validated the growing perception of tourism as a source of national income, a promising alternative to sugar.

Although critics sometimes grumbled about foreigners who wanted to turn Havana into Atlantic City or Palm Beach, most Cubans in a position to benefit from his contribution welcomed Bowman, his friends, and the profits that his activities generated. Indeed, he assumed the sponsorship of Cuban horse racing because a syndicate of Cubans and North Americans invited him to do so, not because he pushed his way in. He agreed to head the exclusive Jockey Club and to direct track operations, with veteran Charles Flynn as day-to-day manager, and the club's officers looked forward to introductions to his affluent and influential associates. The Bowman-led syndicate leased Oriental Park and the Marianao casino, with an option to purchase, from their Cuban owners: Céspedes, Cortina, and de la Cruz. When Bowman and his partners agreed to pay $300,000 annual rent to the three Cs, the syndicate must have anticipated revenues far in excess of that amount. In fact, nearly forty-five thousand tourists visited Cuba just in the four winter months of December through March 1925–26. With the average per person expenditure figured at three hundred dollars, they left approximately $13.5 million in Cuba.[7]

Bowman, the handsome, confident man of affairs, became the genial host of Oriental Park. He welcomed prominent friends from U.S. business and government circles and greeted new and old Cuban acquaintances. Dressed in white flannel pants, straw hat, and blazer with appropriate pocket handkerchief, or three-piece suit with checked cravat and lapel pin, Bowman posed chummily with public officials and theatrical celebrities, businessmen and bankers, for Jockey Club publicity photos, completely at ease in the company of presidents and prima donnas.

Among the Jockey Club's members, probably none saw more promise in Bowman's leadership than its vice president, Frank Steinhart.

Steinhart loved horses; he and Milton Hershey, the chocolate mogul, often sat together and bet their favorites from the club's terrace. If anyone matched Bowman as a hard-working, upwardly mobile Horatio Alger figure, it was Frank Steinhart. Only twelve when his family left Germany for the United States in its centennial year of 1876, with little formal education, Steinhart read law and added language facilities in English and Spanish to his native German. He joined the army at the age of eighteen, earned the rank of sergeant in the infantry at twenty-five, and then worked as a clerk to a succession of generals in the peacetime army. U.S. entry into the Cuban conflict took him to the island, where he served as chief clerk of General Leonard Wood's military occupation government.

Steinhart remained in Cuba when Wood and the troops pulled out and, as the first U.S. consul general, represented the interests of the North American businessmen who rushed to the island. When U.S. forces returned in 1906, people considered Steinhart the manager behind military governor Charles Magoon—not an illogical assumption. Steinhart knew Havana's business community and its public officials. He parlayed business skills, financial resources, and government contacts into a considerable stake in the Cuban economy and a substantial personal fortune. He had invested in Havana's horse-drawn street railway and later spearheaded its conversion to electricity. Extension of the railway tracks required appropriately placed electric lines and paved streets. Wherever the electric railway went, real estate developments sprouted and land values jumped. Complementarily, urban expansion increased tramway ridership and company revenue.[8]

Steinhart became president of the Havana Electric Railway, Light & Power Company, as well as La Alianza and La Cubana insurance companies. He was vice president of the Compañía Cervecería Internacional, producer of the popular Polar beer. He became the first president of the American Chamber of Commerce in Cuba. All of Steinhart's investments benefited as tourism expanded, and not surprisingly, he worked hard for its promotion. Full-page advertisements in guidebooks urged tourists to take Steinhart's inexpensive, safe streetcars to Marianao, site of the casino, the racetrack, and the country club.[9]

✿

TOURISM AND THE COUNTRY CLUB

The Havana Country Club lured wealthy businessmen to its fairways and greens. The unfamiliar game of golf, introduced by foreign residents (some seventeen thousand merchants, bankers, importers, and professionals), attracted only a handful of Cuban aficionados at first. Most *habaneros* retained their long-held affection for cockfights or indulged more recent attachments to baseball and boxing.

Frederick Snare (of Snare and Triest, General Contractors, New York, Havana, and Buenos Aires) became president of Country Club Realty Company and spearheaded the golfers' efforts in 1911. William Whitner, a prosperous insurance man and real estate investor, accompanied Snare in a site search. The two men scoured the Havana countryside for a suitable location and settled on 125 acres of lovely but neglected rolling hills between the urban center of Marianao and its beaches. The realty company purchased the property and then leased it to the Havana Country Club. The board of directors hired a professional greenskeeper to lay out the course, while the club's organizers sold memberships. The twenty-three golfers who founded the club added twelve hundred prominent Cubans and foreigners to their lists in little more than a decade.[10]

The businessmen-golfers had built the Marianao course to satisfy their longing for a game that they had played at home, not as the anchor for a profitable real estate enterprise. However, as tourists arrived in greater numbers, delighted to played their eighteen holes on a sunny afternoon and to down a friendly, thirst-quenching drink or two on the clubhouse terrace, some perceptive club members saw the investment potential in a skillfully marketed residential development alongside the course. Snare and seventeen of his colleagues, including a lumber merchant, two doctors, an advertising agency executive, along with various real estate, insurance, transportation, contracting, and import interests, formed Country Club Park Investment Company. The firm snapped up 425 acres of picturesque land to the south and west of the golf links, between the clubhouse and the beach and near the casino. Workmen widened a small river that ran through the property, turning the waterway into an appealing natural boundary to separate the estate-sized lots and ensure privacy for their owners. Then landscape architects, trained to see the dormant promise in a muddy pool, converted the stagnant pocket of a sluggish stream into an inviting lagoon where ducks paddled on the water and attractive tropical plants crowded the banks. With preparation of the property underway, the developers targeted wealthy North Americans who could afford expensive winter homes, avid golfers whose stateside links lay idle under the snow between November and April.

Country Club Park Investment Company's carefully prepared sales prospectus pitched Havana's "magic spell" and the "mystic beauty" of moonlit shores. A photo montage displayed to full advantage the imposing clubhouse and terrace, surrounded by royal palms. Smiling visitors lounged, danced, socialized, and watched their friends compete at golf. Golfers on the fairways and bathers in the surf at nearby Marianao beaches enjoyed a paradise only ninety miles south of Key West, Florida. Maps, a company history, and purchase details completed the package. Even *Terry's Guide to Cuba* articulated the development's virtues with a salesperson's flourish, describing for its readers a "manorial" clubhouse and exceptional golf course surrounded by the "most artistically satisfying home sites in all Cuba." The *Guide* thoughtfully provided potential purchasers the name and address of the development's Havana agent.[11]

Indeed, many North American visitors found the loveliness of Marianao, Cuba's warm winters, the country club, racetrack, casino, and beaches irresistible. Country Club Park became the prestigious address for wintering foreigners, who made up one-fifth of the country club membership by 1924. The rather small Spanish mission-style cottage of the New York baking company president George Ward still catches the visitor's eye among the trees near the river, an architectural anomaly by size and form among the magnificent, multistory mansions that surround it.

Not all tourists bought homes, of course, but tourism generated customers who helped change the modest municipality of Marianao into an international playground. The Havana Country Club evolved into an institution, a place where businessmen developed or improved critical contacts with important sources of investment capital. By the mid-1920s membership rolls included a Vanderbilt, an Astor, and a Whitney, George Ward and George Loft from the bakery and candy companies that bore their names, candy man Hershey, Coca-Cola's president Robert Woodruff, and Robert Barr of Chase National Bank. Sugar barons were not excluded, of course; Edwin F. Atkins, whose family had entered Cuban sugar production in the 1880s, became a member. Cuban members included the railroad and sugar mogul Josefa Mariana Tarafa and the attorney Juan Arrellano, who became the government's transport commissioner. As the roster of Cuban members increased, the country club published its bulletins in both Spanish and English, and Cuban golfers regularly paired with North Americans in club championships.[12]

Social interaction at the golf course brought permanent and seasonal foreign residents together with native Cubans in ways that extended beyond business deals and golf matches. In fact, they demonstrated a real spirit of civic concern and activism when they established a school for the club's caddies on country club grounds. As the board of governors expressed it, these young men provided an essential service to the members, who in turn had a duty to turn the mostly illiterate youths into responsible Cuban citizens.

The unusual school opened in 1923, and the club levied a ten-cent fee on each golf card to cover the cost of its operation. The racially integrated student body, varying in number from 150 to 250 at any given time, learned to read and write and studied arithmetic and Cuban history. Although attendance often was spotty, the students could caddy only when teachers confirmed acceptable school performance. The country club's board also saw fit to invite the Brothers of LaSalle to provide moral instruction to this group of youngsters, who typically gambled away paychecks before they reached home.[13] At least some of Havana's poorer youngsters gained access to education and to successful businessmen through the country club's efforts, a unique opportunity for upward mobility.

Meanwhile, newspapers publicized Country Club Park as the most prestigious suburban residential location of the era, and many Cubans became owners of architecturally distinctive homes, ranging in style from classical Greece to vine-covered New England. Carlos Miguel de Céspedes's suitably stately home commanded the entrance to the development. Cuban vice president Carlos de la Rosa's residence stood far back from the street, distinguished by a long veranda and double row of palm trees lining the driveway. Rogelio Carvajal, vice president of Country Club Park Investment Company, selected a choice view site that elevated the house above those of his neighbors. A Spanish tile roof extended beyond the large two-story mansion to cover the porches that embellished both ends; a series of classical twinned columns held aloft the balcony that jutted out from the second story.[14] This house broadcast to all viewers the stature of its owner as a member of the fashionable Cuban elite that danced the Charleston as well as the *danzón* at late-afternoon teas on the country club terrace.

✻

OPTIMISM AND OPPORTUNISM

Skeptical observers of Cuban politics might have marked a contradiction represented by the guests of honor on the first two days of the 1925–26 racing season. Gerardo Machado, the Cuban president who only months earlier had swept into office on a wave of fiery flag-waving, held court on opening day alongside the North American investor John Bowman. On the next day, U.S. bankers, despised by many citizens as agents of Cuba's denationalization, took center stage as honored guests. Machado, six feet tall and an image of strength and power, had campaigned on a platform of economic nationalism, promising to protect domestic industries and to boost Cuban self-sufficiency. His speeches had castigated the United States for its penetration of the Cuban economy and for its pernicious meddling in domestic politics, and the candidate had solemnly promised to protect the Cuban patrimony against foreign incursion. Despite the bravura campaign performance, Machado's business and political career had flourished precisely because of ties to U.S. interests. Once elected, he favored foreign investors, repressed striking workers and dissident students, and fostered massive corruption.[15]

When Machado took office the previous May, Cuba had just concluded an extremely successful tourist season. Optimistic tourist promoters counted on his support as they pushed to expand or begin public works projects. Highway construction, for example, promised to spread the benefits of Havana's tourism to the neighboring provinces of Matanzas and Pinar del Río.[16] Public Works Secretary Céspedes inaugurated construction of a highway to run the length of the island, along with the necessary feeder roads. The central highway, Céspedes's best-remembered and probably his most worthwhile effort, had been on the drawing board for some time when he entered office. Frustrated by wartime delays and lack of revenue after the 1921 sugar crisis, the government finally launched the bidding in September 1925. Although eight of the fourteen competing contractors were Cubans,

the contract (worth at least seventy-five million dollars) went to Warren Brothers of Boston, a little-known company with scarcely any experience in Cuba. Warren Brothers, in turn, subcontracted work in
Matanzas and Santa Clara provinces to a Cuban company in which
Machado had a financial interest and simultaneously borrowed ten
million dollars from Chase National Bank through its Cuban manager, Machado's son-in-law, José Emilio Obregón.[17]

If ever a clever fox guarded a well-stocked henhouse, Céspedes held
a critical position in an administration committed to both massive
public projects and tourism. Together, Machado and Céspedes moved
to beautify Havana and improve Cuba's infrastructure. Machado approved plans for an expensive capitol building (modeled after the one
in Washington), a modern national library, and a handsome new museum. Céspedes took bids on some seven hundred projects—water-
ways, sewers, ports, canals, and road paving. He controlled several
hundred million dollars in contracts. The two men funded their ambitious programs through special revenues, such as automobile, gasoline,
and sales taxes, rather than through regular budget appropriations. To
speed the beneficial effects of job creation—beneficial to both workers
and bestowers of favors—the government issued deferred-payment
work certificates to contractors, so that work began even before revenues accumulated in earmarked accounts.[18] Ordinary Cuban citizens,
foreign investors, and visitors benefited from roads and bridges, sanitation and transportation facilities, and good water. However, few users
of public services reaped rewards as substantial as did Machado's political cronies.

Scarcely half a decade after the sugar crisis, Cuba competed with
Florida for the title of America's Riviera. As tourist money perco-
lated through the economy, Cubans across the social spectrum felt its
effects. Merchants hailed tourist profits. Wages and tips, room rents
and meals, postcard and souvenir purchases multiplied their effectiveness in the domestic economy, turning over as food, shelter, entertainment, and services for Cuban families. The hurricane of 1926 helped,
but most of the credit accrued to Cuba's dreamers and schemers.

Céspedes's sizable green stucco Miramar home, its $200,000 mo-
saic shrine brought from India, was a monument to his entrepreneuri-
alism. It stood above a private landing at the edge of the Almendares
River, at one end of the lovely landscaped boulevard called La Quinta,
or Fifth Avenue. Céspedes had overseen construction of the grand

thoroughfare through the Miramar suburb that he had helped to develop. Its western end reached Céspedes's elegant Country Club Park estate, not far from the Oriental Park racetrack, which his company had purchased in 1921, leased to John Bowman in 1925, and would sell for a substantial profit in 1927. The tempestuous twenties were not yet over.

Chapter 4

Tourism Triumphant

Eight lithe young women formed a circle, alternately facing inward and out, their hands lightly clasped around scarves that linked them without impeding movement. Voluptuous bodies in progressive states of abandon—some clothed, others nude—signaled freedom, joy, even ecstasy. Ready to break the bonds of earthly care, recklessly uninhibited, only their toe tips touched the pedestal on which they stood. One figure, with head flung backward and body arched, lifted her breasts toward the sky.

Though cast in stone, the sensuous libertines of the Bacchante fountain captured the very essence of revelry, saluted by the equally high-spirited celebrants who entered Havana's recently refurbished, undeniably elegant Gran Casino Nacional. Major renovations had been underway through most of 1926. For New Year's Eve, a thousand people, sparkling in formal attire and jewels, chatted with friends in the Gran Casino's lavishly appointed dining room. The impressive array of guests enjoyed cuisine carefully supervised by a French chef and served by French-speaking waiters. Several diners carried the titles of European royalty; others were immediately recognizable from society page photographs. Entertainment celebrities came from Hollywood and New York. Sports figures, businessmen, government officials— Cuban, North American, European—carried themselves with the self-congratulatory assurance of acknowledged achievement. The evening was a glorious success.[1]

Whether or not the patrons played in good luck that night, John Bowman certainly considered himself among the most fortunate of gamblers. His Bowman-Biltmore hotel chain stretched from New York to California and included two hotels in Florida and one in Havana. His investment syndicate had leased the Gran Casino as well as the Oriental Park racetrack operation and had totally renewed the faded gambling facility. On New Year's Eve he greeted the glittering assemblage that graced the opening gala. His plans for Cuba were nothing if not grandiose.

Thousands of Havana's merrymakers gladly toasted 1927 with champagne, an illegal commodity in the United States. They overwhelmed the dining rooms at the best hotels: the Sevilla-Biltmore, Plaza, and Almendares counted at least twelve hundred reservations. Hundreds more dined, danced, and drank at the Yacht Club, Jockey Club, and Country Club. Not all of the revelers were tourists, of course. Fashionable *habaneros*, groups of family and friends, also turned out for the occasion.

Tourists and winter residents had needed little persuasion to make Havana their destination for the 1926–27 holiday season. Sensational descriptions of September's disastrous nine-hour hurricane, in which a thousand Floridians died, had bombarded stateside newspaper readers for days. Storm-related damages had cost Miami almost eighty million dollars. In Cuba, the wind blew the roof off the Oriental Park grandstand and broke a few of its windows, nothing that round-the-clock workmen could not fix in time for December's opening day. Many of Florida's hotels, restaurants, and nightclubs remained shuttered as champagne corks popped in Cuba.[2]

Three new Havana hotels opened in December and January, none too soon for the huge contingent of National Cash Register Company supersalesmen, rewarded for their hard work with a sunny vacation. The "Seeing Havana Intelligently" guide listed and explained the city's historical and cultural highlights, most comfortably and conveniently viewed, it proclaimed, from a hired touring car driven by an English-speaking chauffeur. In the increasingly cosmopolitan city, the wives of National Cash Register's strivers could shop for gowns imported from Paris for their evening at the casino, where the five-dollar dinner included a floor show, dancing, and of course, gambling. By season's end, *habaneros* gloated over their good fortune while Florida's dog and horse track owners totaled their losses and called it quits.[3]

THE PLEASURE TRUST TAKES CENTER STAGE

Satisfied patrons marveled at Bowman's redecorated casino and wagered at his repaired racetrack. Then, at the end of January, Havana extended a rousing welcome to Bowman's good friend—everybody's good friend—Jimmy Walker, the popular mayor of New York City, as he steamed into the harbor, accompanied by Bowman's associate, Charles Flynn. Bowman had hosted his prominent guest at the Miami Biltmore hotel at Coral Gables, which had opened in December, after the hurricane, and greeted him warmly at the Sevilla-Biltmore in Havana. The reception committee for a luncheon in Walker's honor, a mix of high-powered entrepreneurs and public officials, included José Emilio Obregón, President Machado's son-in-law and vice president of the Chase National Bank; Carlos Manuel de la Cruz, member of Congress and president of the tourist commission (one of the three Cs); Manuel Pereira, Havana's acting mayor; Miguel Mariano Gómez, mayor elect and son of former president José Miguel Gómez; Miguel Suárez, vice president of the tourist commission; Guillermo de Zaldo Jr., a prominent banker, real estate developer, golfer, and member of the tourist commission; and General Pablo Mendieta, Havana's chief of police. The police chief's presence represented more than a security measure. After lunch a police escort rushed Walker across Havana to Oriental Park for the races. The following day Walker received the key to the city, attended the races, and dined at the casino. John Bowman paid the bills.[4]

If relaxation and friendly camaraderie appeared to be the only reason for Walker's Havana trip, Monday's activities penetrated the facade. After another luncheon for Cuban businessmen and Bowman's New York associates, the whole group motored the few blocks from the Sevilla-Biltmore to the presidential palace for Walker's official welcome to Cuba. Machado then joined the motorcade, and the whole group traveled out to the suburbs, past the yacht club and the country club in Marianao to the still undeveloped beach area at Jaimanitas. There, the entourage watched as Machado and Walker wielded silver shovels and turned the first dirt for construction of the Havana-Biltmore Yacht and Country Club.[5]

Bowman had organized an investment group for this ambitious business deal even before the hurricane hit Florida, encouraged by record-breaking 1925–26 Oriental Park crowds and the oversubscribed membership and limited guest access at the Havana Country Club. Although Cubans had evidenced scant interest in golf at the time of the club's founding, by 1927 many were proficient at the game and avid players. Together with thousands of foreign golfers, they overflowed the course. The Dixie-Cuba Golf Pilgrimage, for example, left Chicago by train on a cold February morning that year. These pilgrims worshiped at the shrine of the manicured green and could afford to spend five hundred dollars for a golf trip (not including tips, souvenirs, gambling, and other personal expenditures), a sum that equaled several months' salary for ordinary workers.

The dedicated devotees and their spouses stopped at Asheville, North Carolina; Charleston, South Carolina; Savannah, Georgia; and Saint Petersburg and Dunedin, Florida. They played golf in each city, then reboarded and moved on. In Havana these indefatigable golfers added a few other entertainments to their eighteen holes. They dined and danced, checked out the cabarets, learned the fine points of jai alai, and shopped. A sightseeing tour preceded lunch and golf, or horse racing at nearby Oriental Park for nongolfers, followed by dinner and dancing and gambling at the Gran Casino on Saturday night. Sufficiently entertained and relieved of a reasonable cash outlay, the group departed and golfed its way back through Key West, Miami, Palm Beach, and Jacksonville, Florida; Atlanta, Georgia; and Chattanooga, Tennessee.[6]

Bowman, who had built the Westchester Country Club outside New York City, speculated that other "pilgrims" would visit Havana and return often. He expected to complete his seafront golf and sailing club within one year and had bought the good-sized piece of land next to the planned yacht and country club grounds for home sites. He and his partners in the Cuban American Realty Company had purchased fifteen hundred undeveloped acres for the substantial sum of $7.7 million from the Sindicato Territorial de Cuba, whose major partners were Carlos Miguel de Céspedes and José Manuel Cortina. Nationalistic legislators tried to prevent foreigners from buying the prime Cuban land but could do little more than shake angry fists against influence brokers, office holders, and real estate moguls such as Machado, Céspedes, Cortina, de la Cruz, and Bowman.[7]

Cuban American Realty Company spawned the Havana Biltmore Yacht and Country Club Company and the Havana Biltmore Realty Company. Parent companies and subsidiaries listed both Cubans and North Americans among the various interlocking officers and directors. Bowman presided over Cuban American, with Charles Flynn as vice president, Cuban transport commissioner Juan Arrellano as secretary, and Rafael Sánchez as treasurer. New York businessman Thomas Pratt and Cuban tourist official Miguel Suárez served as directors.

The Biltmore Yacht and Country Club named Machado kin José Obregón its "commodore" and tourist official Miguel Suárez its treasurer. Two members of the investment/banking/real estate Mendoza clan (father Claudio and six sons) — Fernando and Nestor — were secretary and vice secretary. (Nestor often entertained friends at the Jockey Club with impressions of Broadway stars George M. Cohan and Eddie Cantor.) Alberto Mendoza was a director, along with Machado's friend and political supporter Henry Catlin, the land baron José Gómez Mena (Joseph Barlow's foe in his Havana land fight), the banker Guillermo de Zaldo Jr., and Juan Arrellano. The contracting company of Arrellano and Mendoza supervised construction of the yacht club, first blasting away the shoreline's coral and replacing it with fine sand. When completed, the palatial structure rose above the beach, its wide archways separated by ornate columns, a broad stairway sweeping from the veranda down to the beautiful expanse of white sand. Empty land for future home sites stretched from the club to a roadway in the distance. Palm trees lined the fairways on the nearby golf course. Sand traps interrupted the greens, but no obstruction interfered with the golfer's breathtaking view of the Gulf of Mexico.[8]

The audacious investors projected nothing less than the world's grandest resort, with its own casino and seafront hotel, and vowed to transform Havana into the Riviera of the western hemisphere. Bowman returned to New York after the February groundbreaking but reappeared in March to approve the golf course design and, more importantly, to escort various dignitaries on personal tours of the new property. U.S. vice president Charles Gates Dawes and his wife enjoyed several days as Bowman's guests at the Hotel Sevilla-Biltmore. Mr. and Mrs. Channing Cox basked under his special attention, as did Hugh L. Arson. Hardly your average American tourists, Cox had succeeded Calvin Coolidge in the Massachusetts governor's chair when Coolidge became president, and Arson was vice president of Sundstrand, a major corporation headquartered in the Chicago area. His guests were potential buyers at Biltmore, well worth an investment of time and money to cultivate their interest.

Meanwhile, the Jockey Club, over which Bowman presided, hosted Kentucky Day at Oriental Park, where Kentucky horse owners could legally drink to the health of their state—famous for its bourbon as well as its horses. Bowman moved smoothly through the world of millionaire businessmen and heads of state. A dealmaker, facilitator, and catalyst, he felt as much at home in Havana as in New York or Washington. He shamelessly but charmingly wooed Sevilla-Biltmore patrons as potential residents of Havana-Biltmore. A most obliging host, he gallantly guided his wealthy clientele around the hotel, racetrack, and casino. He even posed for a publicity photograph at the beach, clad in swim trunks, one hand on his hip, all smiles as Mrs. Henry Anderson Gorman, also in a bathing suit, sat astride a bullock—much to the amusement of the grinning Cuban who stood nearby, probably the animal's owner.[9] Cuba most assuredly amused the tourists, but well-to-do North Americans acting like peasants no doubt entertained the Cubans too.

Six months after Bowman and his group of Havana bankers and businessmen inaugurated the Havana-Biltmore venture with great fanfare, they called the journalists together for another announcement. Instead of its original fifteen hundred acres, Cuban American Realty Company now owned two thousand acres, stretching across nearly five miles of ocean front. Moreover, the Bowman-controlled Cuban National Syndicate had exercised its 1925 lease option and had purchased the racetrack and casino. Céspedes and Cortina sold Oriental Park and the Gran Casino Nacional to the syndicate, along with La Playa, the stretch of beach just east of the Havana Yacht Club. The price of the enhanced resort package had climbed from $7.7 million for the original land purchase to $12 million for the package. To accommodate anticipated crowds, the syndicate tripled the seating capacity of the Jockey Club terrace, doubled the size of its restaurant facility, and added a room for gambling. A dozen men worked straight through from Sunday night to Tuesday morning to add seven hundred square feet for the roulette parlor during the weekly off-day at the track to avoid loss of revenue.

The new bathing pavilion at La Playa beach included a thousand cabanas, and the loggia for al fresco dining to the accompaniment of live music contributed to a pleasant afternoon at the shore. Bowman barraged potential buyers with publicity for the Biltmore Yacht and Country Club. With his usual ebullience, his ads trumpeted Cuba as a wonder drug for fatigued executives: SOME DAY BILTMORE-HAVANA WILL BE PRESCRIBED BY PHYSICIANS.[10]

The three Cs, early believers in the prospects of Marianao and tourism, had built their foresight and influence into substantial fortunes. For putting together the most costly real estate deal ever made on the island, Bowman and his syndicate partners—most of them Cubans— earned the pejorative designation of "pleasure trust." The word "trust" telegraphed a familiar political message: powerful men combined to dominate an economic sector. Cubans had learned a lot about trusts when U.S. refiners joined together to control the market and prices for Cuban sugar. They had squeezed Cuban producers and used their political clout to influence U.S. tariff schedules.

In the case of the pleasure trust, however, the term is both apt and misleading. Apt because the biggest, best-known, and potentially most profitable tourist attractions had been brought together under the control of the Cuban National Syndicate, an entity with strong financial backing and political power. The syndicate had advisedly included José Obregón, with his connections to both Chase National Bank and President Machado, among its prime movers. On the other hand, a trust of tourism developers necessarily operated differently from sugar importers. That is, the Bowman group intended to increase tourism in Cuba, not limit Cuba's market to the advantage of U.S. competitors. By making Cuba more attractive, Bowman's group enhanced the incentive of winter vacationers to visit his facilities in both Florida and Cuba and, moreover, to buy homesites in the new development at Jaimanitas. The syndicate profited, of course, but so did the ancillary service and commercial sectors in Cuba, where foreigners spent their money. Furthermore, since the tourist market travels to the producer, the product is not subject to tariffs. The more desirable Cuba became and the more tourists flocked to the island, the more profit for both the trust and Cuba.

Both sugar and tourist consortia wielded political muscle as necessary, of course, and high-level government officials gave them every consideration. For example, when revenues from Machado's special public works fund fell short, syndicate members encouraged U.S. banks to lend money to the Cuban government to advance the central highway. The highway was the keystone of Céspedes's ambitious program of civic improvement and a treasure trove of patronage, as well as a critical factor in tourism's geographical expansion. Céspedes, who had reaped enormous profits from the sale of various properties to Bowman and his partners, completed the broad boulevard that connected Biltmore to Fifth Avenue in Miramar—which in turn connected to the Malecón—just in time for the opening of Bowman's new golf course and yacht club in 1928.

Although the tourist industry demonstrated great potential in 1927, Cuba still depended on sugar for its economic well-being. The official in charge of sugar negotiations with the United States arguably occupied the most critical position in the government, other than the president. Presidential secretary Viriato Gutiérrez held that responsibility under Machado. Gutiérrez fashioned the country's sugar agreements in Washington, where he pressured for favorable tariffs and a guaranteed market share. An extraordinarily capable man and a tenacious bargainer, he labored to beat the U.S. sugar trust with one hand and manipulated pleasure trust aspirations with the other.

The office of presidential secretary had advanced in responsibility and stature under Machado's predecessor Alfredo Zayas, when three Cs partner Cortina held the post. Under Machado's governmental reorganization scheme, reputedly instituted to clean house after the corruption of Zayas's last years in office, the presidential secretary became a virtual czar over government contracts. That is, all government purchases—from food for public institutions to electrical goods for government offices, from boots for the army to medicines for hospitals—passed from lower-level offices in the various ministries up through the bureaucracy by means of recommendation to a Tribunal Superior de Subastas, a board set up to select winning contract bidders. The tribunal operated under Gutiérrez's authority. Thus, in the guise of a reformist watchdog function, Machado centralized both government purchasing procedures and the potential collection of bribes. The openly proclaimed award criterion—the best result for the interests of the state—gave the tribunal great latitude. When the Cuban National Syndicate gained control over five miles of Cuban seacoast, some of which belonged to Céspedes and Cortina and some of it to the government, the deal passed through Gutiérrez's hands. In the process, he acquired a stretch of beachfront adjacent to the Biltmore development, land certain to appreciate in value as the new resort prospered.[11] Bowman's project clearly served the interests of the state, and Gutiérrez benefited as well.

TOURISM AND POLITICAL LEGITIMACY

The 1926 hurricane was not the only force that battered Cuba during the 1920s. The sugar crash had knocked the economy askew on its foundation. Then, university students challenged educational leaders and unleashed a fiercely nationalistic reform movement. Militant laborers demanded higher wages and better working conditions and effected work stoppages to demonstrate their power. Dissidents protested Cuba's unequal distribution of wealth, praised the Russian revolution, and joined the international struggle on behalf of the masses. Afro-Cubans confronted authorities who had turned their backs on long-standing grievances, most painfully the crushing social restrictions and lack of opportunity for people of color. Intellectuals called for uplifted cultural standards to correct a perceived lack of national cohesion.

Unquestionably a milestone in Cuban tourism, 1927 was a pivotal political year as well. Although Machado had taken office in 1925 vowing to protect national interests and cleanse government, corruption continued and foreigners wielded influence at the highest level of power. With presidential elections scheduled for 1928, talk of constitutional changes to permit Machado's continued leadership began to circulate in political circles early in 1927. Some people dreaded the potential disruption of contested elections. Others stood to profit from Machado's policies, lauded his achievements, and wanted him to stay in office. A nascent manufacturing sector welcomed protective tariffs; commercial, real estate, and construction interests benefited from the growth of tourism; and the government poured money into public works.

In April the Cuban Congress formally called for an extension of the presidential term. Legislation to prolong both presidential and congressional terms passed the Cuban Senate in June. A spokesperson for New York bankers assured Machado of continued support: "We care nothing about the method adopted to assure you of continued service, but will welcome the continuation of your administration."[12] A convention stacked in Machado's favor indeed amended the constitution and set the next elections for May 1935.

Many Cubans decried the prorogation as a violation of the public trust. Constitutional procedures in place at the time of the 1924 election required the president to face the electorate after four years. Now a clique of Machado supporters bypassed the public will. When opponents mobilized to challenge Machado's extended rule, the president responded with repressive force, a tactic that he used with increasing regularity and that he justified as the responsible actions of a head of state faced with a disorderly population.

While some Cubans battled the winds of change, others sailed into the gale, relishing an atmosphere of excitement. Members of the pleasure trust, for example, enjoyed positions as political insiders, while a government under increasing pressure and questionable legitimacy reaped the subtle, supportive benefits that accrued to an international playground. Press reports in 1927 of assassinated labor leaders and brutality and persecution of workers did little damage to a tourist industry patronized by royalty, business moguls, foreign officials, clerks, mechanics, Shriners and Rotary Club conventioneers, dowagers, movie stars, and horsemen.[13] In fact, the 1927–28 season clearly thrust Havana into the realm of chic destinations for status-conscious and fun-loving tourists. Counter to more recent experiences in which tourists avoid vacationing in places where potential unrest threatens their ability to enjoy themselves, visitors to Cuba arrived in greater numbers.

High-visibility tourism often serves significant political agendas. The Olympic games, for example, afford an opportunity to display a country's attributes before the entire world. Perhaps most importantly, when the event has proceeded peacefully to its conclusion, the government will have demonstrated its ability and authority to rule. Thousands of exhilarated visitors who return to their homes with enthusiastic reports of good food, comfortable hotels, polite and helpful service personnel, and beautiful surroundings become publicists for the tourist destination and unwitting emissaries for the government. Similarly, cultural festivals and historic commemorations serve as both tourist attractions and props for patriotism. Moreover, travel and sports writers are not political correspondents. Invited to tour a country or cover an event, all expenses paid, they generally write favorable articles emphasizing positive and pleasurable experiences. Wide dissemination of information about a nation's attractions also appeals to potential investors.[14]

Thus governments employ tourism in various ways to gain legitimacy among their own constituents and abroad. Foreigners who feel personally secure and praise a country's amenities, who spend money and provide employment for local residents, justify government expenditures on tourism, even if some of the money is siphoned into the pockets of corrupt politicians. Even harsh repression of political dissidents and labor activists can be — must be — tolerated, because tourists prefer peaceful surroundings and docile workers.

Casual observers most certainly never grasped the importance of the tourist industry to Machado's presidency. When Machado and Ricardo Dolz, former senate president and horsebreeder, headed to Oriental Park's paddock in March 1928 alongside pleasure trust executive Charles Flynn, Cuban Electric Company's Henry Catlin, and Tropical Brewery owner Julio Blanco Herrera (whose beer gardens were an understandably popular tourist attraction in the Prohibition era), the group signaled political power. Although Machado's horse King David finished a close second in the Casino Nacional handicap that day, his triumph came as the cameras turned to a Jockey Club full of notables. Photographers focused on Prince Francisco Rospuli of Rome; Lady Diana Manners, the daughter of the duke of Roxbury; the New York socialites Mrs. Vincent Astor and William Rhinelander; and Otto Kahn, a financier and sponsor of the Metropolitan Opera.[15]

Although Cuba's peak tourist years of 1927–30 accompanied problematic constitutional changes and increased use of force against identified government enemies, thousands of North Americans saw only a well-run country boasting modern amenities. Prominent visitors enjoying themselves conferred approval on a government that many constituents criticized. The New Year's Eve crowds greeted 1928 with joy and good cheer and shook themselves awake in time for the races. The Jockey Club overflowed with stylish fans. Arguably the outstanding headturner that day, Mrs. Frank Hecht arrived at Oriental Park stunningly outfitted in matching coat, purse, and shoes made of Alpina water snake skin, oblivious, of course, to her political utility as she posed for the photographers.

Other prominent holiday season pleasure seekers—all potential Machado publicists—included the respected publisher of the *Atlanta Constitution*, the president of General Outdoor Advertising Company (whose billboards booked one hundred million dollars' worth of advertising yearly), and the world's largest manufacturer of silk. The well-known sculptor Mrs. Harry Payne Whitney, commissioned to do a statue of the late Theodore Roosevelt, relaxed at the races. The radio star Lambdin Kay, "the voice of the south," honeymooned at the Sevilla-Biltmore.[16]

However resplendent, the New Year's crowds were merely the warm-up act. Calvin Coolidge was January's main event. In response to Machado's personal invitation, President Coolidge had agreed to open the sixth Pan American Conference. As the Cuban publicity machine cranked into action in anticipation of the media-capturing event, a dozen young, talented, and beautiful singers and dancers embarked on a thirty-six-city tour of the United States to perform in a show titled simply "Havana." Backed up by attractive scenic repesentations of Havana's casino and jai alai *frontón*, the dancers introduced a hot new number, "La Jota Tangoette," to frost-nipped audiences at New York's Paramount theater and then repeated their warm greetings in equally frigid Chicago, Cleveland, Baltimore, Kansas City, and Washington, DC. Hotel signs in each city asked, "Why Don't You Go to Havana?"

Meanwhile, in Havana erotic Celinda performed her sinuous belly dance in the Spanish-tiled and tropically planted Sevilla-Biltmore patio, undulating before the cameras of a Fox Movietone newsreel crew. Movie theaters all over the United States screened Celinda's performance in time for the conference opening. In Chicago, a one-hour "Tour to Havana, Cuba" rode the radio waves on the night before Coolidge disembarked at Havana harbor. Many of the reporters who accompanied the president to the hemispheric meeting no doubt arrived positively disposed toward the city.[17]

The conference gave Cuba's leadership an unparalleled opportunity to impress foreigners with its achievements. Press courtship and careful preparation paid off handsomely. *New York Times* coverage extolled Havana's cleanliness, efficiency, and friendliness. The *Times* correspondent suggested that New York's mayor might take a few lessons, or even hire the head of Cuba's public works operation, a certain Sr. Céspedes, who most people thought would probably succeed Machado as president.[18] Such praise from North America's most prestigious newspaper was little short of a benediction for the island and its government.

While polo matches and aviation exhibitions entertained conference delegates, members of the press visited tobacco farms, sugar mills, and cement factories. The naval academy showed off its nautical skills. Art expositions and excursions to the imposing Bellamar caves demonstrated Cuba's cultural and natural attractions. Pan American Airways captured press attention, too, timing its inaugural Key West–Havana flight to coincide with the conference. Coolidge and Machado helped to publicize the new route when they greeted Pan Am president Juan T. Trippe at Camp Columbia's airfield. Secretary Céspedes gave the principal welcoming address on behalf of the grateful Cubans.[19] The significance could hardly be missed. Pan American Airways intended to link the hemisphere through the very latest mode of transportation, and Cuba stood at the cutting edge. Havana's early and well-publicized entry into the new era of commercial aviation reinforced the city's image as a major hemispheric capital.

The public relations bonanza satisfied all expectations. Among the many journalists who covered the conference and spread the Cuban message, few could match the impact of the popular satirist Will Rogers. Rogers acknowledged a huge ovation when he was introduced at Oriental Park's Pan American Day festivities, and his syndicated stories placed Havana's attributes under the very noses of opinion makers and the general public in many cities.

January's Pan American conference and presidential handshakes captured headlines around the globe, but February's public relations coup swept *habaneros* into a real frenzy. On 8 February trains left the central Havana street corner of Zanja and Galiano every ten minutes for the trip to Camp Columbia. Exuberant throngs paid the five-cent fare and carried their Lindy dolls to cheer as everyone's hero, the transAtlantic flyer Charles A. Lindbergh, the Lone Eagle, landed at the airfield. During his five-day visit to promote Pan American Airways' new air connection to Havana, Lindbergh graciously accepted greetings from Machado at the presidential palace and then took the head of state aloft for a demonstration flight around the city. The Hotel Almendares staged a gala aviation night in Lindbergh's honor, attended by members of the city's government and business elite. Glowing newspaper reports and photos captured the enthusiastic crowds as they clamored to be near the daring aviator who had flown solo across the Atlantic the previous year. When Lindbergh departed on 14 February, both reporters and admirers breathlessly followed his nonstop, fifteen-hour journey to Saint Louis, Missouri.[20]

The romantic image of the dashing pilot overlay equally romantic visions of Havana, while its air travel facilities confirmed the city's modernity and technical competence. Vacationers could escape from stress and routine, stay in touch by telephone, and return quickly if needed at home. Businessmen could invest with confidence in a country with such obviously effective and efficient governance. Cuba and Pan American Airways staged another important media event the following year when the first lady of flying, Amelia Earhart, opened the airline's new terminal at Havana's airport. Invitees greeted Earhart at a festive luncheon at the Sevilla-Biltmore, where, with the press in attendance, Pan American executives announced a new Miami–Puerto Rico route with stops in the Cuban cities of Havana, Camagüey, and Santiago. They labeled the new schedule a breakthrough for tourism outside the capital and lauded the increased demand for air service between the two countries, while reporters scribbled on their note pads.[21]

EXPANDED OPPORTUNITIES

While Machado presided over public ceremonies, John Bowman greeted his own celebrated guests. He personally welcomed the chemicals magnate Irénée DuPont and his wife to the Sevilla-Biltmore. DuPont shared Bowman's vision of Cuba as a world-class pleasure center, but while Bowman moved tourists to beaches near his resort and residential development west of Havana, DuPont turned eastward. He was converting a neglected spit of sand and rock at Varadero (in neighboring Matanzas province) into an exclusive resort.

Encouraged by travel guides and brochures, more tourists had begun to venture beyond Havana. Three decades before Walt Disney turned name recognition into a profitable tourist attraction, Milton Hershey had invited visitors to tour the facility in Cuba that produced thousands of tons of sugar for his chocolate factory at Hershey, Pennsylvania. A short, pleasant excursion on the Hershey Electric Railway took them to the Hershey sugar mill in Matanzas province. A model town built next to the mill featured theaters, dancing pavilions, an amusement park, and baseball field. Tourists could stay at the Hershey Hotel for six dollars, room and board, or rent one of the two hundred bungalows located in the lushly planted tropical park next to the town.[22] Both Hershey and DuPont positioned themselves to good advantage. As the central highway pushed eastward, the prospects for tourism within motoring distance of the capital increased. By 1931 Ford station-wagon-type buses and Packard touring cars left Havana hourly for a fifteen-dollar, seventeen-hour, island-long trip to Santiago, with multiple stops in between.

For week after glorious week Cuba entertained visitors, who arrived in record-breaking numbers. George Willets, a vice president of Chicago's major meat packer, Armour and Company, played the new Havana-Biltmore golf course. A good real estate prospect for Bowman, Willets could tell his friends about the joys of eighteen scenic holes under bright blue skies overlooking the Gulf of Mexico. His praise probably reached Lake Michigan even before members of an Illinois Chamber of Commerce delegation returned from their February cruise to Havana and the Caribbean. Most visitors hurried down steamship ramps, while a few more adventurous or time-conscious types tried new seaplane and airplane routes. Because so many ships competed in the lucrative New York–Havana route, the Ward Line invested ten million dollars in two new, faster luxury liners that promised to cut run time from seventy-two to sixty hours for the trip. For midwestern tourists, five trains of the Illinois Central Railroad left Chicago daily in the winter months and collected passengers all along the route to New Orleans, where they boarded ships headed for Cuba. The New Dixie Flyer and Dixie Limited trains sped travelers from Chicago, Saint Louis, and other points to Key West for the shorter ninety-mile shipboard ride to Havana. The Pennsylvania Railroad's thousands of travelers read about Havana vacations in paid advertisements on its dining car menu cards.[23]

In the four years between July 1928 and July 1932, Cuba's nearly six hundred thousand tourists included Boy Scouts, doctors, teachers and students on summer holiday, sports figures, scientists, lawyers, salesmen, socialites, honeymooners, and families, enticed by bigger and more sophisticated advertising campaigns, improved access, and more extravagant entertainment. An extended winter season—November through April, rather than December through March—provided the bulk of tourist revenue, but as more conventioneers and middle-class vacationers heard about Havana, they wanted to see the place for themselves and took advantage of cheaper summer rates.

U.S. Chevrolet dealers held their second annual gathering in Cuba at the instigation of Lawrence Ross, the city's major General Motors distributor. The previous year Ross had gathered ninety General Motors subagents from around the island into the Ross Cadillac Company building in Havana, where visiting General Motors officers gave them a pep talk. Ross used this connection to GM's Detroit headquarters to pull the prestigious 1929 meeting to Cuba. The motivational speaker for the occasion was Carlos Miguel de Céspedes, who used the occasion to extoll Cuba's cross-island highway system, which clearly would increase automobile sales when completed. Not only did the Chevy conventioneers contribute their share to the Cuban economy during their stay, but they returned to their respective homes ready to spread Céspedes's optimistic message in casual conversations or through customer banter.

Some conventioneers took their money to Havana and left their inhibitions at home. Shriners invaded the Cuban capital after their annual meeting in Miami and treated an astonished and sometimes bewildered citizenry to a peculiar slice of North American life. *Habaneros* gawked while adults, businessmen for the most part, cavorted on the streets like children, pranksters at play. What must they have thought when groups of grown men in little red hats filled their streets with exuberant antics? Cuban families on Sunday picnics often brought phonographs from home for an afternoon or evening of dancing at Julio Blanco Herrera's beer garden, but the boisterous refugees from stateside Prohibition drank lots of the Tropical Gardens' brew and then sang and frolicked, most likely provoking stares and comments. After the Shriners' animation, visiting Elks appeared so serious that some Cubans mistook them for Canadians. However, those big teeth hanging from watchchains certainly merited a second look. Perplexed though they might have been, Cubans nevertheless understood the significance of an estimated $250,000 left in Havana's hotels, restaurants, and shops.[24]

Hundreds of new businesses and jobs catered to visitors' needs, while established firms flourished. Enterprising peddlers roamed the streets and created their own market niches. New restaurants offered

French, Italian, and Hungarian fare; two eateries even cooked home-style, kosher Jewish food to accommodate the needs of the varied clientele. Thirsty travelers relished the cool refreshment of ice cold beer during and after a day's sightseeing. The Tropical and Tivolí breweries had their own bottle factories and produced 770,000 bottles of beer in ten hours and 840 tons of ice daily by 1929. The Polar brewery built a new ice factory that year, increasing production from 100 to 626 tons daily. Its huge beer garden, featuring one area done in a Japanese motif, one Spanish, and one typically Cuban, drew foreign as well as Cuban customers, and the company used some of its increased revenue to build a children's park and a football stadium. The Bacardí rum company (which also brewed beer under the Hatuey label) built a new million-dollar headquarters building in downtown Havana.[25]

Opportunity sometimes knocked at the wrong door. Al Capone, the notorious Chicago-based mobster, opened a poolroom in tourist-rich Marianao in 1928 but closed it rather quickly and left with the cryptic parting message that Cuba offered no field for his "particular class of business." Maybe Marianao did not need another poolhall; Cubans had played billiards long before Capone arrived. On the other hand, the bootlegger must have had a different enterprise in mind. Intense police scrutiny rather than a poor business climate may have sent him packing.[26]

Capone's experience notwithstanding, myriad legitimate profitable possibilities inspired imaginative entrepreneurs. Lawyers offered advice to Americans on Cuban divorce laws, for example, and doctors advertised their expertise in genito-urinary medicine—specifically, the treatment of syphillis—in newspapers and magazines read by tourists. A "refined" young woman declared her willingness to accompany shoppers through old Havana's maze of commercial enterprises and claimed that her service paid for itself in money not squandered on deceitful shop owners. While many Cubans offered to teach Spanish to Americans, the Cuban merchant José Caseláns tendered a better proposal: he desired to meet an English-speaking lady for the purpose of matrimony.[27]

Habaneros rented rooms in their homes to visitors, and stores rented furniture to long-term tourists who preferred apartments to hotels. So many independent street vendors hawked neckties, knives, beads, and souvenirs that local merchants wanted to license and tax these competitors. Photo studios sold souvenir portraits, film, and photo albums.

Havana, the "Paris of the Antilles," scarcely resembled its namesake in 1923, but travel writers were paid to promote. Travel, December 1923, 8.

Travel magazines portrayed Havana as "quaint" and "foreign" and proved it with photos of street vendors and narrow streets. Travel, above
November 1928, 10;
below
November 1925, 8.

The popular roof garden of the Sevilla-Biltmore Hotel (right) overlooked the Prado and much of Havana. Cuba Review, September 1927, cover.

Spirited maidens of the Bacchante fountain welcomed players at the Gran Casino Nacional. Pan American Union, Bulletin.

The Jockey Club (left) separated the upper classes from the mass of racing fans in the grandstand. Cuba Review, *January 1929, 18.*

The stylish La Playa beach resort belonged to the pleasure trust in the late 1920s. Cuba Review, *March 1929, American Photo Studio.*

Carlos Miguel de Céspedes built Fifth Avenue through Miramar to Marianao, location of the country club, yacht club, racetrack, and casino. Cuba Review, *May 1929, American Photo Studio.*

The ruffled costumes of rumba dancers represented the music and gaiety of Cuba in many tourist brochures. Holiday, December 1952, 69.

Satisfied tourists at
Sloppy Joe's bar, Havana, 1951.
Saturday Evening Post, *31 March 1951, 25.*

Dancers entertained at Sans Souci
nightclub, 1953, where tourists
complained about crooked games
in the casino. Saturday Evening
Post, *28 March 1953, 33, photo by*
Frank Ross.

The Look *magazine photo of Castro's guerrillas skinning a snake for dinner was not the image of Cuba that Fulgencio Batista preferred.* Look, *4 February 1958, 25, photo by Andrew St. George.*

Vendors of postcards, cigars, perfumes, Panama hats, and trinkets earned their living from tourists. The Bazar Inglés carried mantillas, fans, and embroidery. La Belle France offered fine jewelry; Spanish shawls at B. G. Canevares's shop sold for thirty to ninety dollars, a considerable sum in the 1920s. For a less expensive gift, La Casa del Perro sold alligator-leather slippers for two dollars a pair. La Flor de Tokio stocked Asian curiosities, as did La Mariposa, Cuba's largest Chinese store and the place to buy silk goods and kimonos as well as French perfumes. Snider's Antique Store sold furniture and knicknacks (possibly the former possessions of Spaniards who had returned home after independence). Lucerna sold Swiss chocolate. Cecilio Fernández was Havana's exclusive agent for Vigny perfumes of Paris, manufacturer of Le GolliWogg, a favorite fragrance of the time. A music store suggested recorded Cuban songs as the perfect remembrance of a wonderful trip. Tailors offered rapid service for custom-made shirts; opticians replaced lost or broken eyeglasses. A ceramics manufacturer packed and shipped artistic flowerpots and glazed tiles anywhere in the United States for visitors who shopped at his factory. A well-known Cuban race car driver helped to inaugurate the Drive Yourself Garage auto rental company, which placed its agents in most of the big hotels by 1929.[28]

Tourism supported workers who manufactured, transported, and installed goods, as well as bookkeepers who did the paperwork. Seasonal residents, for example, constituted a market for household furnishings; insurance agents sold foreign homeowners protection from losses due to burglary and theft in their absence; warehousemen and shippers packed and shipped household items back to the United States or stored them until the following winter. Hotels and restaurants hired clerks, bellhops, room cleaners, switchboard operators, custodians, cooks, waiters, musicians, entertainers, bartenders, and laundresses, not to mention the thousands of masons, plumbers, electricians, painters, and so on, who built and maintained the facilities. When the Park View Hotel opened, for example, Havana's Independent Electric Company installed the fixtures and sold the lamps and lightbulbs. Manuel Alfonso's factory made the furniture, and the Cuban division of Simmons Mattress Company furnished mattresses and pillows.[29]

Shipping lines needed more dockworkers to load and unload baggage. Tour guides, coach drivers, and interpreters worked for operators of sightseeing excursions and transportation companies. A "high-class" rural hotel advertised for an attractive woman, about thirty years old,

with some ability as a singer and pianist, to act as a hostess. Golf courses
hired caddies and groundskeepers; the racetrack employed grooms,
stable boys, ticket takers, and people who manned betting windows;
casinos needed croupiers and cashiers. Retail stores hired more clerks
to accommodate the crowds as cruise ships turned thousands of people
loose for a day or two of shopping and sightseeing before they moved
on. El Encanto, Havana's premier department store, employed more
than one thousand people in 1927, and management boasted that its
fixed prices prevented the embarrassment of an "unwitting purchase
from unscrupulous dealers," a slap at the owners of small stores who
might charge whatever the transient traffic would pay.[30]

This compilation does not begin to exhaust the job possibilities that
grateful Cubans, perhaps thrown out of work by a stagnating sugar sector, could attribute to the relentless efforts of the quasi-official tourist
commission. Winter residents swelled the number of cooks, servants,
gardeners, drivers, and handymen needed to perform personal and
household services. Since money changed hands in the form of tips as
well as wages, no exact formula could calculate all of the advantages
created by tourists' consumption of goods and services.

As more North Americans came to know Cuba, business and real
estate agents extended services and expertise to visitors who saw in
Cuba a potential market for their manufactured goods, or who considered Havana's real property a better bet than the casino's roulette
wheels. A certain Sr. López, for example, advertised for American
partners with capital to develop copper, lead, and manganese mines.
Several Cubans sought to sell their hotels to Americans who might be
entranced by Cuba's ambience and its potential. One central Havana
hotel owner with a busy bar and an abundant American clientele held
out a promise to some lucky buyer "to get in on the ground floor of
Havana's growth as the resort city of the Americas." [31]

The tourist gamble paid off in profits and benefited a population
beyond investors. Havana's business community and work force increasingly depended on tourism profits to replace customers and jobs
lost in economically crippled, sugar-dependent rural areas. With new
roads and highways, tourist expansion promised to spread Havana's
prosperity outward. Travel writers, invited by the government, lauded
the history, culture, and unique features of Cuba's interior. Tobacco
farms and other typical agricultural enterprises became stops on sightseeing tours. Entrepreneurs turned long-neglected mineral baths into

inviting spas. Hotels, restaurants, and beach development stretched out alongside the incrementally completed highway. Formerly isolated farmland became valuable residential and commercial proper-
ties close to transportation. For a tourist interested in Cuban land, $12,500 cash bought a thousand acres of pasture and coffee land in Santa Clara province, not yet reached by the highway. Closer to the capital, a picturesque 260-acre farm near the highway promised a "pleasure estate" with 30 acres already subdivided to accommodate residential development. With $50,000 down, the balance could be paid in easy terms.[32]

An understandable self-satisfaction characterized the men who had promoted the new economic sector. Their triumph had put Cuba in the forefront of world-class resorts. Cubans and their North American partners traded business information and shared leisure time at the casino, the golf course, or the Jockey Club. They shared profits and satisfactions. If a few threatening shadows crossed the congenial atmosphere, if political tensions bubbled below the surface, if workers struck and students demonstrated, they failed to dampen the optimism and conviviality of the pleasure trust.

Chapter 5

Manufactured Traditions and Cultural Transformations

Under an uncharacteristic, almost perversely cloud-covered Cuban sky, dusky tribal warriors energetically invoked the favors of a seemingly reluctant sun god. Well-built young men, bare-chested but covered from waist to thigh by loosely woven fiber skirts, danced on sandaled feet before a beautiful young maiden seated aloft on a throne. As they twisted and stamped, long dark braids of hair bounced to and fro. Colored headbands held the braids close to the scalp, alongside faces painted in somber colors. Chanting obscure supplications to the deity, they brandished weapons—longbows or machetes—and moved rhythmically toward the place where the Daughter of the Sun presided over the choreographed ceremony. Meanwhile, curious onlookers crowded the stretch of sand between the Havana Yacht Club and the surf. Mostly North Americans, fully clothed and too absorbed in the action to notice the sand that seeped into their shoes, they craned their necks to catch every nuance of the pageant unfolding before their eyes on that March afternoon in 1930. Later in the day several dozen of the spirited young watchers paraded through the nearby streets in the latest bathing costumes. Modern sun worshipers, they warmed to the appreciative applause of friendly onlookers. Despite the scarce sunshine, the day fulfilled its promise: everyone had a wonderful time.[1]

It mattered little that the captivating sun dance, billed as a reenactment of an ancient ritual once practiced by aboriginal Siboney Indians, had no basis in Cuban history. The island's indigenous population had succumbed to disease and harsh treatment in the first years of colonization, and Cubans of the 1920s knew little about the practices and rituals of the long-dead, peaceful shore dwellers. The Siboneys (or Ciboneys) wore no clothing, although they did paint their bodies and used bones and stones for adornment. Their coarse, straight black hair hung freely, not braided, next to light copper-colored (not dark-skinned) faces. The ancient fishermen certainly did not wield machetes, the sharp, broad, metal cutting tools introduced by Europeans in the sixteenth century. Furthermore, no evidence existed that Siboneys worshiped the sun. Though they buried artifacts with their dead in ritual fashion, none vaguely resembled solar images. The conquering Spaniards had replaced native laborers with Africans, whose mixed-race offspring differed dramatically in body size and skin tone from the pre-Columbian population. The dark-skinned pseudo-warriors of 1930, borrowed from the National Theater, descended from those African slaves sent to work on the island's sugar plantations. Never mind; the tourists loved this invented diversion.

Contrived entertainment? Blatantly and unapologetically so. If London and Pamplona promoted palace guards and stampeding bulls, Havana could entice visitors with equal or better lures. Promotional materials portrayed an exotic, erotic, yet familiar island: Spanish food, quaint natives, Afro-Cuban music and dance, romantic moonlight, sensuous women, golf, tennis, country clubs, and racetracks. Cubans modified traditional culture, altered customary behavior, and when necessary, invented new experiences, such as sun worship ceremonials.

CULTURE AS COMMODITY

Cubans stitched together a marketable cultural identity from bits and pieces of island life. They had neither wooden shoes nor windmills, the distinctive artifacts and landmarks whose pictorial reproduction immediately signaled Holland to the reader of a brochure or poster. They had no national costume, no traditional Cuban textiles or ceramic styles, no distinctive religious art, no authentic tribal dances. The dominant, recognizable cultural image—Spanish colonial—was not uniquely Cuban. Lacking authentic Indian ruins or readily identifiable popular arts, they used various Spanish, African, Chinese, and Creole elements. They improvised, revived, adapted, and modified; they sold Spanish castanets as "typical" souvenirs; they manufactured new items and called them folk art. They encouraged tourists to enjoy Holy Week in Matanzas, to watch the monthly religious processions in Regla, and to join carnival celebrations that mixed pagan Afro-Cuban rituals and Cuban frivolity.[2]

Guidebooks lured tourists to Havana's Chinese quarter with accounts of murky opium dens and pungent herbs sold in Oriental markets. Newspapers heightened a sense of mystery tinged with danger in reports of tong wars, assassinations, and acts of terrorism perpetrated by political rivals among naturalized Cuban Chinese and immigrant Chinese nationalists. In the popular imagination, the Chinatown "labyrinth" became an "exotic, impenetrable, obscure" neighborhood.[3] What an extraordinary accumulation of touristic possibilities! Cuba could embellish its identity and character and invent a distinctive personality to enthrall the most jaded foreigner.

Why do tourists seek out and pay for encounters with exotic cultures? Does the experience set them apart from stay-at-home neighbors and contribute to a sense of worldliness or simply satisfy curiosity? Those venturers willing to cross geographic and cultural boundaries perhaps view the unfamiliar as a source of excitement and mystery. Some travelers seek destinations—almost with a religious fervor— that transport them to a world that appears unspoiled or unusual. That appearance is less and less a reality. As the tourist industry expands around the globe, cultures and peoples everywhere are pressed into service as attractions. Tour promoters package lifestyle, artifacts, ritual, and other distinguishible cultural elements in the effort to turn a profit. By endowing everyday activities with exchange value, they commodify (or commoditize) culture for commercial purposes. When tourist boards consciously alter practices and rituals to attract tourists, some residents adapt their behavior to take advantage of new economic opportunities—they become stage actors. On the other hand, less amenable groups or individuals often retreat to protected or inconvenient areas to avoid scrutiny by outsiders.

Tourism-generated intrusions raise concerns about selling folkways as a tourist attraction. Clearly, both traveler and resident are affected by such manipulation, but not equally. Any one tourist spends a short time away from home and returns to familiar routines, while the "entertainers" repeat their activities over and over again until they become part of daily life. As previously remote communities become tourist destinations, fishermen learn to share their beaches with semi-nude bathers, women who typically socialize as they engage in such household tasks as food preparation tolerate camera-wielding gawkers, goods once offered in friendship or enshrined as ritual (such as food and shelter) become salable items.[4] On the stages of the so-called global village, people perform scripts devised by marketing experts. While the traveler succumbs to fantasies of strange customs and exotic inhabitants of distant lands, a successful tourist enterprise brings twentieth-century sophistication to that imagined world.

A group of titillated Europeans and Americans, captured on film in Dennis O'Rourke's provocative documentary *Cannibal Tours*, pursues an illusory primitive society in Papua New Guinea. From the safety of a comfortable riverboat, tour participants search the thick foliage with camera and naked eye for "wild," "savage," and "exotic" natives, although the objects of their gaze no longer practice cannibalism and keep their tourism earnings in banks. They fashion folk art to suit the market; that is, figurines with exaggerated breasts and penises sell rather well but have nothing to do with any local wood-carving tradition. Retail markup for carvings can reach 1,000–2,000 percent. Tourists buy them for souvenirs but haggle over prices. The craftmakers articulate their amazement (and amusement) that people travel great distances just to see them, and they wonder aloud why the obviously affluent strangers are so unwilling to pay a set price for their wares.

Tour companies also steer visitors to New Guinea's ceremonial "sing-sings," where natives play-act themselves. They discard their usual clothing (T-shirts and trousers, for example), paint their bodies, and dress in costume appropriate to expectations. The spectacle is timed for the tour's convenience, not out of ritual necessity. The "primitives," more commercially savvy with each tourist encounter, carefully examine and analyze the voyeurs, maintain an appearance of innocence, and charge what the traffic will bear for performances.[5]

Halfway around the world, equally astute Maasai villagers welcome foreign guests to their homes. Are they really "guests"? The chief has set a price, changing the meaning of hospitality. Householders pose for photos and charge a fee. Tourists want photographs to show to friends, and Maasai villagers want money or the novelties of a distant world that foreigners will exchange. What meaning can we assign to the relationship? Since most of the villagers continue to raise cattle and selectively exploit the tourist market, they appear to have struck a comfortable compromise between foreign intrusion and group cohesion. Farther south, the recently opened Lesedi cultural village affords tourists an opportunity to sleep in thatch-roofed huts with polished cow dung floors, electric lights, and modern bathrooms, surrounded by Xhosa, Sotho, Pedi, or Zulu families brought to the compound to demonstrate daily life, customs, and rituals. Along with diamonds, South Africa now mines the riches of once-scorned native tribes and sells them to fascinated foreigners at one hundred dollars a night.[6]

As the international travel industry grows, tourist bureaus everywhere recognize the attraction of ritual that Cubans had tested in its sun worship ceremonials. In the Amazon basin, the government allowed privileged and paying tourists to observe traditional initiation rites of young Tukuna girls, until the village elders protested the intrusion into one of their most private ceremonies. Indonesia similarly turned ritual into a tourist gem as tour directors arranged for visitors to participate in funerals in remote villages of the Tana Toraja area. Tourists paraded awkwardly in ceremonial circles, wrapped in ankle-length skirts, holding long bamboo stalks, while cameras clicked or whirred to produce souvenir photos. The ritual significance was lost, but the experience was recorded forever.[7]

Ethnicity and exotic culture sell as well in the age of mass tourism as they did in the 1920s. U.S. marketing experts in the 1960s advised Hong Kong officials to organize trips to Macao's fascinating and colorful Chinese quarter, with its unique Oriental-style gambling. They favored Chinese operas as promotional tools and shopping excursions to shops where Chinese ivory and jade carvers and brocade makers sold their products. For Singapore the tourism wizards suggested trips to small villages to exhibit the native way of life. They counseled Cambodians to develop and promote the temples of Angkor Wat, to display elephants at work, birds and monkeys in the jungles, and hooded cobras, folkloric dance programs, and processions depicting events of the Khmer civilization. Vietnam, they argued, similarly possessed great touristic prospects in festivals and colorful events linked to local customs and folklore, as well as sightseeing trips to Confucian temples.[8]

Certainly the travel industry is just one more stimulus in an ongoing process of change and adaptation. Tourism may erode old relationships and substitute new ones, but industrialization similarly moved millions of people about—from rural farm to urban factory—and altered daily routines and creative outlets. Inventions and technological advances continually affect how we order our lives. Electric lights, automobiles, and computers have changed our thinking and behavior in fundamental ways, while leisure activities and entertainment (film, music, television, radio, sports, travel, etc.) influence how we act and interact. Mass tourism added but another dimension to a dialectic of change.

Although we cannot equate the cultural effect of tourism on 1920s Cuba with the introduction of visitors to areas of geographic and technological isolation, tourism did bring new behaviors to Cuba. Chorus girls and tour guides are just two examples of new employment categories. Cubans attended horse, dog, yacht, and airplane races—events organized by the tourist commission. Cubans bought houses along the fairways of golf courses, an innovation designed to appeal to winter residents. Sports-oriented golf and tennis clubs sprang up beside the traditional *centros*, that is, social, recreational, and mutual-assistance associations based on Spanish regional origins (Galicia or Asturias, for example). By the late 1920s Cuban women, as well as men, won golf and tennis championships and danced the fox-trot at the Havana Country Club. Certainly the decade introduced new social patterns, overturned customs, upset traditions, and challenged common sensibilities in many locales. But tourism added a dimension of premeditated promotionalism.

TOURISTIC IMAGES: SOFTLY ROMANTIC
OR HOT AND WILD

Tourist promoters of the 1920s appealed to a numerically significant market that existed within easy reach of the island. Advertisers
had achieved a degree of sophisticated salesmanship, and the United
States had spawned a restless, mobile population. Tourism offered new
frontiers at a time when old ones had been tamed. Wanderers escaped
everyday routine and struck out for new settings. Most of them probably never suspected that tourist industry promoters and advertising
agents had influenced their choices.

Cuba's brochures and publicity carefully interlaced information
and motivation, allurement and assurance. During Cuba's seven fat
years of tourism from 1924 to 1931, the island's image evolved and
the market expanded. Country Club Park sold its fairway estates to a
targeted segment of wealthy individuals and families accustomed to
the luxury spas and resorts of Europe. Thus it was no accident that
Sir Basil Thompson described a muted elegance in his 1923 *Travel*
magazine article. Havana, the White City, glowed like a mysterious,
ghostly bride, exuding a quaint charm. Through languid, romantic
nights of moonlight and guitars, the lights on the Malecón shone "like
a diamond necklace about the throat of a dusky Aphrodite." Affluent travelers who could afford to build a house and spend the whole
winter season in an enchanting, romantic, beautiful setting would appreciate neighbors who observed proper decorum. Thompson's sedate
Cuban householders spent their evenings with family in their parlors
or assembled near the seawall to hear a band or enjoy the breeze. A
dignified bunch who cared little for liquor, they rarely became "up-
roarious."[9]

When John Bowman bought and renovated Havana's Hotel Sevilla,
his socially acclaimed clientele reinforced Thompson's portrait of re-
strained hospitality. Bowman's own leisure pursuits, golf and horsemanship, reflected upper-class interests. But tourist promoters wanted
more: if several thousand tourists poured money into Havana's coffers
in 1923 and 1924, then why not twenty thousand, or one hundred thousand? Foreign visitors, whether riotously rich or modestly middle class,
benefited Cuban entrepreneurs. By 1925 tourism promoters pitched
appeals to a broader market. While some visitors preferred Havana's

quieter charms, others might find hints of Africa more to their taste. If some Cubans sat sedately in sheltered, lamp-lit parlors, others danced erotically in dark shacks. In working-class Regla, across Havana Bay,
the curious tourist meandering through its cramped, crumbling, fly-ridden streets might detect the sounds of Afro-Cuban music emanating from some small house and stop to peek through a ground-floor window to watch dark-skinned dancers rumba to rhythms "more savage than the beat of tom-toms," wild songs and groaning melodies, barbaric jungle music "that awakens a wild desire to join the primitive dancers." [10]

Such provocative descriptions probably set the hearts of 1920s jazz babies pounding. Could an outsider enter this enticing and forbidding world, even vicariously? Regla offered not only an opportunity to ogle but—wait—a hint of participation as well, a chance to exhaust oneself in primitive euphoria. Captivated readers imagined themselves standing at that window. Perhaps someone would invite them inside. Or they might stumble upon some other African ritual, a mysterious "voodoo" ceremonial. Once in a while, the travel adviser confided, some child murder was attributed to these ancient practices.

H. Williams, the author of the 1925 *Travel* article quoted above, invested the island with a pulsating Afro-Cuban beat that demolished images of sobriety and dullness. By 1926, similar purple prose spilled over the *New Republic*'s usually sober pages. For people whose pleasures could not be satisfied by undulating golf courses or ancient Spanish fortresses, Waldo Frank transported his readers to a realm of sexual-racial fantasy. A breathless, sultry slumber enveloped a libertine, dreamlike Havana, where women possessed a venal loveliness, and winds of fancy fanned the desires of visitors who heard its passion-filled songs and sighs of dalliance. Sadly sensuous mahogany-colored men watched passing women: "The hips and the high heels are jazz; . . . breasts swathe her in Andalusian softness; under the blare of her rouge Africa mumbles. . . . The eyes are clouded—A Negress's eyes." [11]

Add savage, wild, barbaric Africa to Spanish food and Cuban customs, and local color exploded from the page. The writer who had stared entranced at the exotic rumba perhaps stumbled across the Afro-Cuban dancers on his own, but more likely tourist officials directed his steps to Regla. They had counted the thousands of yearly visitors to nearby Florida and concluded that novelty and a little extra excitement might draw them to the island. If Washington DC exhibited the war dances of "redskins" in front of the national capitol, Cubans certainly could exploit Afro-Cuban religious rituals.[12]

Promoters worked hard to transform Havana. The only people awake in the wee morning hours, the Cuban novelist Félix Soloni wrote in 1926, were "watchmen, street cleaners, artists suffering from insomnia, bored journalists, chauffeurs, and policemen." The other exceptions were a few ridiculous American tourists who managed to stir up a little excitement. The magnificent lights along the Malecón illuminated an overwhelming ennui, and Havana's mosquitos provided the evening serenade. A derisive *Diario de la Marina* cartoon pictured a robber climbing through a Havana hotel window while a bored tourist, already in bed for the night, grabs his camera and declares, "Oh, hello, Cuban thief, how wonderful. Wait a minute . . . now I'll have something to tell my friends."[13]

The criticism stung, but it also motivated a determined tourist commission. If a dignified, picturesque, and quaint Cuba found a market, a niche also existed for more sensational inducements. Before long, the good-time crowd found Cuba: fun-loving conventioneers and wealthy widows on a fling, thousands of cruise ship excursionists, and serious drinkers escaping Prohibition. The curious and the fantasy-prone, all of them pleasure bound, jammed Havana's new hotels and proclaimed it hot, wet, and wide open. Gray-haired American ladies clung to the rail at Sloppy Joe's bar and sang "maudlin ditties to the tropic night and their bored and slick-haired gigolos." The new racetrack crowd drank, too—grandstand types, not aristocratic Jockey Club members—"hard-looking, ruddy-faced men in expensive loud clothing, with field-glasses on hip, and smartly dressed women who might have been in the chorus fifteen years ago."[14]

Cuba sold whatever tourists would buy. Between 1928 and 1931, each year "outspectacled" the one before. In arguably the most blatant example of pandering to foreign tastes, tourist promoters, with the complicity of municipal officials, merchants, and hotel associations, transformed Havana's annual carnival celebration. Properly handled, carnival had great tourism potential. Mardi Gras, the Fat Tuesday of abandon before the self-denial of Lent, fell conveniently at the height of the tourist season in most years. And if Easter arrived too late in the year, carnival dates need not coincide with an ecclesiastical calendar. Havana's civic fathers, not its priests, convoked the Lenten season and moved it forward to enhance tourist revenues.

Habaneros traditionally partied on four consecutive carnival Sundays. They decorated their houses with bunting and palm leaves, and girls in fancy dresses rode through the thoroughfare alongside the Prado (the wide promenade that extends from the Parque Central to the water's edge) in carriages decorated with paper flowers and bright-colored fabric. Around four o'clock in the afternoon the walkways filled with people in a holiday mood, anticipating the music and laughter. In the houses facing the Prado, residents crowded the balconies and rained serpentine down on the passing carriages. The late-afternoon activity ended as the streetlights came on. Some *habaneros* spent the evening at carnival balls sponsored by various regional and fraternal associations. Meanwhile, on the seaside Malecón, mischievous young boys extended their amusement into the darkness, setting fire to large wads of bright confetti and serpentine collected from the streets.[15]

Carnival had undergone some changes since the early years of the republic. Throwing serpentine and confetti had replaced the practice of tossing flour after a steady drizzle one year turned everything into a sticky mess. Officials had banned costumed street dances (*comparsas*) sponsored by Afro-Cuban social groups after a number of brawls had resulted in at least one death. Automobiles had joined the horse-drawn carriages, conviviality extended into the wee hours, and a carnival queen reigned over the festivities.[16]

Tourism-related carnival entertainment departed dramatically from the laughing, flirting spontaneity of Havana's traditional celebration, however. By 1926 thousands of observers outnumbered participants. They stood along the route of an organized two-and-one-half-hour parade or paid to watch from places in grandstands set up on the Malecón. The seats saved wear and tear on the shoes and feet and afforded better viewing and photo angles. Entries paraded past a reviewing stand where judges awarded forty prizes, from fifty to two hundred dollars, to the winners among exhibiting contestants. One exceptionally elaborate float presented the Spanish court in the fifteenth century, complete with historically accurate costumes. It competed for prizes with a replica of the city of Venice and one of a Nile riverboat whose occupants dressed in the style of ancient Egypt. There was even a slightly risqué human butterfly, a beautiful blond woman dressed in green bodice, lacy gauze wings, and a filmy skirt that exposed her bare legs. Perhaps all of that loveliness could not be graded and ranked adequately, or maybe the judges simply went out of their way to please the foreign viewers. At any rate, they awarded the grand prize to a facsimile World War I trench, complete with barbed wire, machine guns, and several U.S. veterans—members of the American Legion, Havana branch.[17] A for effort; F for gaiety and beauty.

A similarly structured event the following year fell flat; perhaps the formalities of floats and prizes constrained carnival frivolity. Undaunted, the entertainment kings of the tourist commission returned with even more zest in 1928. First of all, they moved the whole season forward and added parades on the Monday and Tuesday before Ash Wednesday to accommodate a bumper crop of tourists. Sponsored floats became little more than commercial advertisements, and shops in the city sold carnival supplies to turn luxurious automobiles into royal chariots. A special concession permitted tourists to join the merrymaking in undecorated rented automobiles, and a beauty contest determined who would reign as carnival queen, replacing the usual popular choice based on a simple vote.

Dances at the Havana Country Club, the Yacht Club, the Vedado Tennis Club, and the National Theater competed with more traditional functions at the various clubs whose membership reflected regional Spanish origins. The ultimate symbol of Americanization came on the third carnival Sunday that year, however, when the visiting vaudevillian Eddie Cantor and his wife occupied a prominent place in the parade.[18] Most assuredly, only a few Cubans recognized the popping eyes of the Ziegfeld Follies star, but carnival had become more of a tourist attraction than a Cuban holiday.

In 1929 the promotion-conscious officials invited beauty contest winners from various cities in the United States to participate in carnival activities along with the Cuban queen and her court. More beauty queens arrived in 1930, and their hometown newspapers predictably carried photographs and stories of the attention lavished by Cubans on the young women.[19] Havana's mayor opened that year's celebration to large crowds that gave no hint of losses suffered in the previous October's stock market crash. As a novel offering, resident North Americans built a miniature Coney Island amusement park on San Rafael Street, and their floats represented various aspects of U.S. history and culture.

Tourists poured into Cuba and made carnival their own. El Encanto, Havana's fanciest department store, sold Spanish-style "quaint and chic" carnival outfits to participating tourists, and vacationers took to the festivities with gusto. The charitable Ball of Nations sponsored by the American colony leaned toward American Indians, Puritans, Pilgrims, and Virginia cavaliers, with lots of fringed buckskin and feathers. A facsimile Powhatan in beads, feathers, and warpaint joined a Pocahontas costumed in long black braids, headband, beaded buckskin, and moccasins. How Cuba had accommodated to tourism! Anglos imitated native North Americans for Havana's carnival, while Cubans pretended to be Siboneys dancing in worship of the sun.[20]

The tourist industry inundated the city with theatrical pageantry, nightclub chorus lines, and a whirlwind of spectacular entertainment. Along the newly opened central highway outside Havana, open-air restaurants such as the Château Madrid offered dining, dancing, and floor shows under the stars. An international lineup of performers mixed rumba dancers, Cuban singers, and jazz orchestras with North American roller skaters and Argentine tango dancers. But Château Madrid's biggest attraction of the 1930 season was Tom Mix, the popular North American cowboy film star.

A competitive frenzy overtook Havana's hotels and nightclubs. The tango dancers Ramón and Rosita made their Havana debut at Sans Soucí's outdoor tropical garden, where the versatile orchestra played syncopated jazz as well as the rhythmic Cuban *son*. The Hotel Plaza's Cuban singers and international dance teams continued to attract a sedate crowd, probably the same people who paid three dollars for orchestra seats to the lavishly costumed Paris–Madrid Revue, designed for American visitors, at the National Theater. At the Sevilla-Biltmore on New Year's Eve, the handsome ballroom dancer Lafayette "hurled his petite partner in a breath-taking swing over the balcony and through the window into the arcade of the hotel. A few minutes later, LaVerne appeared on the dance floor, safe and sound, to the intense relief . . . of all."[21]

Cuba offered something for every taste. Cabaret Infierno featured Mimi, the goddess of rumba, "for a happy night at little cost." Apache dancers Francois and Renée performed a hair-raising routine as Francois flung Renée across the floor under the Club Montmartre's spotlight. Pat Morgan and the Broadway Rhythm Girls entertained at the Tokio Club, which billed itself as the "pleasure seekers' paradise," with hot-sweet music, beautiful girls, and Havana's best floor show. Club Hollywood touted a "gorgeous revue" of "15 * GIRLS * 15" that made "Nights at HOLLYWOOD . . . nights of pleasure." You could take your pick of two hundred pretty girls at the Rex Dancing Club and spend every night in the week listening to jazz. The Black Cat Cabaret welcomed tourists nightly and invited them to dance with its charming hostesses, and El Anón ice cream parlor advertised its own novelty— female waiters. Despite regulations designed to protect young women who worked in cabarets, nightclubs, and dancing academies, various establishments became centers of prostitution.[22]

More than a few enterprising North American ladies of the evening traveled to Havana to compete with the locals. Too voluntaristic to qualify as an organized white slave trade, the traffic nevertheless kept Cuban officials on their guard. With the League of Nations monitoring the international transport of young women for purposes of prostitution, Cubans set a net to catch sex peddlers—or at least to maintain the appearance of doing so. According to one caustic observer, only a "reassuring ugliness," that is, a face judged too unattractive to sell sexual favors, protected single girls traveling alone from the scrutiny of immigration agents. As one savvy traveler remarked, however, "the mesh must still be wide, for many goldfish get through."[23]

Prostitution had preceded tourism to Havana's bustling port area by several hundred years, and Cuban poets enshrined the erotic image of Cuba's *mulatas* (mixed-race women) long before travel writers took note of their presence. Periodic reform movements failed to dampen the ardor of either Cubans or foreigners or to eliminate the exchange of sexual services for hard cash. As Cuba increasingly marketed pleasure to fill its hotels and restaurants, advertising agencies and even tour guides slanted the appeal accordingly. *Terry's Guide to Cuba,* for example, told buyers exactly how to find Havana's officially nonexistent "indecorous quarter," an "unfragrant" section of the old port area, where teenagers who ranged in color from peach to coal roamed the streets alongside ebony antiques. They winked "with incendiary eyes" at passing men. Women who practiced the "scarlet arts of Aspasia" and gladly sacrificed themselves "on the altar of Aphrodite" awaited any tourist willing to seek them out. This "confessedly naughty ward" also accommodated tapestried and mirrored rooms where "the salaciously inclined may witness startling scenes in the flesh or by means of moving pictures. Such places usually are referred to by the cryptic number *soixante-neuf* (Sp., sesenta y nueve, or 69) albeit this number is not that of the houses in question."[24]

In only half a decade, Havana had captured its share of North

Americans with time and money who were looking for relaxation, intoxication, excitement, or thrills. Cuba's tourist industry had fashioned the image of a Latin isle of unfettered pleasure that catered to North American tastes.

TOURISM'S CHALLENGE TO CULTURAL IDENTITY

While tourism promoters remodeled Havana into a pleasure palace for foreigners, many thoughtful Cubans bemoaned the consequences. They had rejected colonial status, but two decades of self-government seemed to have brought corruption and a generation of leaders who valued personal gain over public good. Now they searched for a set of unique and unifying characteristics that might unite them as a nation. Earnest nationalists searched for *cubanidad*, an essence, the foundation of a shared identity, the property that would invest citizens with loyalty and pride and a willingness to adhere to national purpose over particular interests. Cuba could find true nationhood, they concluded, only if people understood what it meant to be Cuban and felt emotionally tied to the *patria* (fatherland).[25] Issues of culture, nationalism, and identity engendered many passionately argued debates.

Foreigners who read the descriptive literature and succumbed to the portrait of a country with an intriguing history and quaint customs, somewhat frivolous and marginally lurid, knew nothing of the patriotic reformers who were trying to create a positive and useful national image. Would tourism erode the Cuban national ethos? Or would it in fact reinvigorate aspects of art, music, dance, and folk culture that were in danger of slipping into oblivion? While Cuba's intellectuals searched for a suitable soul, tourist promoters sliced the body and laid out the entrails. Ironically, Afro-Cuban culture, embodying elements of music, dance, and religion, became essential to both nationalistic and touristic image builders. Romantic patriots located *cubanidad* in the Afro-Cuban subculture, seeing in its music and literature the essence of a unifying culture. Tourism promoters exalted sensual and mystical qualities of Afro-Cubans for purposes of profit, and foreigners saw Cuba as an erotic, exotic island devoted to their pleasure and entertainment.

Chapter 6

Culture and Casinos, Museums and Monte Carlos

Cast Changes and Script Revisions

Tourism collapsed along with the rest of Cuba's economy in the Great Depression. Visitors had spent almost $26 million in 1928–29 but only $9.5 million in 1932–33. Steamship companies optimistically continued their promotional efforts. In the Panama Pacific Lines' 1932 film *Havana, the Siren City,* ship's passengers enjoyed Havana's golf courses and marveled at the city's centuries-old fortresses. "Simple, kindly" Cubans cheerfully performed the rumba, with no hints of hunger or political unrest to mar the image of a romantic island. By the time the message circulated, Cuba offered no carefree escape. Economic depression and political upheaval had taken its toll, and tourism revenues slipped under $5 million in 1933–34.[1]

During the fat years of the late 1920s, visitor-generated earnings had confirmed tourism's value as an economic development strategy and had veiled social concerns about gambling and prostitution. Discussions had centered on attracting more visitors, not what type, and on tapping a growing middle- and working-class market. Most Cubans had encountered few if any tourists in their daily lives; those who did often considered them a pot of gold—strangers with money to spend. Tourist entrepreneurs had introduced casinos as critical to profits, and from the early Monte Carlo bills to the Biltmore Country Club, promoters had insisted on the contribution of gambling to the success of their ventures. If a few unpleasant incidents captured public attention, they added a mere whisper to the cacophony of criticism that began to build around Machado. When a gang of North American poolroom hustlers swooped down on Havana, newspapers denounced them as skillful swindlers, typical of the opportunistic U.S. profiteers who habitually fed on Cuba. Some people might have read this as a swipe at Machado, but police pressure quickly sent the hustlers packing. Undeniably more pernicious than pool hustlers, a narcotics ring operated openly along Dragones Street, the heart of Havana's Chinatown, touted in the tourist guidebooks as the center of the opium, morphine, and cocaine trade. The traffic was an open secret, with hints of involvement by influential politicians, and antigovernment forces might have connected Machado, vice, corrupt officials, narcotics, and tourism.[2]

On the other hand, John Bowman completed his Biltmore Yacht and Country Club and advertised it as the "Greatest Place on Earth," soon to eclipse France's Deauville and other continental showplaces. The casino at Deauville, opened on the eve of World War I, had become a huge success after the war and had remained popular among wealthier Americans. Biltmore, however, had advantages of time and distance, Bowman suggested, only a short thirty-nine hours away from New York by train and seaplane. Guests lounged on its magnificent bathing beach before they scarcely realized they had left home and could even imagine themselves as owners of "aristocratic" Biltmore residences. It certainly did not hurt the Cuban American Realty Company's investment when handsome, smiling John Jacob Astor V smiled at readers from a publicity photograph, stretched out on Cuba's white sands and ready for a game of dominos while on his winter school holiday. Who would not understand the advantages of socializing in such privileged company?

The "who's who" of winter tourists seemed remarkably unaffected by the October 1929 stock market crash. When the Casino Nacional closed at the end of the season, the pleasure trust tallied the profits from a spectacular winter. The Cunard Line broke its previous New York–Havana passenger record when seven hundred visitors arrived on one ship for the Easter holiday, and the P & O line ordered its own seven-hundred-passenger steamer for the Cuba route to compete with Cunard and the Ward Line. Shifting gears expediently, the tourist commission had pitched its message to the business and budgetary concerns of its clientele. Havana became the prudent choice, accessible by telephone and within hours of a hasty return trip, "the logical vacation for this day of changing business conditions and quick moves in industry," with "all the benefits of a warm southern winter . . . without the penalty of being too far from home or incurring excessive expense."[3] Even after the winter vacationers departed, cheaper summer rates at hotels and on ships lured teachers, insurance agents, salespersons, and office workers who sustained an off-season industry for a while.

Tourism's travail became apparent in 1931, however, as both the world's economy and Cuba's domestic situation deteriorated. In the long run the new industry could save neither itself nor the government that promoted it.

DEMISE OF THE DREAM AND THE DREAMERS

A profound discontent had accompanied Machado's 1927–28 electoral manipulations. Intellectuals and reformers who had backed Machado in 1924 publicly aired their antagonism to the power-grabbing president. Angry members of opposition political parties, denied their chance to contest the presidency, moved in the direction of nonelectoral confrontations. Government repression of outspoken dissidents increased their hostility. Labor militants threatened the social peace, and strikes menaced the smooth operation of the utilities, transport, lodging, and food services necessary to tourism. Machado had crushed strikes of railroad and sugar workers in 1926 and then had arrested and deported union activists. When workers unified against his tactics, Machado outlawed the labor confederation. In response, two hundred thousand striking workers paralyzed Havana's commerce and transportation for twenty-four hours at the height of the winter tourist season. The government retaliated and arrested the offending labor leaders.[4]

Tourists apparently took little notice. Two hundred Georgians, guests of the tourist commission, arrived on a four-day goodwill tour the day before the general strike and banqueted contentedly at the Casino Nacional. Visitors may have paid more attention to the "voodoo party" broken up by Havana policemen that day than to the stifling of worker protest. Clashes intensified, but when the Rensselaer Institute held its annual reunion in Havana, their whirlwind tour never missed a beat. No hint of imminent danger or disruption spoiled the good times. After a day at the Hershey sugar mill, the revelers spent the evening at the jai alai palace. The next day they shopped in old Havana and lunched in the Polar Brewery's beer garden. The Cuban Society of Engineers entertained them with a champagne reception. They held their alumni banquet at the Biltmore Yacht and Country Club, and Cuban hosts fêted them at the casino before they left.[5]

While tourists dined under colorful umbrellas on the sun deck at La Playa beach, strolled through cramped streets in colonial Havana, and browsed for souvenirs in the markets, Machado's henchmen murdered workers and assassinated student leaders. When the students protested, Machado closed the university. Meanwhile, Irénée DuPont began construction of a luxury resort for DuPont and General Motors officials next to his palatial Varadero Beach home. He named his beachside mansion Xanadu in anticipation of an earthly Cuban paradise.[6]

Despite the controversy that swirled around his office, Machado signed a contract for a splendid five-hundred-room, four-million-dollar showplace hotel, with Spanish-tiled salons, sumptuous ballroom, gardens, tennis courts, huge swimming pool, and a glorious view of the sea. Big enough to accommodate international meetings and sufficiently majestic to entertain the government's guests, the Hotel Nacional was a fitting monument to the president's surging self-importance, fed by the bankers and businessmen who honored him with banquets and saluted him as he sat in the presidential box at Oriental Park. Four hundred guests in the grand ballroom of New York's Hotel Biltmore praised him as the protector of U.S. interests, a firm leader who maintained stability in the face of daunting social and economic challenges.[7]

So complete was the tourist commission's confidence in Machado's ability to maintain order that it invited a Fox Movietone crew for a six-week filming tour of Cuban attractions. They began in Havana, a frequent site of antigovernment activity and repression, and covered the entire island. Fox distributed the film to its theaters around the country, and residents of the United States saw a tranquil Cuba in celluloid segments shown over a six-month period. Pleasant pictures notwithstanding, economic hardship dried up the tourist market. By the time the luxurious Hotel Nacional opened in 1931, the crisis had considerably diminished the potential guest list and Machado's ability to entertain them.

Machado's longtime supporter and colleague Carlos Miguel de Céspedes resigned his office on 10 December 1930, citing the president's attacks on university students as cause for his departure. Rumors circulated that an empty treasury, rather than humanitarian concerns, prompted his withdrawal. Critics considered Havana's sixteen-million-dollar capitol building, one of Céspedes's projects, a shameful waste of money.[8]

Tourism succumbed to the deepening depression even before bloody street battles and a general strike toppled Machado. Shrinkage in sugar, tobacco, and consumer goods sales had preceded the decline in tourism. Although Machado called on the United States to cut its sugar tariffs, U.S. sugar beet growers successfully argued for protection of their own interests. Unemployment skyrocketed; Cubans experienced grinding poverty, and some channeled their legitimate discontent into violence. They overturned a government that had reneged on its obligations to constituents, and they took revenge on officials who had betrayed their trust. Angry mobs burned Céspedes's house, and he spent several years in self-exile in the United States.

Both John Bowman and Charles Flynn had died before Machado lost power. A pall of sadness had touched Oriental Park in 1930 when Bowman, his eyes brimming with tears, had presented a special prize to the winner of the Charles Flynn Memorial Handicap. Flynn's many friends mourned his passing and paid him homage in this tribute to horsemanship. He had been critical to Cuban tourism, building the racetrack and bringing Bowman to the island.

Eighteen months later Havana's elite mourned Bowman's unexpected and untimely death from complications following relatively routine gall bladder surgery. Some of the most prominent people of New York, Washington, and Havana attended his funeral or sent condolences to his widow and two young children. Obituaries devoted paragraphs to his business and charitable achievements, but the Great Depression had taken its toll on Bowman's personal fortunes. Ever the optimist, he had expanded his interests rapidly and left his heirs more debts than property. Six months before Bowman's death, a Cuban court order had tied up the holdings and revenues of the Cuban National Syndicate—the pleasure trust—pending payment of several million dollars in mortgages. Probate officers valued Bowman's shares in the syndicate at $892. His dream of a fabulous beach resort fell to economic hard times and revolution, and his hotels passed to other owners.[9]

In the depression-plagued early 1930s, when dissidents focused on the highly visible alliance between a corrupt and increasingly repressive leadership and foreign interests, tourism in fact played a minor role. Despite the enthusiasm and optimism of its backers, the industry had never come close to challenging sugar as the island's economic mainstay. Tourism's entrepreneurs had not replaced sugar refiners as political bêtes noires to be blamed for Cuba's sorry decline. Nevertheless, the pleasure trust had entwined its ambitions around Machado and his associates, some of whom had become partners in the National Casino and the Oriental Park racetrack, in country clubs and exclusive seaside communities.

When the Cubans ousted Machado, he and several top officials headed for Miami or Nassau in the Bahamas. People reacted with joy at the success of their uprising, anger at the pain inflicted by the Machado administration, and a sense of disappointment that the leadership had escaped. Vengeful crowds rampaged in the streets, vandalized buildings, and attacked members of Machado's hated goon squads. An enraged mob sacked former presidential secretary Viriato Gutiérrez's house. They also seized stretches of beach at the Biltmore, along with Gutiérrez's adjacent Playa Viriato. Rebels charged Gutiérrez with ceding the beaches to private interests for personal profit and insisted that the new government return the coastline to its rightful owners, the Cuban people. Finally, in 1941, the city council of Marianao made Viriato Beach public property. Five years later, when the citizens of Marianao learned that Gutiérrez had appealed for financial compensation, they wrote a bitter, six-page condemnation of the "usurper of beaches," typed in red ink to symbolize the blood that they had spilled to defeat Machado and his supporters.[10]

A CRIPPLED INDUSTRY REBORN

Tourism, like Cuba's other trade items, depended on the economic health of the market place. The enterprise had generated profits and employment and, for a while, had shielded Havana from the most extreme financial repercussions of the island's reliance on agriculture. However, it was not indestructible. The island's foreign trade in 1933 was about one-quarter of what it had been in 1928. The equivalent of more than $400 million in U.S. currency circulated through the Cuban economy in 1926, but only $32 million greased the wheels of commerce in 1934. People earned little money to pay for purchases. A public works plan could not begin to soak up the ranks of the unemployed; even government employees went unpaid. Sugar workers' salaries averaged eighty-three cents a day, and circumstances forced many workers to accept thirty cents if that was all the mill owner offered. Tourist sector employment languished too, as hotels and restaurants closed. Tour bus and car services lost their passengers. Cuban manufacturers of soap and sweets, perfume and paint, cement and crystal, souvenirs and straw hats felt the pinch as tourists disappeared. Breweries and distilleries certainly felt the loss. Business in cafés and bars deteriorated to such a degree that unemployed cabaret musicians strolled from place to place and performed for whatever the patrons were willing to give them.[11]

Entrepreneurs and employees all had a stake in tourism's revival. Unfortunately, no overwhelmingly popular leader could harness the energy of rebellion and unite Cubans in a regenerative effort. Dissidents ranged the political spectrum, and no ideological consensus underlay their opposition to Machado. The post-Machado leadership changed hands rapidly from moderate reformist in August 1933 to more radical reformist in September to authoritarian populist in January 1934. While Machado's enemies fought among themselves, Fulgencio Batista, an obscure army sargeant, stepped out of the shadows as the leader of a discontented military faction. Sensing a commonality of outsider status, university student rebels turned to Batista and signed an agreement on 4 September to form a new government. A university professor, Ramón Grau San Martín, became president in September 1933 and launched a four-month legislative blitz. Protective of its own interests, the United States refused to recognize Grau's nationalist, reformist government. Roosevelt withheld economic assistance, encouraged political opposition, and pursued Fulgencia Batista as Grau's successor. Grau's activist regime ended in January 1934.

The volcano of discontent spewed a terrain-altering seriousness across the pleasure-bent tourist landscape when it finally erupted. Earnest reformers debated the social utility of tourism. Did a successful industry require Cuba to cater to the base desires of the marketplace, or could tourism be used to uplift and educate, to achieve desirable cultural gains; that is, could Cuba market tourism that elevated and enlightened as well as entertained? Cubans found a powerful supporter for the idea of socially beneficial tourism in Franklin D. Roosevelt. When a 1935 delegation to Washington met with Roosevelt to discuss economic assistance, the president advised them to expand tourism. But forget gamblers and patrons of cabarets, he admonished; move away from horseracing and casinos. Appeal to families who would appreciate the island's beaches, historical sites, and natural beauty. In Roosevelt's view, a country concerned with its well-being had to attract responsible persons, using entertainment compatible with human dignity.[12]

In fact, FDR preached to the converted. Almost as soon as Grau San Martín had taken power, a group of manufacturers, merchants, small businessmen, and other interested parties had solicited his help on behalf of the troubled tourist industry. The group's goals signaled a tourism recast to meet new cultural and nationalist standards in a proposal designed to construct exhibit halls; move the historical museum, fine arts museum, and national library to locations more accessible to tourists; organize a fine arts salon and open-air painting classes; improve the botanical garden; and open the Institute of Natural History to tourists at hours when visitors would not interfere with the institute's work. In the new scheme, the government became a partner in a resurgence of cultural, as well as economic, tourism.[13]

Thus the successors to the pleasure trust chose not to eliminate tourism but to change its nature, to replace casinos with culture, substitute museums for Monte Carlo. If the old partnership of real estate speculators and public officials had bent tourism to its needs in the 1920s, a more enlightened and responsible stewardship could fashion an agency to serve social purposes. If the former tourist commission had turned carnival into a glorification of commercialism and concocted inauthentic rituals to please foreigners, a postrevolutionary authority, sensitive to Cuban needs, could devise a program to define national identity in a positive way, could recapture aspects of culture and use them to inspire citizens as well as to attract tourists. North Americans traveled to Italy or Greece to admire classical art and history. Why not encourage them to undertake similar pursuits in Cuba while encouraging Cubans to appreciate their own heritage?

Champions of an enlightened tourism argued that the industry need not be the captive of profiteers nor capitulate to the tastes of the widest market. They injected a tourist populism into the debate, a concern for the social well-being of popular classes as well as the satisfactions of businessmen and financiers, and determined to leverage the revenue-producing benefits of tourism into support for museums, parks, art, music, and the preservation and promotion of Cuba's cultural legacy. The new breed of tourist promoters—civic-minded businessmen and cultural activists—tried to fit tourism into an ideal of responsible government that satisfied intellectual, aesthetic, and spiritual hungers as well as physical and commercial needs. Museums, concerts, art exhibits, and community festivals entertained but also educated. Historical displays, painting, sculpture, music—appropriately selected and arranged—fostered an appreciation of a shared past and encouraged an emotional attachment to the land and its institutions, in short, a beneficial nationalism. Tangible, constructive projects would bring the government closer to the people and begin to erode the distrust and distaste that years of corruption and repression had generated.

Culture advocates supported expansion and renovation of the National Museum. Visitors averaged 400–600 monthly but increased to 1,500–2,000 during the winter tourist months. The old-fashioned repository for artworks and historical artifacts had opened in 1909 in a former jai alai *frontón* and then moved to larger quarters in the 1920s. Many exhibits were of questionable merit, however, such as the skeleton of the horse from whose back the independence hero Máximo Gómez had fought. Other items remained awkwardly displayed in crowded, unattractive cases.[14] Clearly, an improved museum could facilitate intellectual and cultural growth, promote nationalism, and entertain tourists, both foreign and Cuban. Reformers freely employed the profit motive as leverage to gain social objectives in a time of scarce financial resources. That is, improved cultural institutions not only served the public interest but brought dollars into the country that turned over many times in the local economy.

Compelling arguments prompted government action, and a National Tourist Corporation emerged, with fifteen thousand dollars in start-up money and additional revenue authorized from a newly created tax on visitor entries. Spokespersons for the agency acted like missionaries responsible for the soul of the country and promised economic, cultural, and social development for the good of all citizens. Their enthusiasm conceded little to their boosterish predecessors of the 1920s. More than just an industry, they proclaimed, tourism was a diamond in the rough, a generative motor force, a creative power.[15]

A new, multifaceted tourist bureaucracy encompassed Rotarians, bus drivers, journalists, theatrical booking agents, architects, tobacco harvesters, musicians, and hotel, restaurant, and café owners and workers, as well as social and recreational associations, feminist organizations, the Franco-American committee of Havana, the Automobile Club, and wholesalers and retailers of clothes, silks, furs, and jewelry. Juan Sábates of the Cuban Chamber of Commerce presided over an unwieldy group of volunteers who tried to cover all eventualities as they deliberated issues of finance, communication, transportation, tourist protection, receptions and courtesies, lodging, programs and general attractions, motor and air tours, research and statistics, official relations, publicity, public decoration, port relations, tourism education, water tourism, price control, cultural attractions, public monuments, and thermal springs.

The tourists began to return in 1935, despite sporadic political violence as Batista consolidated his authority. Cruise ships advertised trips to Havana with the disclaimer "if conditions permit." Newspaper articles about street violence prompted letters to the U.S. Embassy from fearful potential travelers. Because so many tourists worried about safety, boxing promoters launched a full-scale publicity campaign in December to ensure a crowded arena for the Christmastime match between Joe Louis and Izzy Gastanaga. Despite heavy advance ticket sales, the fight's promoter, Mike Jacobs, postponed the match at the last minute. He told inquiring reporters that machine gun–toting Cubans had met him when he arrived at Havana's airport and he felt compelled to delay the fight in order to protect the fighters and the fans. Jacobs's charges infuriated Cubans who had counted on the popular "Brown Bomber" to attract big holiday crowds. They claimed that Jacobs had backed out because Louis was out of condition, not because of any imminent danger. Jacobs, of course, denied the accusation.[16] Whatever the truth of the contretemps, it had little apparent effect. The number of visitors increased by 85 percent between 1933–34 and 1935–36. The tourist corporation launched summer school classes for foreign students and packaged low-cost summertime tours for hunters and fisherman, and traffic increased by another 60 percent in the 1936–37 season.

An upturn in the sugar trade prompted talk of recovery, and tourist promoters shared the optimism, encouraged by the arrival, aboard their private yachts, of the well-known North Americans millionaires W. K. Vanderbilt and Vincent Astor and the distinguished and popular actor John Barrymore. The appearance of these celebrities anywhere attracted publicity, and photos from Havana in the social columns of major U.S. newspapers would help to dispel fear. The New York and Cuba Mail Steamship Company made a new film for stateside promotion, and increased traffic between Miami and Havana required daily departures by October 1936.[17]

Concerned with Mexican competition for the North American market, the tourist corporation stirred up a hornet's nest when it tried to revive the colorful spectacle of the bullfight. Offended Cubans did not deny that the *corrida* was part of their Spanish cultural heritage; however, it represented a past that they had rejected in 1898. Supporters countered that their narrow-minded, hypocrital opponents ate steaks with gusto and cheered at boxing matches while they scorned the beauty, skill, and courage displayed in the bullring. If vacationers willingly shot animals and hooked fish for sport, why exclude the drama of matador and bull? A brave death in the arena, they insisted, conferred a nobility on the animal that the anonymity of the slaughterhouse denied.[18] Whatever logic underlay the arguments, the critics prevailed: tourists did without bullfights.

Controversy also surrounded the outlawed Afro-Cuban street parades known as *comparsas*, a blend of European and Creole music and dance with drumming rhythms and movements brought from Africa. More uniquely Cuban than bullfights, carnival *comparsas* would attract tourists and, at the same time, preserve Cuban culture for its citizens. But the processions had been forbidden by law years before, on the grounds that they had encouraged a rowdiness that resulted in violence. A number of highly vocal *habaneros* attacked the parades as reminders of earlier racial discord and thus contrary to the best interests of popular education and culture. "Foreigners do not look to Cuba for what they can find in their own country," Havana's mayor countered. "A program of festivals . . . could put foreigners in touch with our colonial past, our distinctiveness, with the practices of the distinct races in Cuba and with their art." The mayor persisted and gained a powerful advocate in the respected anthropologist Fernando Ortiz. Ortiz argued passionately on behalf of the musical processions as worthy representatives of popular Cuban culture. The colorful costumes, floats, lanterns, music, songs, and dances certainly would impress foreigners, Ortiz asserted, but more importantly, Cubans would enjoy themselves and learn about their background. Opponents finally capitulated, and Havana's city council allocated funds for the dance groups.[19]

99
Culture and Casinos

Having navigated the rough waters of bullfights and *comparsas* with mixed success, the tourist corporation and its allies took up the cause of conservation and preservation and moved the concept of public culture beyond museums, music, and art to include national parks and public recreation areas. A responsive government carved one nature refuge out of the Zapata Swamp, on the island's south shore, and another in the province of Santa Clara. Officials also brought a recreational parkland to Havana, at the city's edge along the Río Almendares. Plans for the park included conservation of trees and vegetation to inspire an appreciation of nature, with balconies overlooking the river for relaxation and quiet contemplation. Recreational areas for family outings included space for team sports. Along with an open-air theater, planners also designed a golf course—for tourists and those Cubans who had an interest in the game. The social utilitarians had prevailed: beautiful cities not only attracted tourists but benefited its residents. The Bosque de la Habana would stand as visible proof that the government cared for its people. When work began on the park in 1937, Fulgencio Batista made a well-publicized visit to the site.[20]

RETURN OF THE CASINOS

The battle between culture and casinos was far from over. The upheaval of 1933 hardly refashioned all Cubans into secular saints, selfless idealists, and good Samaritans. No revolution eradicates self-

interest, and Cuba had its share of pragmatists, opportunists, particu-
laristic profiteers, ambitious social climbers, larcenous businessmen,
and petty thieves, as well as honest workers and do-gooders. As in most
societies most of the time, Cubans tried to maintain a balance between individual advantage and collective public welfare.

A businessman-politician spearheaded the return of the casinos.
Alfredo Hornedo, owner of the newspaper *El país*, built a gaming
establishment. After he was elected to represent Havana Province in
the Senate, the government legalized card playing and other games
of chance in certain identified clubs and casinos. Before long, casino
operations were transferred from civilian to military control, with Fulgencio Batista in charge. Batista, familiar with the acquisitiveness of
his colleagues, suspected that managers at the government's Casino
Nacional underreported gambling revenues. And the earnings potential was considerable. For example, three familiar figures from the
1920s signed hefty IOUs in the resuscitated Casino Nacional on New
Year's Eve, the biggest betting night of the 1937 holiday season: the
Havana car dealer Lawrence Ross, who had brought the Chevrolet
meeting to Havana in the 1920s, gambled alongside the landowner-
speculator Alberto Gómez Mena and the real estate developer Nicolás
Mendoza.[21]

Concerned also that dishonest dealers might discourage tourists,
Batista looked to North Americans to ensure the reputability of the
casino and to protect his own interests. The gambling expert Meyer
Lansky was an old friend from Prohibition days. Lansky, well known
to U.S. federal and state authorities for his bootlegging activities in the
1920s, more recently had acquired a reputation for turning gaming
profits. At the end of Prohibition he and his fellow liquor transporters
had realized that a burgeoning demand for legal whiskey would fall
behind supplies, making a move into liquor manufacturing extremely
lucrative. Lansky became a partner in a company formed to import
molasses, used in dehydrated, powdered form by distilleries during
the fermenting process. The Molaska Corporation registered in Ohio
on 25 November 1933; Prohibition ended 5 December 1933; Batista
led the ouster of Grau San Martín in January 1934. Lansky went to
Cuba shortly thereafter and concluded a deal to buy the raw material—molasses—needed for his dehydration plants. When competition crowded the liquor business, Lansky moved on to illicit, profitable
gambling.[22]

Whether Batista turned to Lansky for help only after Cuban gaming had been reestablished, or had intended to include Lansky all along, remains unclear. Nevertheless, when Batista put out a call for help, Lansky rounded up his pit crews and went to Havana. There he could run card games, dice tables, and roulette wheels openly, in a town where gambling was legal. Lansky regularized casino operations, and Cuba looked forward to a tourist resurgence.

MAKING THE BEST OF IT

By the end of the 1930s Cuba offered tourists both culture and casinos. They traveled to parks, nature preserves, and beaches; they visited the giant rock formations at Viñales, created thousands of years earlier by the earth's movement, and enjoyed the centuries-old colonial city of Trinidad. But they also frequented the racetrack and gambling rooms. Visitors doted on rumba and conga lines and watched in fascination as Afro-Cuban *comparsas* filled the carnival nights with music and dance. They dined magnificently in elegant supper clubs or cheaply in cafés, listened to music in theaters as well as cabarets, or sat around plain wooden tables in a typical dive, watching Cuban couples move sinuously to Latin rhythms under bare light bulbs that cast shadows on plain or garishly painted cinder block walls. Tourists left fourteen million dollars in Cuba in 1941; but the United States entered World War II at the end of the year, and the market disappeared once more.[23]

Warning signs of wartime exigencies had appeared even before any official declaration of hostilities. For example, military exercises prevented U.S. participation in Cuba's 1939 competitive winter aviation meet, intended as a tourist attraction. Cuba offered to host the Pan American games in February and March of 1940 as a replacement for the war-interrupted Olympiad but had to abandon the plan in favor of a small-scale sports carnival. When the tourist commission sponsored the midwinter championship for star class yachts (held every January since 1926), the U.S. Yacht Racing Association declined to enter, citing wartime conditions in the Atlantic Ocean and the folly of unnecessary civilian risk. Moreover, commercial aircraft and ships that formerly transported tourists increasingly served military purposes, taking matériel to European allies even before they carried troops. Visitors to

Florida feared setting out for Cuba by way of the Atlantic even when transportation was available.[24]

Trying to paint a bright lining on an ominous cloud, tourist officials labeled the war a "pause," a time to prepare for a postwar inundation when North Americans would head south. They formed local committees and discussed the construction of small airfields and quality hotels and the development of curative mineral springs in anticipation of increased travel and fierce competition. Unfortunately for the enthusiastic tourism planners, sugar proved a great seducer of private capital and public concern. For the duration of the war and even after, as the market expanded and prices held, workers labored in the cane fields and sugar mills, not on accommodations for tourists. Facilities should have been built or refurbished, but they deteriorated instead. At war's end, Cuba was ill prepared for a tourist boom.

Chapter 7

Intermission in Cuba and a
Sea Change in Tourism

In the frosty cold of November 1941, with news from Europe
adding a further chill, the film *Week-end in Havana* opened in New
York City, promising to exchange biting winter winds and nagging
worries for tropical sunshine and romance:

FADE IN	Long shot, New York skyline; snow falls
DISSOLVE TO	Montage shot of pamphlets, literature
SUPERIMPOSED	"Cuba—The Holiday Isle of the Tropics"
DISSOLVE TO	Long shot, office building
CLOSE UP	Sign, "McCracken Steamship Co"
MOVE TO	Sign in window, "Sail to Romance"
DISSOLVE TO	Hotel interior, supper club
CLOSE UP	Nightclub singer, Carmen Miranda, singing:

How would you like to spend the weekend in Havana?

How would you like to see the Caribbean shore?
How would you like to go where nights are so romantic?
. . .

If you would like to spend a week-end in Havana
You better pack up all your summer clothes
See you down at Sloppy Joe's
So long boy and ship ahoy—Havana![1]

Box office favorites Alice Faye and John Payne dangled a lot of desires from a meager plot line. A young, beautiful Macy's sales girl resolutely saves part of her meager salary for a dream vacation in Havana. On the way the ship runs aground under questionable circumstances, so McCracken Steamship sends Mr. Payne to show Miss Faye a good time in Havana to forestall legal procedures against the company. Carmen Miranda and Cesar Romero spark the action with romantic fireworks, Latin style.

Glamorously gowned for nightclub scenes, tastefully attired for daytime, Faye samples picturesque Havana, excursions punctuated by such songs as "Tropical Magic" and "Romance and Rumba." The thrifty working girl contentedly returns to New York, more than sufficiently rewarded for every self-denial required to purchase her ticket.

Travelers finally returned to Cuba five years after Alice Faye's screen image had shown them Havana, but that half-decade break might well have been a Rip van Winkle slumber. Hollywood's salute to Cuba hit the movie theaters just before Japanese bombs struck Pearl Harbor, and World War II altered the tourist trade forever. First of all, aircraft capacity expanded in size and range to meet wartime needs for military personnel and equipment on battlefields reaching from the North Atlantic to the South Pacific. Improved communications kept track of planes, people, and matériel. After the war, those planes would lose their primary mission but remain fully functional. Moreover, the economically significant aircraft industry on the west coast of the United States would be in need of a new market in order to maintain profits and keep its labor force employed.

Secondly, many people who had had neither the expectation nor inclination to travel before the war now found themselves moving around—or moved against their will. Hundreds of thousands of people traveled overseas, courtesy of the U.S. military; civilians traversed the country, following family members or jobs. The United States experienced a major population shift from east to west, with California absorbing the lion's share of new residents. Displaced persons and war refugees with ties to other homelands would settle in the United States after the war.

Thirdly, in addition to physical movement from place to place, wartime photography and news stories imparted vicarious experiences and stirred curiosity about countries, cities, and seacoasts where battles had taken place. The names of islands that were little more than specks on a map became familiar through headlines, newsreels, and feature films. Returning GIs brought stories, memories, and even wives to share with their families. They created new ties with previously ignored locations in Europe and Asia and new incentives to travel.

HEMISPHERIC SOLIDARITY AND
LATIN AMERICAN TOURISM

Even before the war began, President Roosevelt had had a firm grasp of tourism's economic and political potential. Encourage visitors, he had told the Cuban delegation in 1935, but lure their dollars with family travel and natural attractions, not casinos and gambling. Cuba's earnings represented only a tiny portion ($13.6 million) of the $5.7 billion spent worldwide on travel in 1939. A considerable proportion of those billions generally found its way to Europe in response to both traditional travel patterns and effective promotional campaigns. European nations deluged America, both north and south, with literature that made the continent's appeal compelling. Because of the renewed threat to trans-Atlantic travel, as well as actual and threatened acts of war on the continent, FDR and his advisers reasoned that the tourist stream could be diverted to the Americas to strengthen hemispheric ties. Most Latin American governments had pledged their nations to a united front against fascism, but subversion and erosion of commitment remained a constant threat. Since the hemisphere had long served as a source of raw materials for Europe's industries, and access to minerals, fibers, and food would be critical in an attenuated conflict, the U.S. prepared to foil enemy penetration in all forms, whether clandestine operations involving acts of sabotage, infiltration into government ranks, or propaganda.

Roosevelt declared 1940 "Travel America Year" and actively entered the field of travel promotion. He urged completion of the long-planned Pan American highway as a stimulus to the inter-American tourist trade. (He knew, of course, that the highway also would be a necessary transportation artery in the event of war.) Planners projected a string of hotels and camps rising alongside the motorway, a paved ribbon that would wind its way through the hemisphere's natural beauty and tie countries together for friendly visits among neighbors. In the spirit of the times, representatives of leading hotel operators established the Inter-America Hotel Federation and planned ways to increase travel, shelter the weary tourist, and—not incidentally—capture the financial benefits.[2]

To achieve hemispheric solidarity, Roosevelt created the office of Coordinator of Inter-American Affairs (CIAA) and selected as its leader Nelson A. Rockefeller, a young man whose family business interests had given him a familiarity with, and concern for, Latin America. Rockefeller assumed responsibility for commercial and cultural aspects of hemispheric defense, reporting directly to the president and coordinating activities with the State Department. The CIAA countered actual and potential Axis propaganda with its own media blitz of newsreels, documentaries, travelogues, and feature films. Rockefeller kept the cameras grinding out such films as *Viva Mexico, Highway to Friendship, Gaucho Sports,* and *Cuba: Land of Romance and Adventure.* By the time *Week-end in Havana* opened, Washington and Hollywood had formed a mutually beneficial patriotic alliance. Moviemakers mobilized to counter enemy subversion and mentally prepare citizens to defend Latin America in the event of armed conflict in the hemisphere. Film studio executives also looked to Latin Americans to replace the fast-disappearing European market. They accepted Washington's directives, including a measure of censorship, and depicted Latin America as friendly territory.[3]

Hollywood sent moviegoers on dozens of imaginary trips to Latin America. Through such musical comedies as *Down Argentine Way, Fiesta, That Night in Rio, They Met in Argentina, Carnival in Costa Rica, Holiday in Mexico,* and *Luxury Liner,* movie fans learned to rumba, samba, and conga. Even feature films set in the United States offered elaborate musical production numbers with a Latin beat. Xavier Cugat was as well known an orchestra leader as Harry James. In Walt Disney's *Saludos Amigos* popular cartoon characters cavorted to Latin rhythms through Peru, Argentina, and Brazil.[4] Entertainment films, cleverly crafted to carry the government's wartime message, undoubtedly roused some viewers to head south of the border as soon as the war ended.

As early as 1943 Rockefeller began to evaluate peacetime objectives in Latin America and concluded that the primacy of U.S. influence there must be maintained. Several European nations already were discussing postwar economic relations with Latin America, including industrialization schemes. Once reestablished in the hemisphere, Rockefeller reasoned, Europeans might influence client nations to drastically restrict their imports of U.S. manufactures. Since European competition might prove detrimental to U.S. interests on the economic battleground of Latin America, the CIAA, under Rockefeller's direction, linked private U.S. industrialists with the appropriate business sectors in twenty American republics. The resulting Inter-American Development Commission studied issues relevant to postwar economic prospects: finance, power and communications, raw materials development, manufacturing, transportation — and tourism. The commission specifically recommended tourist promotion and construction of the airports, roads, ports, and other facilities requisite to mass travel.[5]

At the same time, Roosevelt called Pan American Airways president Juan T. Trippe to the White House one morning and, over breakfast, thrashed out Trippe's role in the postwar economic picture. Roosevelt pictured Europe, its war-ravaged countries incapable immediately of absorbing substantial amounts of U.S. goods. Inevitable cutbacks in U.S. production would coincide with the return of hundreds of thousands of military personnel to the civilian labor force, a sure formula for unemployment and an economic downturn. Clearly, the country needed rapid market expansion to avoid repetition of the country's post–World War I experience.

Trippe and his company figured significantly in Roosevelt's economic plans; that is, businessmen and tourists could put dollars in the hands of Latin Americans who would use them to buy U.S.-produced goods, such as equipment for new industries or consumer goods that had been unavailable during the war. In the circularity of hemispheric commerce, traveling Americans would put dollars in the hands of Latin Americans whose purchases would, in turn, sustain U.S. factory operations. Thus high-volume, low-cost air travel would maintain profits for the airline and the factory owner and contribute to prosperity. Tourists and businessmen would likely fly on Pan American, the airline that had pioneered hemispheric passenger and cargo flights to Havana and beyond in the 1920s. But where would they find the comforts of home when they arrived in distant Latin American cities? Pan American's airline business needed a hotel component, FDR advised, and in the best interest of the country, he would help. Trippe, swayed by the logic of Roosevelt's arguments and the promise of government backing, sent a company representative to South America in search of local capital and official support. When he secured sufficient interest, PAA spawned the "hotel chain with wings," Intercontinental Hotel Corporation (IHC). The company put up only one million dollars of its own funds in 1946, while the Export-Import Bank, founded by Roosevelt in 1934, extended twenty-five million dollars in credit to launch the venture.[6]

Roosevelt and Trippe hatched a chick, and the hatchling fattened into a bird that produced golden eggs. By 1950 IHC planned one hundred million dollars' worth of construction, including hotels in Bogotá, Colombia; San Juan, Puerto Rico; Mexico City, Mexico; and Santo Domingo, Dominican Republic. Pan American Airways' hotel subsidiary mobilized local funds for construction financing and collected substantial fees to supervise the architectural and engineering functions. Once completed, IHC operated each hotel under a management fee, and its parent airline promoted air travel with the promise of pure water, ice, and air conditioning at the end of the flight. Moreover, the airline used its worldwide network of ticket offices to generate hotel traffic.[7]

Thus tourism emerged as an economic development strategy after the war, and its nature changed as the industry gained importance and became enmeshed in transnational corporate and institutional networks. Many countries learned to appreciate the contribution of foreign travelers to domestic revenue and employment. The International Bank for Reconstruction and Development (World Bank) loaned money for tourism infrastructure projects, and the United Nations Economic and Social Council (UNESCO) assisted in the rehabilitation of historical and cultural attractions in economically vulnerable nations. While Europe struggled to regain economic and social stability, Soviet advances and the subsequent Cold War polarized the world into capitalist and communist camps.

A powerful United States, moving quickly to rebuild Europe,

launched development schemes elsewhere to alleviate the poverty that might invite communist subversion. Tourism figured prominently in both efforts, a relatively quick way to infuse economies with needed hard currency. Few if any pleasure travelers saw themselves as soldiers in the Cold War, but U.S. citizens had saved money when there was little to buy and, properly motivated, would spend it where it was needed. Working people, not unlike Alice Faye's fictional salesgirl, became a prime target for tour packagers who turned a week's paid vacation into a fantasy journey. A *Washington Post* film critic had predicted in 1941 that "Technicolor Havana . . . will set the tourist trade about the thrifty business of saving their pennies . . . to spend gaily in a . . . quest of some such prodigious pastel Paradise." Four years of deprivation, saving, and better-paying jobs had built a market, and Hollywood fantasies served peacetime as well as wartime goals.[8]

Cuba's tourism promoters woke up to a changed environment that swept the once-unique island into a Latin American/Caribbean tourist region, one corner of a worldwide pleasure-oriented travel business. Tourism's expansion was good for the United States but not necessarily best for Cuba. True, FDR had stamped his approval on Latin American tourism and had put public monies behind its growth; but for Cuba, the president's actions meant increased competition from other destinations. Although the major thrust of development policy pushed industrialization, shortages of natural resources and small domestic markets propelled a number of Caribbean islands into tourism instead. Beach resorts could be developed profitably with lower investment costs and less imported machinery than required to start factories. As vacation destinations, Jamaica, Haiti, the Dominican Republic, the Bahamas, Bermuda, the Virgin Islands, Puerto Rico, and other islands enjoyed the same attractions as Cuba: tropical climate, sandy beaches, and warm, blue sea. Once they recognized the potential for jobs and profits in vacation resorts, island governments pursued tourists in an organized, aggressive fashion.

The tourist commission had spent the early 1940s in eager anticipation of a postwar influx. Members held conferences and established local bureaus to coordinate public and private efforts. In their analysis, postwar chaos would impede travel to Europe, and the flow of U.S. tourists, who had spent some hundred million dollars in pursuit of relaxation and new experiences on the continent before the war, could—and must—be channeled in their direction. An abundance of military aircraft converted to peacetime use would keep fares in the affordable range. Despite fierce competition from other Latin American countries, Cubans reasoned, their location, reputation, and years of experience represented a decided advantage for local entrepreneurs.[9]

Many Cubans expressed less enthusiasm than the tourist backers, however, as they evaluated the overall aims of U.S. recovery programs. The enhanced world stature of their neighbor worried them, and they asked themselves to what degree might they control their own destiny in the postwar power configuration. Although humanitarians applauded the dismantling of colonial empires in Africa and Asia, they tended to overlook the less formalized domination that the United States exercised over Latin America. Cubans weighed their options. Since U.S. banks had accumulated wartime savings, perhaps Cubans could leverage the need for capital investment into industrialization schemes geared to national interests. On the other hand, new industries would require protection to compete with cheaply produced imported goods. High tariffs raised prices, hurt mass consumers, and might encourage U.S. retaliation against Cuban sugar. Furthermore, would industrialization in a free market system help Cuba economically if a mechanized sugar industry fueled unemployment?[10]

Uncertainty generated more questions than answers for the troubled Cubans. The war's end might signal a real opportunity if they gained control over the process of economic development and channeled investment to suit their own needs, but was that possible if U.S. financial interests supplied the capital? If anything, the wartime economy had tightened the U.S.-Cuban relationship. Cuba still depended on sugar and tobacco exports to the United States. How did tourism fit into the equation? It represented diversity but not self-sufficiency. Cubans could run the business, but with Europe not yet recovered, a resurgent industry counted on even closer relations with the United States.

Moreover, foreign investors might hesitate to put their money in Cuba under a leadership remembered for its nationalist leanings. The reformist generation of 1933 had triumphed in Cuba's 1944 presidential elections, with Ramón Grau San Martín as the new chief executive. Grau's presidency had drawn Roosevelt's disapproval in 1934, and in 1944 U.S. business executives feared that his leadership signaled more government regulation, labor power, and a detrimental collusion between Cuban-born company supervisors and nationalistic public officials. When it came time to hold presidential elections in 1948, however, two of the three candidates announced clear intentions to protect foreign interests. The winner, Carlos Prío Socarrás, unequivocally declared that he intended to "provide every practical facility for the investment of foreign capital in Cuba, especially American."[11]

While U.S. and Cuban public officials and businessmen sniffed each other warily, uncertain who was predator and who the prey, ordinary North Americans joyously greeted the end of the war with vacation plans. By the late 1940s, at least thirty-six million U.S. wage earners enjoyed paid vacations. Moreover, some two million farmers earned a comfortable annual income of five thousand dollars or more, and their work load diminished at the height of the Caribbean winter season. Unfortunately for Cuba's 1945–46 winter season, plans for tourist-related investment in airport and highway construction, hotels, park development, museums, and public monuments still lay on the drawing board. A desperate tourist bureaucracy pleaded with residents in Havana and Marianao to rent rooms in their homes to visitors and urged small investors to develop low-cost tent camps. Despite hotel room, food, and gasoline shortages, crowded bus and train facilities, and inflation-driven high prices, Cuba quickly inaugurated new campaigns to capture vacationers, mindful of the expanded market and fearful of growing competition.[12] (Direct flights from New York to Havana cost $150 round trip, but plane fare to Bermuda cost only $124.)

VIPERS IN A TOURIST EDEN

Holiday tourists added thirty-seven million dollars to Cuba's foreign exchange earnings in 1947, but Mexico also advanced its tourism plans. The Mexican government turned Acapulco into a world-class recreational complex for affluent vacationers and outlined proposals for a large-scale tourist industry. When significantly large numbers of North Americans headed for the heavily promoted Mexico City summer schools in 1948, Cuba dropped its summer hotel rates, solicited more convention business, turned up the pressure on investors to build hotels, and advertised for fearless explorers willing to fly to picturesque foreign cities, namely, historic interior towns such as Bayamo and Trinidad.[13] In 1951, when Cuba captured some fifty million of the nineteen billion dollars that U.S. residents spent on travel, Mexico took in three hundred million dollars. Furthermore, the Caribe Hilton opened in Puerto Rico, and Jamaica's Montego Bay filled with beachside hotels nestled among the palm trees. Vacationers visited Cuba, but they also went to neighboring islands, where they stretched out under the same sun, swam among tropical fish in the same aquamarine Caribbean sea, and drank rum punch from coconut shells.

While Havana had much to offer, its mostly urban hotels badly needed refurbishing, and they had no inviting sandy beaches just outside their doors. Much of the city's shoreline is rocky and hardly suitable for lounging or frolics in the surf. La Playa, the attractive, sandy public beach at Marianao, lay about ten miles from the downtown area. Varadero did not begin to emerge as an international playground until air taxis from Havana put tourists on its beaches in half an hour. While Cuban capitalists invested millions of dollars in hotels and apartments in Florida, North Americans invested two million dollars in Varadero's International Hotel. The tourist commission howled in outrage. Why were Cubans sending their money abroad, when they had not built a single hotel in Havana in fifteen years?[14]

Moreover, Hilton and Intercontinental, hotel chains that mobilized local capital in other countries, bypassed Cuba. Some analysts and critics blamed politically powerful, militant labor unions for investor caution. Batista had traded his permission to unionize workers for labor's support in the 1940 elections. He had won the presidency, and organized labor had gained political clout. Successive governments mandated industrywide wage increases for purposes of political mobilization, often at the expense of economic rationality, and job protection legislation made dismissals difficult. No wonder hotel chains and independent entrepreneurs hesitated to take on the challenge of doing business in Cuba.

The presidential election campaign of 1948 found Cubans more cynical than ever about their corrupt politicians. The elected officials who gained power in 1944 proved themselves one more phalanx of greedy officeholders. With high sugar demand and prices sustained by European production shortages (and later by the outbreak of hostilities in Korea), money flowed into government coffers. Public payrolls swelled, and lucrative contracts once again filled private pockets. Elected and appointed guardians of Cuba's patrimony embezzled and stole at a level that would have reddened the faces of even the most profligate office holders in Cuba's long history of abuse. A 1947 *New*

York Times headline blared, "Grau Losing Grip on Cuban Public," as the Auténticos, the authentic heirs of the 1933 revolution, alienated even ardent supporters with exceptional graft, corruption, and scandal.[15] Despite record-breaking government revenues and millions of dollars expended on public works, the vital connecting highway between Havana and Varadero Beach still had not been completed.

Moreover, Grau had not kept his promise to remove the war taxes that artificially elevated prices and made Cuba less competitive in the tourist industry. Meat, butter, lard, rice, beans, and other essential items brought outrageous prices in the black market. When the government granted workers across-the-board increases to maintain real wage rates, the concession raised hotel and restaurant prices accordingly. Did Cuba have sufficient tourist attractions to overcome price differentials? Or would budget-conscious vacationers—the wage-earning mass market—go to other places with equivalent appeal?

Already subject to economic and political handicaps, the tourist industry reeled when reports connected the U.S. mobster Charles "Lucky" Luciano (Salvatore Lucania) with gambling activities at the Jockey Club and Casino Nacional, two critical centers of tourist activity. Luciano, a veteran of the prostitution and bootlegging eras of U.S. organized criminal activities, had been sent to prison on drug-trafficking charges in 1936 and was paroled and deported to his native Italy a decade later. Shortly after Luciano's departure, the U.S. Bureau of Narcotics noted an increase of Turkish heroin on the streets and traced its route through Italy. When Luciano showed up in Havana late in 1946, U.S. narcotics agents consulted their files. Accumulated information on his Cuban connections convinced them that he intended to establish Havana as a transfer point for the hugely profitable heroin trade into the United States.

Once in Cuba, Luciano rented a home in suburban Miramar and met with old friends and colleagues from Havana and the United States during a six-month period while the U.S. unsuccessfully pressured Cuban officials to oust him. *Habaneros* complained that the longtime Mafia boss enjoyed protection from high Cuban officials. The interior minister refused to order Luciano's appearance for a hearing on illicit drug trafficking charges, most likely to avoid revealing the names of his Cuban associates. Only when the U.S. Narcotics Bureau threatened to cut off supplies of legitimate medical narcotics did the Cubans arrest Luciano and send him back to Italy. Facing expulsion early in 1947, Luciano called his Mafia subordinates to a meeting in Havana and told them to obey Meyer Lansky, the man in charge of Luciano's interests in the United States.[16]

By 1947 Lansky and many other organized crime figures in the United States were heavily involved in lucrative illegal gambling establishments and were moving into legal casino investments in Nevada. It was generally assumed that Havana was Lansky territory because of his casino activities there in the 1930s. Rumors circulated that Luciano wanted a piece of the postwar Cuban casino action and that Lansky sent an informer to talk with an agent of the Narcotics Bureau, who passed the word to Harry Anslinger, commissioner of narcotics. Anslinger contacted the Cuban ambassador to the United States, who telephoned Cuban president Grau San Martín and advised deportation. According to this scenario, Grau consulted with Lansky, who advised him to wait for a good excuse, which Anslinger provided with the threat to withhold medical narcotics.[17]

If Luciano's activities helped to focus Cubans' rage on the venality of the Grau presidency, it certainly offered no relief to know that the mobster enjoyed a long-established relationship with Francisco Prío Socarrás, whose brother Carlos followed Grau to the presidency after the 1948 election. Cubans had publicly laundered a great deal of dirty linen during that election campaign. Newspaper editorials blamed bribable officials for the lack of enthusiasm among honest investors. Moreover, government regulations and decrees favorable to labor daunted capitalists. Skittish entrepreneurs and financiers needed reassurances of an equitable business climate. If Cubans would not invest in their own economy, why should foreigners assume risks? Understandably, when the newly elected Carlos Prío Socarrás visited the United States in December 1948, he made a crucial pilgrimage to Wall Street as well as to Washington.[18]

Harry Truman, buoyed by his own upset electoral victory, extended Prío a warm welcome. In his response, Prío emphasized Cuba's importance to the United States; that is, the island remained the world's per capita leader in consumption of U.S. products. Truman's display of support was intended to boost Prío's stature with his Cuban constituents, as well as to impress and encourage financiers and industrialists. Mounting inflation and rising world production of sugar in 1948 made Cubans uneasy. Even the most prosperous year in Cuba's history could not overcome nagging uncertainties. After all, sugar had failed them before. Tourism hovered offstage, the stand-in waiting to substitute for an ailing star. While Prío courted approval and investment, a Cuban couple in ruffled rumba costumes smiled broadly at New Yorkers from the pages of their newspapers and wooed them to a tropical holiday isle, billed as a gayer-than-ever land of sunshine and adventure.[19]

The 1948–49 winter tourist season lagged, however, plagued by high prices, inadequate accommodations, and competition. Even moderately priced tours—under $30 a day, including air fare—failed to attract the desired crowds. Mexico had opened seventeen new hotels in 1947, spent $400,000 for publicity in the United States in 1948, and pulled in some 235,000 visitors. Although the market base clearly had expanded, Cuba barely surpassed its prewar peak of 162,300. In fact, tourist dollars flowed out rather than in, as Cubans with money in their pockets and looking for good times spent more on foreign trips than visitors left in Cuba.

Havana's top nightclubs, Tropicana and Sans Souci, struggling to cover their inflation-burdened overhead, threatened to close their doors unless the government permitted them to open gaming rooms. Under considerable pressure, Prío opened the doors to gambling, although the Luciano affair, still fresh in most people's memories, stirred the local cynics. Did Prío concede to the nightclub owners out of a genuine concern for business prospects, or did the decree really reflect the heavy hand of foreign gambling interests? Prío had served as Grau's labor minister and prime minister and might prove as corruptible as his predecessor. While critics carped about his motives, hotel and restaurant owners welcomed the potential boost to their incomes. Convinced that gambling would increase their profitability, hotels cut room rates, and bars and restaurants installed air conditioners to lure summer visitors.[20]

Prío's concession in fact positioned Cuba to take advantage of a shift in U.S. tourism policy. Late in 1950 the Commerce Department officially endorsed a campaign to encourage American pleasure travel to Latin America. Despite Washington's enthusiasm for hemispheric tourism when the war ended, Soviet expansion into Eastern Europe necessarily had shifted the leadership's emphasis. Responding to fears that the Soviet Union might overrun all of Europe, the Commerce Department's International Travel Office urged travelers to spend their dollars on the continent to aid European recovery.[21] By 1950 Western Europe appeared less threatened, while Latin America loomed as a Cold War battleground. The alchemists of tourism moved to convert sun and sand into gold and to keep the hemisphere from turning red.

Few people outside government circles and the travel industry followed the evolution of tourism into a global phenomenon. Package tours made international travel a viable and desirable vacation option, even for the working classes of the industrial societies of Europe and North America. The well-ingrained consumer culture had survived the economic restrictions of the Great Depression and the patriotic sacrifices of the war effort. Indeed, while the war altered peoples' lives and outlook in many ways, desires had been deferred, not interred. New hungers, new curiosities, new demands piled atop the old ones. Foreign travel for pleasure was among the many items on consumers' wish lists, but homes and cars, clothing and appliances, no doubt, came first. What factors shaped the 1950s travel market in the United States and moved people in Cuba's direction? As with the tourist boom of the 1920s, aspects of popular culture, along with promotional materials, communicated the island's temptations, and hundreds of thousands of tourists fulfilled vacation dreams.

Chapter 8

Blue Water, Green Money
Act 2, Curtain Up

On polished ballroom floors and on worn linoleum with rugs rolled back against the wall, pairs of feet in all sizes cut new figures timed to an irresistible Cuban beat. "What the heck is a mambo?" Vaughn Monroe inquired musically on his best-selling 1954 record. From New York to California, the insistent rhythm propelled dancers into action. They knew little or nothing about Cuba, but they danced the mambo. People for whom the word *vacation* signaled a break from routine, but rarely conjured up images of tropical islands and plea- sure, caught "mambomania." Legions of Arthur Murray dance studio instructors taught their eager pupils *mambiar*, to dance the mambo.[1]

Dance crazes had swept the nation before. The fox-trot, Charles- ton, and jitterbug had snared devotees in their times and offended the sensibilities of genteel traditionalists. Latin America had contributed more than its share of sensational musical kinetics. Rudolph Valentino's sinuous tango captured the sexuality of dance in a physical embrace that chased sedate waltzers off the floor. Tourists of the 1920s taught their stay-at-home neighbors and friends how to rumba, dancing to records that they carried home from Cuba as souvenirs. The lively Brazilian samba pulsated its way northward. Long lines of gleeful dancers snaked in and out of dance halls and high school gymnasiums, bouncing to a one-two-three-kick Americanized version of the Cuban conga.

Mambo had swept Havana in the 1940s and had entered the United States along with thousands of emigrating and visiting Cubans late in the decade. Pérez Prado shook the usually decorous Waldorf Astoria ballroom, while well-known Broadway dance spots featured "mamboramas" and hired hefty bouncers to keep the boisterous crowds in line. Meanwhile, the cha-cha waited to catch the next wave north. For dancers and lovers of good times, why not dance in Cuba if you could afford the trip?

Arguably, a trip to Cuba may have assuaged nagging worries. Any identifiable decade or similarly delimited period of time exhibits continuities and changes, familiar patterns and distinctive characteristics. Remembered through the distorting blur of the chaotic 1960s, the immediate postwar years may appear to have been a relatively benign calm between two upheavals. In reality, people in the 1950s tried to cope with wrenching disruptions: communism's spread, the threat of nuclear annihilation, and challenges to the racial status quo.

China's revolution generated fears of a communist "yellow peril" after 1949. Would war in the Korean peninsula spread to the rest of Asia or perhaps precipitate nuclear confrontation? Children dropped to classroom floors with their hands over their heads and practiced their responses to a nuclear attack. Julius and Ethel Rosenberg lost their lives to fears of atomic weaponry, communist subversion, and a general unease. Veterans had barely finished school on the GI Bill, settled down, and started families, when a spate of war novels crystalized their shared experience of tenuous existence—life one moment, death the next. On the other hand, some men and women shoved the pain and sacrifice of World War II to the sidelines of memory and looked back at the war years with a touch of nostalgia for the possibility of extraordinary personal encounters in exotic places, for the sense of risk and discovery away from home, for the challenge of the unfamiliar.

Not everyone donned gray flannel suits with ease or found apron strings comfortable. When the harness of propriety chafed, beatniks went on the road and teenagers rebelled without cause. Racial minorities, excluded from suburban dreams, questioned the comfort that seemed to come at their expense and demanded long-delayed civil rights. African Americans walked through the doors of previously segregated schools, sat down at forbidden lunch counters and in the front of the bus. Clearly, times were changing.

The 1950s brought television into people's homes, a box that opened the world in the middle of their living rooms and rattled complacency. News that a major crime was committed every fifteen seconds menaced the personal security of those suburban homeowners more interested in kitchen curtains than Iron Curtains. The U.S. Senate investigated the insidious influence of organized crime in local government and then plumbed the subversive influence of communism in the military and diplomatic ranks. And they did it all on television. Concerned citizens drew the wagons in a circle; whoever was different was dangerous. Conform to some poorly defined standard of conduct or risk suspicion and ostracism.

Television entertained as well as informed and frightened. In fact, the most talked about, most watched show of the decade introduced families in the United States to a Cuban-born bandleader who frequently pounded a tall drum and called out "Babalú." Uninitiated North American viewers understandably overlooked this reference to a high priest of *santería*. The whole country loved Ricky and Lucy Ricardo. Every week the funny, often sentimental, antics of Desi Arnaz's nightclub owner and Lucille Ball's restive housewife rewarded viewers' devotion.

I Love Lucy captivated its first television audience in 1951, the same year that a New York working girl, Barbara Dubivsky, took her dream vacation and fulfilled the prewar promise of *Week-end in Havana*. "Along about this time every year," Dubivsky wrote in a *New York Times* essay, "hundreds of briefly liberated young working ladies stagger up the gangplanks of cruise ships, bringing their savings in the form of new clothes and a round-trip passage to southern places. Most of them are fully prepared to meet loads of interesting people."[2] For about five hundred dollars, two months' pay for the average secretary, Dubivsky had her fling and then returned to work, just like Alice Faye. Single working women—most of whom lived at home until they married—could afford to travel and dared to venture out alone in search of interesting people. But did the phrase "briefly liberated" extend to married women like the fictional Lucy Ricardo?

Much of the humor of *I Love Lucy* derived from a basic plot line—a husband who wants a traditional wife is married to a stagestruck spouse who tries to break into show business. He spends his working hours in a nightclub and wants her to be at home; she yearns for the spotlight and a little glamour. Ricky won the battle of the sexes each episode, but never the war. The half-hour show about love and family reached ten million homes in 1952, and the characters struck a chord that vibrated in many American kitchens. Once a week, Lucy pushed the parameters of acceptable behavior, offered vicarious experiences, enjoyed occasional fun-filled triumphs, tolerated weekly frustrations. Occasionally penitent, she never gave up. Lucy's public pregnancy broke television barriers, but for the most part, the Ricardos' marriage remained within the cultural norms.

HAPPINESS IS HAVANA

The Cuban tourist commission could not have written a better script. Like characters in one of Cecil B. DeMille's 1920s movie plots (before his epic period), Lucy and Ricky breathed a little madness into their marital relationship and improved the bond. And like the Ricardos, vacationers briefly challenged restraints or tried to recapture romance or a sense of freedom lost to household responsibilities. Seeking, yearning, escaping, affirming, rejecting, repressed or hedonistic, they reflected the ambivalence of the 1950s. A UCLA coed, asked by a magazine pollster what she wanted out of life, responded, "Why, a good sensible life." Then she quickly added, "But, you know, of course, not too darned sensible."[3]

Few Americans ever heard of that University of California student, but many of them identified with her fictional alter ego in the popular Broadway musical and film *Guys and Dolls*. Who could have been more sensible than Sister Sarah Brown, Damon Runyon's covered-to-the-neck, oxford-shod proselytizer from the Save Your Soul Mission? In Runyon's short story the proper Miss Brown implausibly fell for the gambler Sky Masterson and he for her. In an unpredictable fantasy world, love tamed and redeemed an offbeat Broadway character. The theatrical version of Sarah Brown let loose and bent standards of conduct without really breaking them. Audiences loved this battle of the sexes fought with 1950s temptations—gambling and trips to Havana.

Confident, swaggering Sky Masterson bets on anything. He even wagers that he can take the buttoned-up mission sister to Havana. Havana, the sin capital of the hemisphere; surely she will never consent. Masterson wins, of course, providing an opportunity for a rousing, colorful dance number set in Cuba. Sarah Brown does the rumba, falls in love in the sensual tropics, but keeps her virginity. Redeeming love gains a steamy physical passion, and gamblers are, by turn, tough and touchingly romantic. At the end of the show, Brown and Masterson marry and, one assumes, live traditionally ever after—the acceptable conclusion for 1950s entertainment being first wed, then bed.

Who needed a better reason to try Havana? Cuba brought a do-gooder to life without robbing her of virtue. In most cases, the sexual double standard that prevailed in the United States followed travelers to the tropics, that is, romance for single women, with sex as an option for men. The show opened in 1950, and Barbara Dubivsky bought her steamship ticket in 1951.

Trips to Cuba brought *I Love Lucy* and *Guys and Dolls* to life, as they had fleshed out filmed Latin romantics of the 1920s. Tourists may have followed the mambo or the Ricardos or Sarah Brown to Cuba, but once there they were greeted by serious, self-congratulatory tourism promoters who had cajoled officials, laid plans, struggled against economic odds, fashioned an image, and cultivated the contemporary North American market. Consider an ordinary young adult celebrating a twenty-first birthday in 1957, the high point of the tourist boom. A recent entry into the responsibilities of the workplace and the burdens of family, he or she began life during the Great Depression, attended elementary school accompanied by war bulletins, and graduated high school to a world of atomic threats, loyalty oaths, red tides, and yellow perils. Why wouldn't such a person translate lascivious La Habana as Spanish for "letting go" and regard a visit to Cuba as well-deserved relaxation?

In the transitional era between the clumsy groping of the drive-in movie and the boastful sexuality of the hot tub, Cuba offered tourists an acceptable way to succumb to temptation without scandalizing the neighbors. The suburban striver removed his necktie; the PTA president hid her hat and gloves. Offered many temptations, they might visit a reasonable facsimile of Ricky Ricardo's nightclub, open up to the tropics like Sarah Brown, change personality, find (or become) the equivalent of a Playboy centerfold, and learn for themselves what Kinsey reported on human sexuality. Then they returned home to respectability.

Some tourists spelled Cuba s-e-x. Havana's more than ten thousand prostitutes openly solicited visiting conventioneers, college students, or any unaccompanied male. Some of them whispered invitations from behind shuttered windows; others accosted men on the streets and in small, dark bars where liaisons could be arranged easily. Havana's prostitutes shifted their locations with the market, moving from seamen who prowled the dock areas to the abundance of tourists staked out alongside the newer hotels. It would be stretching the evidence to suggest that closing the door to Cuba in 1961 encouraged more openness at home. Though the thought of a connection between political revolution in Cuba and sexual revolution in the United States is intriguing, the introduction of birth control pills probably figured more prominently in changed attitudes and behaviors.

LAS VEGAS IN THE CARIBBEAN

Aspirations of turning Havana into a cultured Paris or a sophisticated Monte Carlo dimmed; instead a proliferation of casinos transformed Havana into an ersatz Las Vegas. While Cuba's temptations perhaps reflect the temper of the United States in the 1950s, they also reveal much about Cuba. A few years of profitable frivolity ensured its lasting reputation as the premier pleasure island of the time and offered a rallying cry and a focal point for antigovernment rebels.

In some ways Havana in 1959 caricatured the aspirations of the tourism visionaries of 1919. When Céspedes, de la Cruz, and Cortina herded the first casino bill through the Cuban legislature, they pictured a dignified, decorous, wealthy clientele who wagered large sums of money in the plush salons of Oriental Park's Jockey Club or the Casino Nacional. Cosmopolitan travelers of the upper classes could afford to winter in Cuba in the pleasant comfort of a home built on land purchased from Cuban-owned development companies, preferably theirs. By the 1950s wealthy Cubans owned the overwhelming majority of the 1920s-era homes around the Havana and Biltmore country clubs. Real estate profits figured less prominently, if at all, in tourist promotion, and the raucous cacaphony of coins in slot machines filled gaming rooms that had sacrificed the quiet elegance of an earlier era to mass marketing. More than a dozen casinos raked in the losses of fun seekers who scrambled off airplanes for a weekend or longer. Talk to some aging bons vivants who visited Havana in the 1950s. Listen to the chuckle, catch the wink of persons reliving stolen moments in a wide-open city, eyes misty with blissful memories of indulgence. The Cuban legislator German Wólter del Río had warned his colleagues in 1919 that casinos and gambling would turn Havana into a toilet. Forty years later, Fidel Castro declared that indeed they had.

John Bowman had taken into consideration the attraction of horse racing and casinos, as well as readily available liquor, when he invested in the Sevilla-Biltmore in 1919. Gambling entertained the clientele, but hotels were his primary business. The reverse was true in the 1950s: hotel and nightclub owners counted on gaming profits to pay their bills. You need not even spend the night; high-stakes players might want to catch a little sleep, though ideally not too much.

The founders of Cuban tourism might have lamented the distortions of their dream, but they surely would have applauded its overwhelming financial success. Everything that tourists had enjoyed in the 1920s reappeared in the 1950s, and more. More events, more sights to see, livelier bars for drinking, a greater variety of restaurants and places to eat—from the pedestrian fare at Woolworth's lunch counter to Russian food at Boris's, Chinese at the New Mandarin, the strictly kosher menu at Moishe Pipik's, and gourmet continental cuisine at numerous elegant dining rooms. Bowman's ten-story hotel tower and roof garden entertainment had created a sensation in 1924; hotels built in the 1950s boasted twenty air-conditioned stories and rooftop swimming pools. When Bowman cheered the horses at a track in Miami, boarded a plane, and caught the last races at Oriental Park on the same day in 1928, the feat was newsworthy. By 1958 most travelers reached Cuba by plane, many just for the evening, with sixty to eighty Miami–Havana flights a week, depending on the season, and convenient flights from many other large cities. A dozen U.S., European, and Latin American carriers touched down at Havana's airport or flew directly to Varadero Beach.

Oriental Park had been refurbished several times since Bowman's syndicate bought the racing facility in 1927. Another investment group, the Cuban Racing Company, purchased the down-at-the-heels track and overhauled it yet again for a gala reopening in December 1955. The new owner, Joseph Lease, almost lost his life, however, when he installed a totalizator (the mechanical apparatus that updates the sums of money bet on a race) to replace the hand-manipulated pari-mutuel boards. Two racketeers slipped into Havana, beat Lease over the head with blackjacks in his hotel room, and hopped the next plane back to Miami. Police speculated that the assailants wanted Lease to dismantle the betting equipment, which threatened their ability to manipulate the stateside numbers racket payoff.[4]

Marianao still drew crowds of tourists to the beach attractions that Bowman's pleasure trust had consolidated under its ownership in 1927. The Biltmore Country Club of the 1950s counted mostly wealthy *habaneros*, not prominent New Yorkers, on its membership rolls. The planned residential community that Bowman had advertised to his associates became a suburb for affluent Havana professionals and businessmen, convenient for an endless round of social engagements. They entertained each other at birthday dinners, holiday parties, and Saturday night soirées held at the Biltmore and Havana country clubs.

There were new attractions in the Marianao neighborhood too. A track for dog races opened near the Havana Yacht Club in 1951, its nighttime entertainment augmenting the daylight horse competitions. In 1928 a popular Cuban magazine had commended the pleasures that Brooklyn's Coney Island brought to New York's multitudes. In the 1950s *habaneros* enjoyed their own Coney Island, a similarly named, though much smaller, amusement park alongside La Playa beach. Havana's Coney Island attracted crowds with its miniature railroad and other rides, a children's theater, circuslike exhibits of dwarfs, giants, and other people with unusual physical attributes, plus bingo.

And, of course, Marianao boasted the swank Tropicana nightclub, where spectacular stage shows featured lavishly costumed, statuesque Cuban showgirls. Set in the gardens of a mansion that once had housed the U.S. ambassador, the Tropicana had missed the 1920s boom altogether. The open-air theater had opened in 1939 and quickly eclipsed the 1920s clubs in grandeur and imaginative productions. Abundant tropical foliage formed part of the staged extravaganzas. At capacity, some twelve hundred to fourteen hundred people applauded the show and danced all night for less than five dollars each. For another dollar or so, a roving photographer captured the evening's festivities in a personalized souvenir.

Internationally famous stars such as Josephine Baker and Nat "King" Cole, Xavier Cugat and Carmen Miranda headlined Tropicana shows that put a company of at least fifty dancers through their paces in elaborate production numbers. Roderico Neyra (Rodney) choreographed dozens of thematically distinctive shows, performed two each night, every night for eight weeks. Japanese and "voodoo" productions might be followed by a dramatic Greek piece and Latin American love songs, each with appropriate costumes, settings, music, and dance.

The Tropicana management took exquisite pains to create the proper atmosphere for their exotic theatricals, consulting an army of musicians, artists, and folklore experts on the music, costumes, and makeup. For one elaborate Asian number, two Japanese professors coached the dancers for hours just to create a distinctive rhythmic sound with their feet, made by moving stalks of sugarcane located on the stage floor. Twelve full-time seamstresses sewed fanciful costumes and created imaginative headdresses; shoemakers constantly replaced dancing slippers. Special effects, accomplished with lighting, waterfalls, and colored smoke, embellished the various moods created by the orchestra and the performers. The shows' producers hunted for their beautiful showgirls and dancers in Havana's ballet schools and lower-class neighborhoods; they held talent contests and picked the most striking young women for the shows. While most middle- and upper-class families frowned on show business as employment for their daughters, nightclub work claimed many pretty and talented young women.

The club became a veritable entertainment factory with four hundred employees. Well-regarded nightclubs of the 1920s had employed two orchestras and several featured artists; clubs of less stature boasted showgirls but no headliners. Club owners had paid their bills from food and liquor sales. That type of operation persisted in the 1950s, but nightly revenues at the Tropicana had to top $5,000 just to break even, and gambling made the difference between profits and loss. The Tropicana spent $200,000 a year on advertising and publicity alone. An office in Miami booked tourists on the nightly round-trip flight aboard the fifty-passenger "Tropicana Special," and the entertainment started with an onboard show that set the tone for a high-rolling evening in the casino.[5]

During the relatively short boom in the 1950s, Havana's casinos

offered employment to hundreds of young Cubans at wages high
enough to persuade some professionals to switch to the gaming rooms.
Unionized workers dealt twenty-one or turned the roulette wheel,
thanks to some family member or friend who could recommend them
to the casino manager. Many casino workers remained loyal to their
old bosses after the 1959 revolution.

Exciting, cynical, sinful Havana wooed and won its northern neighbors. A typical carouser's evening might start rather casually at one of
the pleasant outdoor cafés in central Havana. All-girl rumba bands,
an unknown treat in the 1920s, serenaded the drinkers, some of them
theater and sports figures who were appearing or vacationing on the
island. The rude attentions of uninhibited male customers caused one
female orchestra to perform inside a glass cage, but most played in the
open to appreciative audiences of both genders.

Then what? The Colonial Club, "dingy and dark, but reeking with
the color of Far Eastern ports," where the show featured torrid rum-
bas and a female impersonator or two. Chinatown at night offered the
Teatro Shanghai, with its own version of burlesque—no stripping, but
a shifting of tightly wrapped satin sashes that crept higher with each
undulating hip movement. A tourist who "cannot be satisfied unless he
has had a glimpse of degradation," wrote W. Adolphe Roberts in 1953,
need go no farther than the open bars in the very heart of Havana.
Marijuana addicts and drunkards hung out there, lost souls who used
the "easiest and cheapest means of stunning their nerves." Not far away,
garish electric signs marked the small bars known for their smoky back-
rooms where men danced to jukebox music with hostesses that could
be enticed away from the premises with the right offer.[6]

When in 1950 the government unexpectedly cracked down on
known houses of prostitution (the same reformist wave that temporarily ended gambling), some cynics charged that practicality had
superseded morality, since the property in the red-light district west of
the lower Prado had become valuable in the tight housing market of
a growing city. Whatever the explanation, hundreds of dwellings va-
cated by brothels quickly turned into residences for more respectable
tenants. Prostitutes then swarmed the sidewalks and violated the law
against streetwalking. Some of them drifted temporarily into the bars
as hostesses, but it wasn't long before houses at new addresses recap-
tured old clients.[7]

Exciting, wonderful, and foreign, the city became the "coolest" place because it was the hottest. Havana cultivated its reputation for sinfulness and capitalized on the customers' willingness to pay for prurience. On the other hand, not everyone prowled for action; thousands of tourists enjoyed entertainment that diverted or titillated but gave a wide berth to outright obscenity or purchased sex. Perhaps they ogled the girlie show at Sans Soucí and gambled at the Casino Nacional or the greyhound track, then took a quick cab ride to Las Fritas, Marianao's three-block-long strip of food stands, shooting galleries, peep shows and beer parlors, cabarets, and restaurants. The area reminded many visitors of New Orleans' Bourbon and Basin Streets, with rumba substituted for jazz.

A night on the town might conclude sometime before dawn after one last drink at Sloppy Joe's Bar, formerly La Victoria, a venerable institution given its new name in the 1920s by an angry, inebriated Havana journalist, rebuffed by the owner in his quest for a fifty-dollar loan. His vengeful editorial denounced a certain saloon on Zulueta Street and urged police to investigate violations of the city's sanitary code, claiming the joint should be called "Sloppy Joe's." When the free publicity increased business among dedicated drinkers—escapees from Prohibition for whom the thoughtful owner had crafted belts holding miniature liquor bottles to be smuggled into the United States—the wily proprietor changed the name and his bar became an institution.[8] Sloppy Joe's retained its appeal into the 1950s, even without the thrill of defying antiliquor laws.

Some 1950s tourists followed worshipfully in the footsteps of the novelist, avid sportsman, and prodigious drinker Ernest Hemingway as they made the rounds of Havana's restaurants and bars. Hemingway often had lingered over drinks at Bodeguita del Medio or Floridita and had made them famous by his patronage. He had crafted novels in a room at Havana's Ambos Mundos Hotel; later, he bought his Cuban country home with profits earned from the sales of *For Whom the Bell Tolls*. Was it Hemingway's influence that prompted one travel writer to label Havana a man's city, where wolves on every corner regarded unaccompanied women as fair game?[9] Hemingway's lifestyle and work made him a legend to Cubans and a benefactor of Cuban tourism. He lent his name to fishing tournaments in the 1950s, and Cuban tours still guide thousands of pilgrims to his San Francisco de Paula estate, now government owned and frozen in time as a monument to a favorite son. Not allowed inside the house, tourists gaze through the windows at the author's typewriter and the hunting trophies that had surrounded him at work and play.

Only the Tropicana, Casino Nacional, Jockey Club, and the summer casino had had permission for gaming rooms before 1949. Sans Soucí and Montmartre joined the group shortly before social reformers convinced the government to close cabaret gambling in 1950. When owners complained that only the financial cushion of legalized betting kept them afloat, the government relented. The infusion of foreign capital that built Havana's Las Vegas–type hotel casino and its reputation did not arrive until the mid-1950s, however. Casinos built by and for high-rolling professional gamblers made a huge media splash, but in fact they lasted a very short time, less than two years in some cases.

ALTERNATE ATTRACTIONS

If it appeared that folly and frolic completely triumphed over culture and nature—after all, one writer called Havana the New World's tropical version of wicked old Pompeii—the crassness and glitter overshadowed, but did not obliterate, the efforts of 1930s reformers.[10] Those idealistic uplifters fought for and in fact achieved many of their goals. Vacationing families with children went to Cuba and played on the white sand of beaches made accessible by new roads or direct airplane connections. Some of them packed up the car at home and motored to Key West to take the car ferry to the Cuban city of Cárdenas, disembarking only a short distance from Varadero Beach.

Varadero rose from the neglected, marshy spit of land of the 1920s like a mirage. The national government finally completed the long-planned highways and feeder roads and improved the airport, while local civic committees solved sanitation problems and freed the beach of pesky mosquitos, flies, and other insects. Private investment in hotels and yacht harbors spiraled upward from $245,000 in 1951 to $3.5 million in 1957. Flourishing bars, restaurants, hotels, and shops changed the character of the once-impoverished area. Travel folders proclaimed the resort a "playground of the international set," but you could get there cheaply, by car or bus, as well as by yacht. Happy Pete's inexpensive Hotel Happiness shared the long stretch of beach with William Liebow's International Hotel and Casino. Xanadu, Irénée

DuPont's 1920s mansion, stood far up the peninsula. The Kawama Club and a millionaire's row of palatial homes overlooked the beach, not far from President Fulgencio Batista's vacation retreat. Middle-class Cuban families vacationed in Varadero, and on most Sundays groups of Havana teenagers rode buses to their favorite site.[11] Other beaches and small harbors along the coast between Havana and Vara-dero lured skin divers, spear and line fishermen, water skiers, and sun-bathers. Vacationers also tried the motels that sprouted along new highways and the government-sponsored campgrounds.

Tourists who drove the northern coastal stretch between Havana and Varadero stopped and marveled at the same limestone caves near the city of Matanzas that had awed visitors in the 1920s. But by the 1950s the government had illuminated the pathways through the cav-erns and provided guides who explained areas of geological interest. A national culture institute in the Education Ministry extended govern-ment sponsorship to a wide variety of artistic, literary, and musical ac-tivities and institutions. Officials had spruced up old museums, adding an Afro-Cuban collection to the relics and paintings at the National Museum, and had inaugurated new historical exhibits, like the one devoted to the life and achievements of the patriot José Martí.

Cubans and foreigners alike enjoyed Havana's many theaters. The ornately decorated National Theater in the center of Havana, built in the nineteenth century, hosted most major cultural productions. Alfredo Hornedo, a supporter of casinos in the 1930s, opened the ultra-modern Blanquita Theater in suburban Miramar in December 1949 with a three-week run of the New York Latin Quarter review "From Paris to New York." The astounding Blanquita, a three-million-dollar, air-conditioned building that accommodated almost seven thousand patrons, matched Hornedo's confidence and exuberance. Three adja-cent parking lots had room for more than a thousand cars. The stage measured 60 by 120 feet and was equipped with a freezing mechanism that could cover the entire surface for ice shows in fifteen to eighteen hours. Hornedo planned to use the facility as a public skating rink when no theatrical attractions had booked the numerically intimidat-ing showplace. It hardly mattered that very few heat-loving Cubans knew how to ice skate. They could learn, and many of them did.[12]

By the end of the 1950s Cuba boasted an internationally acclaimed ballet company and an accomplished national symphony orchestra, botanical and zoological gardens, a new museum of fine arts, a privately organized sales center for arts and crafts, and impressive sports centers. The island put itself on display for people who found pleasure in intellectual and artistic impulses, in investigating the history of another country, or in gaining a sense of *cubanidad,* the spirit of being Cuban—as well as for visitors whose pleasures lay in more earthy pursuits.

Cuba also soothed the aches and pains of tourists who found relief in the mineral springs and baths of newly renovated spas. The five bubbling springs at San Miguel de los Baños earned the title "Vichy of the Americas," after the famous French health resort. Frequent bus service and a mere thirty-minute ride made Santa María del Rosario convenient to Havana's visitors and residents who enjoyed the beautiful paintings in the town's colonial church, as well as its mineral baths. The four hotels at San Diego de los Baños outside Havana were frequently fully booked. Farther from the tourist hub, Pinar del Río's San Vicente de los Baños and Las Villas's Ciego Montero pulled their share of clients and helped to spread the health seekers' dollars around the island, at last fulfilling the projections of successive tourist commissions.

Colorful events filled a year-round calendar of pageantry that encouraged tourists to see all of Cuba—from Holy Week in Trinidad, celebrated in the old colonial town with passion plays and processions, to the cowboy atmosphere of summertime carnival in the cattle-raising center of Camagüey or Santiago's three days and nights of revelry in July. Urged on by anticipated revenues and enthusiastic tourist promoters, many cities in the island's interior expanded their own unique celebrations of saints' days. After all, forty-three million believers in the United States and nine million more in Canada constituted a marketing gold mine for Cuba's colorful Catholic pageantry.[13]

Havana's own carnival had long since lost its religious significance and moved even further from tradition. The 1957 festivities, for example, included an acrobatic team from the Miami Police Department motorcycle corps who performed intricate maneuvers at high speed. The high school band from Cocoa, Florida, and the drum majorettes from Miami's Jackson High School participated in the parade. The Cuban armed forces float featured a dozen girls dressed as Roman soldiers mounted on replicas of ancient chariots, and the Public Works Ministry publicized Havana's zoological garden. Scantily clad young girls danced the mambo and cha-cha aboard commercially sponsored floats and competed for applause with the rhythmic gyrations of the *comparsas*.[14]

The public officials and social scientists who had revived this example of Cuban folklore and culture in the 1930s had unleashed a cyclone of creative energy. The two *comparsas* sponsored by the city fathers in 1938 had expanded to at least ten dance groups in the 1950s. Los Dandies de Belén, Los Marqueses de Atares, Los Jardineros, and Los Guajiros del Batey mesmerized carnival participants and onlookers with their colorful and imaginative costumes and the intricacies of their dances. Unsuspecting parade watchers audibly gasped, however, as Los Alacranes (the Scorpions) unleashed their elaborate ritual on Havana's streets. As dark-skinned dancers ringed a huge black papier-mâché scorpion, musicians quickened their tempo; throbbing drums intensified in sonority. Following the lead of the music, dancers grew more abandoned. Suddenly a painted-faced high priest bounded onto the scene. Brandishing a sword, he danced sinuously, then leaped into the air and twisted his body in violent contortions. At the high point of this sensational performance, he spied a fair-skinned, light-haired young woman among the many darker bodies that surrounded the black scorpion. As the viewers held their breath, the priest pressed his sword against the girl's white throat and choked off cries for mercy. All at once the band burst into a blazing, mood-breaking rumba. The laughing, fair-skinned "victim" rejoined the group and danced on down the street while stricken onlookers struggled to regain their composure.[15] The compelling pseudo-ritual danced by Los Alacranes undoubtedly surpassed the Siboney sun worshipers of the 1920s as a breathtaking memory preserved in some tourists' diaries.

Memories were not the only souvenirs, of course. Since the 1920s Cuba had introduced a greater variety of domestically produced items for tourists to take home to friends and relatives. A dozen or more souvenir shops flourished in the downtown area, most of them owned by members of Havana's small Jewish community. Stores such as the French Doll, Oriental Bazaar, King Solomon, and Havana City Store sold alligator handbags, belts, and wallets; hand-embroidered dresses, blouses, children's clothes, and tablecloths; mahogany cigarette boxes, candy dishes, and bookends; costume jewelry; ornamental tiles; dolls made from shells; carved maracas; and of course, Havana's famous cigars and rum, as well as imported perfumes. Cruise ships emptied hundreds of passengers onto the streets of Havana every day during the season. Most of them headed for the shops close to the harbor, where they often stood in line to make their purchases. Stores also opened in Vedado or occupied space in the newer hotels. In the best years at the height of the tourist season, some merchants took in two hundred to three hundred dollars a day. Sidewalk vendors also prospered from their postcards, sunglasses, cheap necklaces, religious charms, and pornographic photographs.

Tourism provided souvenir sellers a good living for a dozen years, earnings that turned over in the economy as wages for employees and payments to suppliers. The tourist left his or her money at the cash register, but that was just a point of dissemination for tourist dollars. Stores paid for merchandise and hired salespeople, maintenance crews, and people to make deliveries. Home industries flourished, as craftspersons sold their embroidery, woodworking, shell dolls, and maracas directly to store owners. Owners of small factories manufactured leather and other goods. One entrepreneur bought basic earrings in the United States for between 35 and 50 cents a pair, paid young women in Havana 10 cents a pair to paint them by hand, and sold the "Cuban" jewelry to tourists for $1.99. Tour guides who steered customers to particular stores earned a 10 percent commission. Some shopkeepers set up small bars where tourists sampled various brands of rum. After the owner educated novices on differences in taste and quality, their selections—by the bottle or case—were packaged and delivered to the hotel or ship.[16]

Similarly, cigar factories invited tourists to observe deft master cigar makers expertly roll tobacco leaves. Employees escorted the watchers through a museum that displayed centuries-old smoking pipes used by pre-Columbian Cuban natives and other artifacts of the tobacco trade, then sold cigars in the factory's gift shop. Rum distillers and beer brewers encouraged tour groups and made their products available. Few merchandisers accomplished their aims with more flair than the Habif family, importers of perfumes for its Havana shops since the 1920s. When the Habifs began to manufacture their own perfumes, soaps, and lotions, they reversed the spelling of the family name and launched Perfumería Fibah. In 1949 Mauricio Habif purchased Château Madrid, well remembered as a 1920s-era nightclub that had offered quality entertainment under the stars. Habif resurrected the Château Madrid's reputation as a garden showplace, with birds and monkeys in cages, a fishpond, and peacocks parading on the lawns. As many as a thousand visitors wandered the grounds in a single day. Tour groups and individuals enjoyed the ambience, the restaurant, and of course, the gift shop.[17]

Cuba's second tourist boom peaked amid highly dramatic political conflicts, and it disintegrated before the eyes of its faithful backers, as revolutionaries took center stage. In 1957, when tourism appeared to have fulfilled its economic promise, Cuban rebels escalated their challenge to Fulgencia Batista's government and began to hurl the island's Las Vegas image like a grenade at the leaders who had fashioned it.

Chapter 9

Shady Business in the Tropical Sun
The Mafia and Gambling

Underneath banner headlines, dramatic photos of Cuba's revolution captured cheering crowds and triumphant rebels, as well as angry citizens flinging slot machines, roulette wheels, and broken blackjack tables into Havana's streets.[1] Readers who linked visual and verbal images justifiably concluded that Cubans had tied Batista to gambling interests. Organized crime figures from the United States did indeed operate many of Havana's casinos in conjunction with Cuban leaders, and rebels had exploited this connection to galvanize opposition to the regime. However, disgust with government excesses preceded and outstripped outrage over casinos. Jubilant citizens celebrating Batista's downfall also looted shops and department stores and broke into streetfront offices and locally owned businesses in a generally destructive rampage. Revolutionaries charged Batista henchmen with torture and murder—not casino operations—when they put them on trial.

135
*Shady
Business
in the
Tropical
Sun*

PROFESSIONAL GAMBLERS AND CUBAN POLITICIANS

Before we critique the play, we will venture behind the scenes to see who designed the sets and wrote the script. One need not be an apologist for corrupt politicians nor condone criminal activity to acknowledge that casinos are big business. The last two decades of the twentieth century have witnessed a rush to share the multibillion-dollar annual revenues generated by gamblers in the United States, as civic leaders and Native American tribal councils bring the gambling industry's revenue- and employment-producing potential to decaying or impoverished communities. Hired consultants set up and run the casinos; hired lobbyists protect interests in the halls of government.[2] Trade journals track the market and consumer trends; Wall Street analysts advise investors when to buy and sell gaming-related stocks.

With similar expectations of legitimate profits and jobs (as well as opportunities for unreported gain), Batista encouraged high-finance, high-risk resort gambling. He had recognized the potential contribution of gambling to his political and personal fortunes long before his 1952 coup. When he had assumed power in 1934, Cuba's national lottery had long been a source of patronage and pocket money. Instead of the weekly drawings authorized by his predecessors, Batista had inaugurated daily games. Cuban radio stations had announced winning numbers to an eager audience every night at 9:30. Moreover, he had allowed private lotteries, known as *bolita*, to flourish. *Bolita* paid off on the same numbers that were drawn officially, and policemen took a cut of the informal action. Encouragement of the private gambling sector gained Batista a considerable contingent of loyal followers among the people who secured new sources of income through both lottery and casino.[3]

In the 1950s dice, cards, and roulette wheels contributed to Cuba's prosperity as they did in Las Vegas. The Nevada city had legalized casino gaming and wrapped it in a glamorous vacation package of bright lights, showgirls, and lavish entertainment at reasonable prices. Cuba offered tropical nights, beautiful beaches, and a taste of foreign

136
*Shady
Business
in the
Tropical
Sun*

culture as well. Gamblers bet thousands of dollars a night. Sometimes they won; sometimes they lost. But the odds always favored the house. Thus a combination of practical statecraft and personal greed tied Batista to foreign casino operators, some of whose histories were less than wholesome.

When the United States outlawed the production and sale of alcoholic beverages in 1919, the undiminished desire for liquor produced an entrepreneurial clique that was willing to risk prison and bodily harm to pursue riches. Liquor profits increased when the government criminalized the trade, and organized groups of purveyors competed ruthlessly and violently to control lucrative markets. Prohibition also fostered tourist opportunities in Cuba. A similar U.S. inclination to legislate morality and eliminate gambling boosted Cuba's aspiration to become the Las Vegas of the Caribbean. While a portion of the electorate decried games of chance, many people loved to gamble.

The trajectory of organized criminal activities in the United States, in fact, traces the profitability of society's forbidden fruit: prostitution, liquor, gambling, and narcotics. Before World War I the gangs made their money in prostitution. Just as changing sexual mores and a softening of public opinion made prostitution less profitable than the risks warranted, prohibited liquor offered an alternative enterprise. When Prohibition ended, gangs turned to slot machines, punch boards, numbers, and casinos, with narcotics traffic contributing a share of the revenue. By the late 1940s an estimated twenty billion dollars changed hands every year in the United States as a result of organized, illegal gambling—the most profitable enterprise in mob history to that time.

Syndicates that engaged in the illicit businesses adopted a corporate structure, with centralized direction over nationwide operations. To end the deadly competition that had characterized the bootlegging era, they divided territories, made deals, and reached decisions through deliberations rather than vengeance and confrontation. They also paid out millions of dollars to local officials to avoid arrest and prosecution. When social reformers turned up the heat, operators of highly profitable, illegal gaming rooms sought new, legitimate venues. Some went to Las Vegas; others saw similar prospects in such emerging Caribbean tourist destinations as Puerto Rico, Haiti, the Bahamas, and Cuba.

By the 1950s the line between organized criminal activity and legitimate business interests had begun to blur. The hands of professional gamblers signed the paychecks of ordinary workers—waitresses, electricians, gardeners, barbers, room clerks, and so on—in hotels and casinos in Las Vegas and Cuba. Moreover, the syndicates invested gambling profits in such enterprises as advertising, banking, coal, restaurants, bars, laundries, gas stations, cigarette distribution, news services, the garment industry, and real estate. Gamblers—and gambling—turned a corner toward social acceptance. The Las Vegas crap shooter was your vacationing neighbor. The roulette enthusiast belonged to the Rotary Club.

137
Shady
Business
in the
Tropical
Sun

By the time Batista brought big-time casinos to Havana, Cuba's consumerist upper and middle sectors had grown fond of imported automobiles, television sets, and electric appliances. They also traveled abroad. The drain on currency reserves warranted tourism as an economic development scheme. Tourism's revitalization required capital for new hotels, however, and foreign investors who surveyed the Cuban business climate—powerful unions, high labor costs, political uncertainty, corrupt officials—hesitated to commit their resources. As an incentive in an increasingly competitive industry, Batista offered to lend funds from state-sponsored development banks to build hotels, structures that could house casinos as well as guests. When he enticed foreign entrepreneurs with Cuban capital, North American gambling and hotel interests responded favorably. If prospects for growth required deals with businessmen whose experience recognized political payoffs as legitimate expenses, Batista had no qualms about such transactions. Kickbacks and political patronage, longtime Cuban practices, distributed profits to a broad circle of colleagues but were most lucrative for those at the top. The partnership was as much a marriage of convenience as a love match: casino operation, the key to hotel profitability, required expertise, and the mobsters had it.

Casino owners did not strew North American garbage across a pristine Cuban landscape. Foreign gamblers introduced neither gangsterism nor vice to the island, nor did they necessarily corrupt righteous islanders. Cubans themselves scoffed at the idea that the mob could "march into Cuba and start giving orders like Little Caesar," a reference to actor Edward G. Robinson's ruthless celluloid character. "You just go ahead and send your toughest gangster down here," one Cuban challenged an American journalist. "I guarantee you that even a second-rate Cuban politician will run rings around him."[4] The mob was playing ball with seasoned veterans, not second-stringers.

Cubans did not need foreign gangsters to teach them the intrica-

138
Shady
Business
in the
Tropical
Sun

cies of extortion rackets and payoffs from gambling and prostitution. Policemen throughout the country made their rounds daily to collect an unauthorized "tax" from even the smallest of businesses; Cubans called it *el forrajeo*. Payments in cash and merchandise accrued to officers at the precinct level and climbed up the chain of command. Peacekeepers in patrol cars extracted daily payments from prostitutes, drug traffickers, and gambling operations. Havana's houses of prostitution paid the local patrolman, on a sliding scale according to the number of clients and the house's fee scale. The most active and luxurious establishments paid between two thousand and five thousand dollars per night. Some policemen started their own operations, using young rural-urban migrants who worked as poorly paid maids in middle-class homes during the day.[5] Simply stated, *el forrajeo* underwrote an informal redistribution of income and a form of political patronage. However, the endemic petty chiseling and extortion contributed to many Cubans' sense of alienation and injustice.

High-ranking government officials, including the heads of the Cuban army, navy, and police, enjoyed other sources of illegal funds. Accusations of narcotics trafficking had circulated since the 1920s and appeared confirmed when Lucky Luciano showed up in Havana and gathered together old friends from the United States and well-placed Cuban politicians. Under Batista, some of Luciano's old friends became new partners in high-stakes casinos.

Although rebels effectively propagandized Batista's underworld connections in a moralistic, nationalistic call to arms, the uprising sprang from other roots. Rampant corruption and deadly rivalries had brutalized Cuban politics between 1944 and 1952—the formative university years for a generation of rebels, including Fidel Castro. Havana University undergraduates with political aspirations joined student movements or affiliated with political parties to gain acceptance in government circles. Government-sponsored "action groups" often settled ideological and personal differences with guns. Enemies stalked each other, and bloody confrontations between rivals were routine. Cubans labeled the politics of the period *gangsterismo*. Carlos Prío Socarrás, elected president in 1948, tendered an agreement to end the violence: government appointments with possibilities for bribes and kickbacks to all university-based supporters. Some youthful militants grabbed the olive branch; others denounced the pact. Meanwhile, the predatory political scene continued to deteriorate.[6]

When Batista left the presidency in 1944, he retired to Daytona Beach, up the coast from Meyer Lansky's flourishing, illegal casino business along Florida's eastern Gold Coast. Gambling and real estate opportunities had attracted its share of former bootleggers after World War II, a time when Miami's tourist and gambling prospects far outstripped Cuba's. Florida reigned as the gambling capital of the nation, particularly active in the winter tourist months. Crap games, roulette, and blackjack appealed to thousands of sun seekers. The so-called carpet joints, or roadhouses with gambling, featured dinner, dancing, floor shows, and casinos. Many of the nightclubs on the edges of towns had opened in the 1930s and had remained in business after liquor became legal once more. Owners of outlawed backroom games of chance bribed the same local officials who formerly turned a blind eye to illegal drinking.

Lansky had opened several clubs north of Miami in the mid-1930s, about the same time that he had cleaned up Cuba's race track and casino operations for Batista. Hallandale, just over the Broward County line from Miami, became a haven for horse players and crap shooters. By the late 1940s Lansky shared the ownership of Club Boheme, Greenacres, and Colonial Inn in Broward County; the Colonial Inn in Miami; Arrowhead Inn and Piping Rock Casino in Saratoga Springs, New York; the Flamingo Hotel in Las Vegas, Nevada; and the Beverly Club in New Orleans, Louisiana. Greenacres and Club Boheme reported net gambling profits of some $349,000 in 1948 and $599,000 in 1949. Lefty Clark (William Bischoff), who later operated the casino at Havana's Tropicana nightclub, ran the extremely lucrative crap game at Greenacres.[7] While no documents point to Batista's financial involvement in Lansky's Florida enterprises, we can assume that he was at least an interested bystander, perhaps a player.

Gambling acquired tacit acceptance in southern Florida as a tourist attraction. A few residents expressed outrage at the gaming centers and the horse-betting parlors in their midst, but most people winked at the lax law enforcement. In wide-open Hollywood, Florida, no one spent time in jail either for betting or taking bets, despite several citizen-led efforts to shut down gambling operations. When an outspoken attorney charged that local officials ignored the gambling that oper-

140
Shady
Business
in the
Tropical
Sun

ated out of every tavern, poolroom, and nightclub in town, the mayor passed the buck to the police chief, who ducked the issue, as did the Broward County sheriff. (Sheriff Walter Clark was himself a partner in Broward Novelty Company, which operated an illegal slot machine business.) One city commissioner, a septic tank installer with political ambitions, jumped on what he falsely perceived as a campaign issue, but his attempt to outlaw gambling suffered a resounding rejection.

When the hint of discontent reached neighboring Hallandale, an assistant state's attorney applied for an injunction to restrain a nuisance, a move directed against gambling at Lansky's Colonial Inn. Ten prominent citizens offered to testify against the casino's owners, and the injunction was granted. The Colonial Inn opened for business that night; guests dined and danced but did not gamble. Lansky evaluated the situation, decided he could not operate without gaming profits, sold the Colonial Inn to John Minsky of New York burlesque fame, and concentrated his efforts on his injunction-free Greenacres and Boheme clubs.[8]

Estimates of revenues at the seven gambling venues of Dade County (Miami) ran between thirty million and forty million dollars a year, and casino operators invested a portion of their substantial profits in oceanfront real estate and other legitimate businesses. After they paid off local law enforcement and civic officials, they donated generously to the campaigns of elected statewide officeholders. The ties between organized crime figures and government angered many citizens more than gambling per se. That connection also attracted the attention of an ambitious young U.S. senator named Estes Kefauver, who rode their indignation to fame, then routed the gamblers and drove them to consider Cuba their home.

Both the United States and Cuba held elections in 1948. Thomas Dewey lost a squeaker to Harry Truman. Carlos Prío Socarrás succeeded his 1930s comrade in arms, Grau San Martín, as president. But the more important races for the future of Cuban tourism were senatorial. Batista made his political comeback as a senator from Las Villas province, elected in absentia from his home in Florida; and the lanky, soft-spoken, congenial Kefauver became one of Tennessee's two senators. As citizens increasingly vocalized their concerns about the ethics of local politicians, some U.S. newspapers launched front-page crusades, attacking the power of the payoff to influence legislation and law enforcement. Alarmed by an inability to control the insidious penetration of interstate crime figures into local politics, the American Municipal Association called for federal action to stop an internal peril as potentially dangerous as global communism. Moreover, juvenile narcotics use had increased notably, and questions arose about suppliers. For years the federal government's Bureau of Narcotics had tracked a shadowy international organization centered in Sicily. Investigators concluded that the secretive Mafia stood behind a number of organized criminal activities in the United States, not just narcotics traffic. In response to public outcries, the U.S. attorney general called a conference on organized crime in February 1950, and the audacious freshman Senator Kefauver doggedly fought for and won the right to conduct a full-scale congressional inquiry.[9]

The Senate Crime Committee, with Kefauver as its chair, held hearings over the course of a year, from May 1950 to May 1951. Testimony from law enforcement officials and suspected racketeers covered activities in Miami, Kansas City, Saint Louis, Philadelphia, Chicago, Tampa, Cleveland, Detroit, New Orleans, Las Vegas, San Francisco, Los Angeles, Saratoga, New York, and New York City. Kefauver probed connections between crime syndicates, gambling, narcotics, and politicians, and the committee concluded that cities and states needed help. Only federal agencies could exclude the aliens who became members of "predatory criminal groups," and only Congress could close the legal loopholes that allowed the guilty to escape punishment. Since nationwide crime organizations did indeed conduct business in interstate commerce, the federal government had an obligation to pursue violators of federal laws.

The committee's legislative recommendations signaled an imminent crackdown on lucrative mob-controlled gambling. First of all, a federal rackets squad in the Justice Department would be authorized to investigate mob activities. Second, legislation would make it a felony offense not to keep adequate records of income and expenses for tax purposes, and gambling casinos would be required to maintain daily records of money won and lost (to be filed with the Bureau of Internal Revenue). Third, interstate transmission of gambling information by means of telephone, telegraph, radio, and so on, would be a federal offense, and the law against interstate transport of slot machines would be extended to other gaming equipment.

The Senate investigation spurred local civic organizations to action. The glare of the national spotlight and the unrelenting eye of the

142

*Shady
Business
in the
Tropical
Sun*

television camera exposed crooks and politicians in their cities and started a chain reaction. Angry citizens swept complacent law enforcement officials out of office and closed down many gambling casinos. Even Florida's governor felt the heat and arrested friends of the New York crime boss Frank Costello. Grand juries issued indictments in three Florida counties. Meyer and Jake Lansky, William Bischoff, and Vincent Alo faced charges of operating illegal gambling establishments in Broward County. A Dade County grand jury seized the records of the hugely profitable S. and G. syndicate, whose wire services carried race results to a nationwide network of bookmakers. Furthermore, the Dade County sheriff raided and seized records in an office identified by Kefauver as belonging to the syndicate's accountant. When the crime probe clamped the lid on Florida's coastal playland, a considerable amount of elaborate gaming equipment, made useless in Florida, found its way to Cuba.[10]

THE CAST ASSEMBLED

Batista's coup sounded a clarion call to Florida's retreating gamblers. After he seized power, he suspended the Cuban Congress, gave legislative power to a council of loyal ministers, prohibited strikes for forty-five days, and promised the fullest protection of the government to all foreign capital already invested in Cuba or that might subsequently enter the island. As soon as air and sea traffic resumed normal operations, Batista placed the retired sugar baron Marcial Facio in charge of a newly constituted tourist commission and placed its functions in the hands of his own hand-picked team.[11]

In a short space of time Batista also accelerated plans for motels in the provinces and gas stations with clean restrooms that would accommodate travelers along the highways. He ordered street repairs and authorized his health minister to prosecute commercial establishments for violation of sanitation codes. He modernized and expanded the airport at Rancho Boyeros to accommodate the influx of visitors stimulated by airlines' package tour bargains. Work finally began on a museum of fine arts not far from the presidential palace. The tourist commission organized a special corps of police to answer the usual tourist complaints about taxi drivers or street vendors or unauthorized guides who overcharged gullible customers. Taxis had to post printed price lists, and inspectors checked the pay-off mechanism of gambling devices in nightclubs.

The new president found the gambling establishment in sad shape. The lottery ran only once a week, as in 1934. Prío had closed down the casinos from time to time, and those that operated at the Tropicana, Sans Soucí, and Montmartre barely made their payrolls—even when they cheated the customers.

If satisfied customers and good publicity are the nourishing lifeblood of a healthy casino industry, then disgruntled visitors and bad publicity might be compared to an infection that carries a threat of gangrene. Thus Batista could ill afford the flood of angry complaints that threatened to reach epidemic proportions in the first winter tourist season of his administration. In the most menacing incident, Dana C. Smith, highly regarded Pasadena, California, lawyer and good friend of then-Senator Richard M. Nixon, denounced Cuba's gambling casinos. One of the sponsors of Nixon's controversial senatorial expense fund, Smith challenged the legitimacy of his Havana gambling losses. He and his wife had dined at the Sans Soucí nightclub; as they were leaving, a member of the staff approached and urged Smith to participate in a "free game" in the casino as a courtesy of the house. Curious, and told that he could not possibly lose, Smith tried his luck. Despite the assurances, he dropped several thousand dollars in a very short time, withdrew from the game, and wrote a check to cover the loss. Agitated and probably angry at himself, Smith made a few inquiries and learned that the game he had played was not sanctioned under Cuban laws. When he returned home, he stopped payment on the check.

Norman Rothman, formerly of Mother Kelly's nightclub in Miami Beach but more recently manager of the Sans Soucí, assigned the Beverly Credit Service of Miami Beach to collect Smith's forty-two hundred dollars, and Beverly Credit Service brought suit. Smith, his sophisticated lawyerly self having supplanted the carefree vacationer, refused responsibility for losses on an illegal game. He also telephoned his friend Richard Nixon. Meanwhile, Rothman denied knowledge of the matter, even though he had reendorsed the check originally payable to cash and endorsed by Smith.

Nixon inquired at the U.S. Embassy in Havana and requested that the embassy clarify the status of the fast-paced, tricky game descriptively called "razzle-dazzle." As embassy personnel checked with Ba-

144
*Shady
Business
in the
Tropical
Sun*

tista's representative on behalf of Smith and other indignant North Americans (one of whom claimed to have lost twenty thousand dollars), rumors sped through hotel lobbies, restaurants, and bars: tourists were being fleeced; the government might have to halt gambling. With the winter season set to begin in December, Batista quickly released an official statement to the press: "razzle" was illegal. Then he ordered the police to protect foreign tourists and make sure that the casinos played fair.[12]

That prompt and forceful assault on casino cheaters probably saved the season and deflected the potentially damaging March 1953 *Saturday Evening Post* exposé "Suckers in Paradise." According to the widely read chronicle of middle America, predatory U.S. gamblers in Cuba skillfully plucked flocks of golden geese, that is, the tourists. "Muscles" Martin had brought razzle to Sans Soucí, where Sammy Mannerino, an ex-Pittsburgh rackets boss, also hung out. Billie Bloom ran the game at the Tropicana, now owned by Cubans who had amassed their financial stake running *bolita*, the numbers game that Batista had initiated in the 1930s.

Meanwhile, Cuba faced stiff competition. Both Puerto Rico and the Bahamas boasted thriving casinos and expanded tourist business. So Batista and his newly installed team embarked on a campaign to clean up and enliven Havana's nightlife. Clubs refurbished their gaming rooms to resemble the fantasies of moviemakers, and Meyer Lansky headed south.[13]

Cuba's revitalized casino operations had every reason to love Senator Kefauver. Successful casinos require skilled managers, not amateurs. Also, casinos do experience occasional bad nights and need a substantial bankroll to cover losses. Laws of probability underpin the gaming business, and profits depend on a calculated margin of advantage. Given enough bettors and playing time, the percentage favors the house, and mass tourism generates the flow of gamblers needed to work in the casino's favor. Furthermore, lack of control spells disaster. Thousands of dollars change hands in minutes, and management's share has to be collected several times during the course of the evening. Owners might skim money off the top, but not employees. Surround players with glamour and an atmosphere of calm professionalism, but maintain discipline, restraint, and a business mentality behind the scenes. Gamblers play; everyone else works.[14]

Professional casino managers take fast action against cheaters. They know the clientele, that is, those who play on credit and those who do not. In Cuba, for example, a courier rushed personal checks from Havana to Florida as soon as the casino closed. Checks were cleared the following day, and the casino manager confronted suspected welshers that very night. No Cubans had the stateside connections to run that kind of service. It required a nationwide network in the United States, such as that built during the mob's years of illegal gambling operations.

Displaced American mobsters became partners in four of Havana's five casinos. Meyer Lansky bought a share in the popular Montmartre club, and partners in Miami's defunct S. and G. race wire syndicate (Kefauver victims, also) operated the Casino Nacional. Lansky operated a school to train and screen casino employees. Only trustworthy individuals gained access to the privileged world of blackjack dealers, croupiers, and roulette stickmen. Instead of diplomas, graduates earned their tuxedos, the proper attire to create an atmosphere of comfortable gentility. Since the selected cohort of gaming "technicians" earned excellent wages, applicants even included university graduates.[15]

Certainly, racketeers operated casinos in Cuba; were they welcome? Yes and no. When razzle failed to disappear immediately after the government had ordered operations stopped, tourist chief Facio sent troops into the gaming rooms. One month after the March 1953 *Saturday Evening Post* hit the newsstands, Cuba's military intelligence forces (Servicio de Inteligencia Militar, or SIM) arrested a dozen North Americans suspected of running crooked games at the Tropicana, Sans Soucí, and Jockey Club. The government deported eleven of the offenders and announced the problem resolved.[16]

While petty chiselers would not be tolerated, Lansky ran an efficient operation and attracted big-time professional players to his crap tables, gamblers whose trust in the fairness of the games would draw others and improve Cuba's competitive position among Caribbean resorts. At his Montmartre club in Vedado, businesslike table crews conducted the games. Employees dealt blackjack from a box, not from the hand, and floormen watched the action for any signs of impropriety. Lansky watched over Havana's casinos. He knew how to run them and whom to trust. His brother Jake, for example, worked as floor manager in the Hotel Nacional's casino.[17]

The last thing Cuba needed was tourists complaining about gam-

146

*Shady
Business
in the
Tropical
Sun*

bling losses to their elected representatives, or the media's portrayal of Cuba as a haven for Kefauver refugees. Batista held power without the benefit of elections, and his opponents threatened to take the political contest into the streets. He wanted North Americans to enjoy their stay and to see Cuba in the most positive terms, as a boost to both tourism and his political legitimacy. Complaints about crooked gambling became a rarity, and Batista launched a frenetic period of hotel and casino building with Lansky at his side. They never imagined that their gambling empire would survive scarcely half a decade.

Chapter 10

Batista Stages a Tourist Boom

Between 1953 and 1959, Cuban tourism truly prefigured Michael Frayn's chaotic *Noises Off* third act. The stage was set for pleasure, but behind the scenery, the action centered on a violent political struggle. As actors moved between the worlds of tourism and insurrection, the stage became a battleground. Fulgencia Batista, as tourism's producer, director, and stage manager, dealt with questions of money and scripts, always with an eye to the critics, at the same time fending off challenges to his authority. Then, in a plot twist, successful rebels took center stage. For a while they were the tourist attraction; they also were proprietors of hotels and business partners with gamblers. It was a play filled with dramatic irony.

Revenue potential and economic diversification justified tourist development in the 1950s, just as they had in the 1920s. A market existed, ready to be tapped. By 1950 seventy-five million North Americans took annual vacations and were spending nineteen billion dollars for travel every year, almost two-thirds of it in the Americas. One-third of U.S.

families earned annual incomes of at least five thousand dollars, compared to just 2 percent of such families in 1920–23 and 4 percent in 1941. Clearly, U.S. workers enjoyed sufficient free time and disposable income for vacation travel. Like Machado, Batista understood that a successful tourist industry required planning and a considerable dedication of public resources. Like Machado, he enjoyed close relations with the U.S. government and strong ties to North American business interests and counted on both to back his plans.[1]

Casinos represented as sound a public policy and business decision in Cuba as they did in Nevada. Profits accrued to investors, and the government took its legitimate contractual cut in fees and taxes. In the competitive Caribbean market, the alliance between the Cuban government and U.S. gamblers cast adrift by Estes Kefauver also made economic sense. Despite real growth in annual income from its hotel, restaurant, entertainment, commercial, transportation, and tourist service sector, the island's share of the Caribbean market actually declined between 1949 and 1954, from 43 percent to 31 percent. Cuba recorded a 30 percent increase in tourist arrivals, but Puerto Rico doubled and Haiti quintupled the number of their respective visitors. Tourist income expanded, but too many of the dollars sailed past Cuba's shores.[2]

Gambling casinos and nightclub extravaganzas served another purpose as well. Like bread and circuses, they diverted attention from authoritarian, arbitrary governance. To counter persistent political rumblings after 1953, Batista strengthened his hold through forceful restraint of militant dissidents and questionable elections. He responded to real and rumored conspiracies against his leadership with roundups of suspects, followed by physical punishment or incarceration. When a determined young lawyer, Fidel Castro, led an attack on an army post near Santiago de Cuba on 26 July 1953, Batista's forces quickly brought the situation under control. They captured and executed seventy of Castro's followers and tried, convicted, and imprisoned the rest, including Castro. The unsuccessful Moncada Barracks attack had threatened to crack the façade of political peace, but Batista's rapid, decisive, albeit brutal response reassured potential visitors and investors that he was in control. With militants imprisoned and dissidents chastened, Cuba awaited the tourists.

By the 1953–54 winter season Batista had jailed the political activists, had deported the razzle operators, and had put Meyer Lansky on the payroll as his gambling supervisor. U.S. authorities, in fact, had delayed Lansky's return to Havana but ensured his commitment to Cuba. Several years earlier, when he and his wife had traveled to Europe, he had acknowledged to authorities that he expected to visit Lucky Luciano in Italy. Whether that contact or Kefauver's 1950–51 inquiry triggered the indictment, the state of New York charged Lansky with conspiracy, gambling, and forgery. He pled guilty, probably to avoid having to testify under oath about his activities (and those of his associates) and to escape the publicity of a trial. Sentenced in May 1953, he served his time in the county jail in Saratoga, New York. His conviction precluded open participation in casino operations in Las Vegas, so when he left jail two months later, his future lay in Cuba.[3] Lansky had mastered the art of profitable casino operations, including the skim, that is, removing part of the cash that crossed the tables before the figures went into the books. Experienced professional that he was, he expected to share that revenue with public officials. He could be sure that Batista would tolerate no Kefauver-like investigations.

Sugar sales slumped as the Korean War ended, and with some half million unemployed workers on his hands, Batista needed tourist dollars as an economic and political bulwark against enemies inside and outside the island. The army and police intimidated internal dissidents with officially sanctioned strong-arm tactics, but self-exiled opponents were raising money and buying guns. News of arms seizures in New York reminded both Cubans and North Americans of the deadly serious intent of Batista's antagonists. In March 1954 the United States charged ex-president Prío with conspiracy to violate the Neutrality Act by shipping weapons to Cuba.[4] The accusation recalled the customary practices of antigovernment Cuban militants through a century of colonial and national history. That is, they went into exile and organized armed invasions to oust the government. In presidential elections held later that year, all opposition candidates withdrew, and thousands of cynical or apathetic voters simply stayed away from the polls. Batista's dubious electoral victory satisfied few dissidents.

Habaneros nonetheless rallied their enthusiasm for carnival in February and joined crowds of tourists who lined the streets and filled the bleachers along the Prado and in front of the presidential palace. An estimated quarter of a million spirited onlookers clapped and cheered and soaked up the atmosphere. Street vendors hawked confetti, caps, and whistles, while many a viewer—moved by the intoxicating music and dance—turned into a convivial participant. Night-clubs and casinos, some of them under new ownership, enjoyed brisk business. Both Cubans and North Americans patronized the cafés and nightclubs to eat, dance, and see the shows. Lansky's Montmartre Club treated its guests to a sophisticated, somewhat sedate musical production. The Sans Souci's showgirls performed in the more typically colorful "A Thousand and One Nights" and "Serenata mulata." In the advertisements, Sans Souci's dancers shared space with a roulette wheel positioned in front of an easily identifiable King of Hearts caricature. The King held a drink in one hand, playing cards in the other, and winked one eye.[5]

Carnival festivities and cabaret merriment perhaps veiled, but could not dispel, the tension that surrounded Batista's 25 February inaugural, a well-orchestrated celebration held despite—or because of—the equivocal election it confirmed. Frustrated political opponents renewed efforts to topple the president, and the racket of exploding bombs periodically punctuated the hubbub of Havana's daily activities and nighttime festivities. On the lookout for political enemies who might disrupt the inaugural, police happened upon a suspicious pair—two men injured by a bomb that had exploded prematurely in their hands. Interrogation led the officers to a cache of rifles, machine guns, and hand grenades and to two women who directed them to Orlando León Lemus, who had headed the Socialist Revolutionary Movement (MSR) in the 1940s. Veteran of that era's political gangsterism, León Lemus—popularly known as "El Colorado"—was Public Enemy Number One to the police. He died in a bloody gun battle that belied the carefree carnival atmosphere of the streets, the stylish congeniality of the nightclubs, and the solemnity of the inaugural. After the deadly exchange of gunfire, police officers bragged of having prevented Batista's assassination. They had, they claimed, uncovered such a plot while extracting confessions from those arrested.[6]

Perhaps encouraged by the effective police work, a confident Batista granted amnesty to political prisoners. Within weeks of his release from prison, Fidel Castro departed for Mexico to train his followers for an armed uprising. Carlos Prío Socarrás returned to Cuba to organize the political opposition, and university students, marching to honor the memory of a student revolutionary hero killed by Machado, demonstrated their mobilization potential.

Batista's economic efforts probably attenuated discontent in some circles but did not co-opt his most dedicated opponents. Antigovernment agitation flared as the 1955–56 winter tourist season opened. Students rioted in Santiago de Cuba, and signs of general unrest flickered in numerous cities in the interior. Police arrested several Havana University students at the Carmen Café, not far from the steps where most university political rallies took place, and charged them with a conspiracy to place bombs throughout the city. When police arrested José Antonio Echevarría, president of the university's student federation, demonstrators stoned passing vehicles and lit bonfires in the middle of the street. Then they declared a strike and called for new presidential elections. Echevarría made it clear that the student federation, given no alternative, would support armed insurrection.

Batista accused Prío Socarrás of fomenting rebellion and deported him to Miami. Then he court-martialed and imprisoned Colonel Ramón Barquín López, military attaché of the Cuban Embassy in Washington, for conspiracy against the government. In the escalating conflict, military forces gunned down fifteen young men who attacked a rural guard post in Matanzas.[7] Batista underscored his authority with a generous dose of police power; nevertheless, in the midst of the threats and counterthreats, Oriental Park racetrack opened its season with great fanfare.

HOTELS, BANKS, AND PUBLIC ENTERPRISE

If voter apathy and sporadic violence cast doubts on Batista's legitimacy, the flattery of contented tourists and an influx of dollars circulating through the economy might fix him more firmly in the presidential chair. To boost the sluggish economy, he courted foreign investment. Joint ventures between the Cuban government and foreign industrialists brought cement, rubber tires, paper, fertilizer, steel products, glass, nickel, and food production to the island.[8] The government also issued $350 million in bonds to finance roads, aqueducts, and agricultural and industrial projects, including the long-awaited tunnel under Havana Bay. Batista tried to restrain organized labor and to restore the right of owners to dismiss workers as necessary until vehement union protests forced him to back down. His policies nonetheless spurred economic growth and fueled a period of prosperity, however skewed the benefits.

Although a thriving tourist industry might add luster to a tarnished regime, a fundamental problem had yet to be resolved. Havana lacked sufficient hotel rooms, and investment was not forthcoming. Batista devised an incentive: if investors committed at least one million dollars to build a hotel, the government would authorize the inclusion of a casino. Licenses could be obtained for twenty-five thousand dollars, and casino operators would pay an additional two-thousand-dollar monthly fee, plus a percentage of the take (money bet minus payout). To deflect critics, Batista followed the example set by the 1919 tourism legislation: a portion of the casino fee would benefit charitable work carried out by Sra. Marta Fernández de Batista, the president's wife. (Batista may have capitalized on the experience of his contemporary, the Argentine dictator Juan Perón, whose wife Evita Perón had garnered the gratitude of Argentina's poor through state-sponsored charities.)

While Havana unquestionably needed hotel rooms to increase tourist revenue, construction contracts and operating permits also had co-optive properties; that is, profits might turn known or suspected enemies into allies. Fat payrolls would be shared by entrepreneurs and thousands of laborers, engineers, and office workers. The coordinated effort of capital formation and hotel construction began in 1955 and practically doubled room capacity by 1958. Project by project, hotels and motels emerged under the impetus and watchful eye of public financial institutions. The government's intention was not to operate hotels but rather to facilitate and encourage private investment.

Although Carlos Prío Socarrás had inaugurated the publicly funded Banco de Fomento Agrícola e Industrial de Cuba (Banfaic) in 1950 to facilitate agricultural and industrial development, Batista redirected the bank's financing capabilities toward hotel projects, specifically those large enough to warrant the granting of casino licenses. When the Intercontinental Hotel Corporation (IHC) finally moved into the Cuban market, a decade after Juan Trippe's conversation with Roosevelt, the company purchased the management contract to operate the government-owned Hotel Nacional, and Banfaic loaned IHC the substantial sum needed to rehabilitate the 1920s-era landmark. Thoroughly familiar with business practices in Latin America, IHC advisedly gave a 20 percent share in the Hotel Nacional contract to Cubans who had helped to arrange the finance agreement with Banfaic.

The elaborately detailed, Spanish-style Hotel Nacional had passed through a series of lessees and badly needed refurbishing. The Chicago hotelman and real estate entrepreneur Arnold Kirkeby had acquired the Nacional's lease in the 1940s. Kirkeby's wife came from a family of Cuban cigar manufacturers. When his brothers-in-law expressed uncertainty about Fidel Castro's activities, Kirkeby sold the operating rights to the New York magnate William Zeckendorf. In 1955, on the eve of the tourist boom, Zeckendorf sold the management contract to IHC for a hefty profit.[9]

When Meyer Lansky proposed a deluxe Las Vegas–type casino for the Hotel Nacional and suggested converting some of the rooms into elegant suites for wealthy gamblers, Batista concurred. The government leased the hotel's casino to Wilbur Clark, familiar to many Las Vegas gamblers. Clark opened the Nacional's gaming room with considerable fanfare in December 1955. The governor of Nevada and the president of Cuba shared the spotlight. Batista had made his point: Cuba stood on a par with Las Vegas. He scored again in the stature of the Nacional's internationally acclaimed cabaret headliner. Few of the patrons who applauded the popular songstress and Broadway star Eartha Kitt at the grand opening cared that Jake Lansky, Meyer's brother, directed casino operations. They enjoyed the show, praised the ambiance, and judged Cuba a wonderful place to vacation.[10]

Financial institutions formed an administrative heart through which the government pumped capital and credit into Cuba's tourist economy. Batista had inaugurated the Financiera Nacional de Cuba (National Finance Company) in 1953 to fund self-liquidating public works projects and to assist private groups in various ventures. The company mobilized capital resources by contracting loans from insurance companies, pension funds, and commercial banks and issuing its own bonds. The Banco Nacional de Cuba held half of the Financiera's shares, plus one, and thus controlled lending policies. For example, to build the long-awaited tunnel under Havana Bay, the Financiera issued tax-free Tunnel of Havana bonds, backed by a mortgage on future tunnel revenues. A French firm won the construction contract by agreeing to accept partial payment in Cuban sugar, which the government had been unable to unload on a glutted market. The Financiera also backed a new tourist complex, including motels and recreational beach facilities, near the site of John Bowman's 1920s Havana-Biltmore Yacht Club, west of the city.

The president of the Banco Nacional also managed the Banco de

Desarrollo Económico y Social (Bandes), established in 1955 and capitalized in part with government funds. Bandes loans built cargo ships, railroad and airline facilities, a paper mill, match factory, and copper mine, and they ensured the operation of the Compañía Cubana de Aviación, Cuba's principal airline and carrier of thousands of tourists. But Bandes money contributed to hotel construction as well, including the Havana Riviera and the Havana Hilton (later the Havana Libre). Ironically, because of Batista's efforts, the revolutionaries who deposed him in 1959 found themselves committed to the financial soundness of foreign-owned enterprises that they scorned ideologically, as well as several hotels in which U.S. gamblers ran the casinos.

The Havana Hilton: Owned by Its Workers

Batista's financial creativity brought IHC to Cuba, and the hotel and restaurant workers union captured Hilton Hotels International (HHI). Domestic capital—thirty-two million dollars in Bandes loans and the union's pension funds—built the Hilton.[11] When the culinary workers' union (more than six thousand cooks, waiters, bartenders, and so on) established their pension fund in 1952, no major hotel had opened in Havana for twenty years. In a classic contradiction, the reluctance of investors reflected the power of the union itself. For example, just as the 1952 winter tourist season got under way, the Gastronómico, as the union generally was known, staged a twenty-four-hour strike to pressure for a substantial 30 percent wage increase. They shut down thirty-two hotels, seventy-five restaurants, eight hundred cafés and soda fountains, and seven cabarets. The owners promptly announced a lockout and threatened to fire all workers who had participated in the labor action. Florida newspapers quickly picked up the story. Their own tourist industry could benefit from the extra few days' lodging and meals for people who had intended to spend part of their time in Cuba. In the deliberately gloomy pictures painted by the press, tourists in Havana had to carry their own bags and make their own beds. They found neither decent places to eat nor telephone service. In short, they had no fun.[12]

With the rest of the Caribbean competing for hotel investment and tourists, the Gastronómico leaders and pension fund board members finally saw the light: new hotels created jobs for union members, added to members' contributions, and provided income for the retirement fund.[13] For Bandes, the Gastronómico's loan application carried a compelling logic. The union would not shut down a hotel that its pension fund owned nor set wage rates that would reduce profits needed to repay its loan. The government facilitated the union's effort by expanding allowable pension fund investment to include a hotel. Thus the pension fund became not only a valuable source of investment capital but also an assurance of labor peace.

With financing in place, the pension fund board pursued various potential partners with hotel operating experience. They settled on Hilton Hotels International. Many governments and private investors looked to U.S. hotel chains for guidance as they built facilities to accommodate North Americans. Hotel companies entering foreign markets agreed to supervise design, construction, furnishing, and staff training on a fee basis, and then to operate the hotel on a long-term contract. HHI's capital investment for the Havana Hilton was modest, a little over one million dollars, but its capability to direct guests to the new hotel was invaluable. Hilton had a reputation for generating tourists accustomed to paying high room rates. Moreover, guests would gamble at the Havana Hilton casino and thereby increase the revenue needed by the union to refill its pension fund coffers and to repay its Bandes loans.

Cuban officials considered the culinary workers–Hilton agreement so significant that Batista himself called in the press to announce the loan authorization and to praise the project's social benefits. During the construction phase alone, Hilton would hire almost 1,300 workers directly; subcontractors would employ another 440. In fact, salaries estimated at some seven million dollars would boost the economy even before the hotel opened.[14]

Construction began in 1955 and took more than two years. The Frederick Snare Corporation, whose founder had spearheaded the Havana Country Club development in the 1920s, acted as general contractor. When Hilton prepared for its 1958 grand opening, however, two potential conflicts threatened its management contract. The Gastronómico, as owner of the hotel and protector of its members' well-being, expected to maintain the customary Cuban practice of employing young men to prepare and clean guests' rooms. HHI strongly objected; American women—a substantial percentage of anticipated guests—might balk at chambermaids who were in fact chamber males. They were accustomed to seeing females in that role, and the Hilton name assured its guests the comforts of home. Furthermore, Hilton insisted on hiring fifteen Swiss cooks, a violation of labor legislation that reserved at least half of the positions for Cubans. However, since HHI's worldwide reservation facilities were critical to the union's long-range objective, the hotel company won. Weighing the interest of thousands of workers who would share benefits against the rights of a handful of union members, the leadership granted the exemptions. In the end, Hilton held the upper hand with its promise of affluent clients and a smooth-running operation.[15] The hotel opened its doors for business less than a year before revolutionaries swept into Havana and camped in the lobby. The pension fund had scarcely made a dent in its multimillion dollar debt, and the new government, as guarantor of bonds issued by Bandes (the mortgage holder), joined the culinary workers in their gratitude for the patronage of North American tourists.

The Havana Riviera: Las Vegas Chic

The Havana Riviera belonged to Meyer Lansky, even though the incorporation papers for the Compañía de Hoteles La Riviera de Cuba, SA, listed the names of Miami hotel operators, a Canadian textile and real estate family, and several other investors instead. Company shareholders invested eight million dollars to build the hotel and applied to Bandes for a six-million-dollar loan. The investor group included several identifiable Lansky associates, some of them Prohibition-era friends with whom he shared other investments. An old chum, Hyman Abrams, had participated in the group that built the Flamingo Hotel in Las Vegas, along with Lansky associate Benjamin "Bugsy" Siegel. Morris Rosen also invested in the Flamingo Hotel and became one of the hotel's bosses after Siegel caught a bullet in the head in Beverly Hills in 1947. Riviera Hotel partner Sam Garfield had gone to elementary school in Detroit with Moe Dalitz and later smuggled liquor across the Canadian border with Dalitz during Prohibition. Dalitz invested with Lansky in the post-Prohibition Molaska Corporation, which manufactured legal booze, and in the 1950s he had an interest in Wilbur Clark's Desert Inn in Las Vegas. Garfield had invested money in oil and gas production with Lansky as a partner, and now Lansky returned the favor.[16]

Harry and Ben Smith owned half the company's shares. They were Canadians, involved in their family's knitting mills and a real estate holding company in Toronto. They vacationed in Florida, where Lansky had owned several gambling clubs, and they controlled considerable assets in that state. Harry served as the Riviera's president through the construction phase, and Ben was treasurer. After the hotel opened in December 1957, the brothers resigned from the board, although they apparently retained some financial stake in the company.[17]

Work on the Riviera Hotel began in December 1956. Joaquín Martínez Sáenz, president of the National Bank of Cuba and a director of Bandes (years earlier a youthful rebel who had fought against Machado), praised the Riviera project for its role as an employer, a producer of foreign exchange, and a stimulus to the tourist industry. "With this operation," he wrote glowingly in a Bandes report, "will be confirmed one more time the steps toward positive advancement that this institution makes possible for the economy of the country, situating Cuba among the top centers of tourist attraction."[18] Despite his enthusiasm, Martínez Sáenz scrupulously examined construction accounts for signs that the company might use loan funds improperly. After all, the principals had no credentials to match those of the Hilton or Intercontinental hotel chains. The Riviera Corporation brought in a contractor of its own choosing, and given the reputations of its board members, Bandes auditors watched lest they skim construction funds as they did gambling receipts.

As the project moved along, the notation "ojo" in the margins of financial transaction records signaled the bank's surveillance; that is, they kept an eye on certain expenditures. Auditors continually questioned unexplained fees and checks payable to corporate executives unaccompanied by documentation. Gutman Skrande, the Bandes official who administered the Riviera loan, complained constantly about the absence of receipts and failure to annotate operations in accordance with acceptable accounting practices. He questioned differences in payment authorizations and check amounts, and payments for gambling equipment that had no accompanying invoices. He challenged Irving Feldman, a Miami building contractor and company stockholder who with his architect son, Irving Jr., oversaw a team of six hundred workers on the project. When Feldman collected a total of $375,000 in checks with no documentation, the frustrated bank officer learned only that, by verbal agreement, Feldman's fee would not exceed a reasonable percentage of the total cost of construction. On another occasion, a skeptical Skrande sought an explanation for six-figure checks payable to "bearer." A company representative coolly replied that the checks reimbursed advances extended by corporate president Harry Smith before the company had available funds, although no one could say exactly how much the company owed Mr. Smith. In the blizzard of paper, the bank even questioned snowflakes, for example, an $1,880 payment to Lansky for travel expenses.[19]

Like other hotel projects, the Riviera generated significant economic activity long before the doors opened. In April 1957 the construction team marked the ahead-of-schedule completion of the hotel's steel skeleton with a "roof party." By September the company had spent $7.5 million on land, structure, electrical work, air conditioning, plumbing, wood, refrigerators, elevators, casino equipment, telephone service, and workers' insurance.[20]

The Y-shaped tower, Havana's first major building with central air conditioning, rose majestically from a site next to the sea and close to the fashionable Miramar suburb. Entering the front door, patrons encountered a world of marble, mosaics, and futuristic furnishings, evidence of great expense, if not to everyone's taste. The round, windowless casino afforded a cloistered haven for gamblers on one side of the block-long lobby. On the other, the Copa Room, with its floor shows and famous feature artists, awaited diners and dancers. When the Riviera opened in December (Ginger Rogers headlined at the Copa), the management lavished luxury on its pampered guests, and they filled the hotel for the next five months. Lansky insisted on the best of everything for his clients, especially the high-stakes gamblers.

Riviera shareholders congratulated themselves as the money began to pour in. Three weeks after opening night, when they closed the books on 31 December 1957, revenues from hotel and casino operations totaled almost three-quarters of a million dollars. For the three months from 1 January to 31 March 1958, income from the hotel and casino reached over $4 million. April–June figures made the owners even happier: $4.9 million in income and $3.4 million in operating expenses. The casino was the core of the operation. A ratio of $3 earned from the casino for every $2 from hotel rooms, cabaret, restaurant, and shops confirmed that gambling, more than hotel rooms, rewarded investors with profits. The formula had built Las Vegas and clearly would work for Cuba, too. Give the guests well-appointed rooms, extravagant shows, and good food, but most importantly, attract gamblers who left big money at the tables.

Not only was the Riviera profitable for its investors, but the operation also redistributed hotel income to a variety of large and small Cuban businesses. Operating expenses for the month of June 1958, for example, at the tail end of the hotel's first tourist season, included $15,500 in auto services paid to drivers, mechanics, and service station owners and $77,580 in repair and maintenance expenses to electricians, carpenters, plumbers, and general repairmen. A $55,000 laundry bill paid for workers and supplies. General administrative expenses of $183,000 and salaries and publicity totaling $136,000 provided fees for various professionals, technicians, and consultants, as well as salaries and miscellaneous goods and services. An employer's contribution of $4,000 went to the Gastronómico's pension fund, and the hotel paid more than $10,000 in taxes. These figures did not include tips, which went unrecorded but circulated in the local economy. Some of the revenue left the country, of course, to purchase goods and to pay shareholders, but countless Cubans enjoyed the benefits of tourist dollars spent at the Riviera.[21]

Other Hotel Developments

Batista's policies turned a paucity of hotel investment into an avalanche of loan applications. The new Hotel Caprí, with its fancy casino and flashy rooftop swimming pool, held its own opening gala at the same time that planeloads of celebrities glamorized the Riviera's inaugural ceremonies. North American hotelman Julius (Skip) Shepard leased the Hotel Caprí from its Cuban owner and, in turn, sublet the hotel's commercial space. Some fifteen thousand dollars in rentals accrued to the Compañía Hotelera Shepard each month from Cubans who ran the profitable barbershop, beauty salon, and souvenir store. Santo Trafficante Jr., a fixture in the Havana gambling scene, managed the casino. (His father had gained considerable notoriety running numbers in Tampa, Florida, in the 1930s and 1940s.) The film star George Raft, known for portrayals of suave gangsters in the movies and a familiar figure in Cuba, served as genial greeter of gamblers and hotel guests.[22]

While the Hilton, Riviera, and Caprí shared the publicity spotlight, casinos also opened at the old, established Sevilla-Biltmore Hotel downtown and the brand new Comodoro Hotel in the suburbs. Between the Hotel Nacional on its elevated site overlooking the water and the Hilton at the top of the incline that followed Twenty-third Street (La Rampa) inland, several new small hotels, like the Vedado, St. John's, and Flamingo, accommodated a less affluent clientele. New restaurants sprang up, and older ones redecorated and installed air conditioning for the comfort of summer patrons. Dozens of little clubs and bars opened all around town.

Despite rebel guerrillas camped in the Sierra Maestra and increased urban violence around the island, prospective resort builders maintained their confidence in Batista's leadership and ability to maintain control. The Antillean Hotel Corporation applied to build a twenty-eight-million-dollar, six-hundred-room luxury hotel and asked Bandes for eighteen million dollars for construction expenses and furnishings. The investors' application form listed experience "in the southwest of the United States," which probably indicated Las Vegas affiliations. As the loan request went forward, however, a politically sensitive issue threatened to derail the project. The proposed hotel property was occupied by a popular children's park, one named in honor of the independence hero José Martí. Although the government had used the land for decades, title to the property remained vested in the heirs of the deceased owners of record, along with an unsettled claim against the government for compensation.

Cuban lawyers intervened and successfully protected their foreign clients' interests against local critics. Well connected in Havana's business and government circles, Mario Lazo and Jorge E. Cubás gained a favorable court ruling: possession of the land would be transferred to the recorded owners, but the hotel concessionaires could have the land on payment of a "just price" to the owners, with $500,000 going to the Ministry of Education for a new playground. Rather than a corporate contribution, however, the half million dollars came from the owners' share. The court justified Antillean's right to the property on the grounds that the planned hotel was a public utility needed for tourism. As in the 1920s, tourist promoters had powerful friends.

Backers also considered the Santa Ana de Soroa resort a patriotic labor: their multimillion-dollar project would promote the economic and social development of Pinar del Río province, to the west of Havana. The seven Cuban investors asked for five million dollars in government-backed loans so that Montañas Occidentales, SA, could build a 225-room hotel with a casino, cabaret, swimming pools, golf course, an artificial lake for fishing, and equestrian trails. The developers also intended to construct 650 high-priced homes for a quiet residential retreat not far from noisy, hectic Havana—another public service, no doubt.[23]

The proliferation of new and proposed hotels signaled Cuba's emergence as a world-class tourist center, in contention for international conventions of Lions and Rotarians who contributed millions of dollars to a country's economy. A persistent lobbying campaign persuaded the American Society of Travel Agents (ASTA) to schedule its 1959 overseas convention in Havana, a meeting that usually drew more than two thousand visitors. ASTA's 1949 Mexico City meeting had boosted Mexico's tourism after inspired travel agents returned home and sold the country's attractions to their clients. *Habaneros* anticipated a similar stimulus to their own industry and immediately began to plan facilities for plenary sessions and business meetings, nightclub visits, golf and fishing tours, guides, stenographers, and other services.[24]

If Europe's royalty had made Monte Carlo's casino into a synonym for nineteenth-century glamour, Havana in the 1950s showcased an elite that traded more on celebrity than claims to aristocracy. John Kennedy, a U.S. senator and rising political star, spent three days in Havana in December 1957, while the boxing champion Jack Dempsey lounged among other sunbathers at the Hotel Nacional's swimming pool. That same month, some thirty top U.S., Canadian, and Cuban golfers matched their skills in Havana's tenth invitational open. Competition among professional women golfers, the Proette Open, took place in the spring. In January the popular television show host Steve Allen moved his whole production crew to Havana to stage an hourlong variety show. The Sunday-night broadcast was a real tribute to the Riviera Hotel's publicity operation, the first time that any North American entertainer had telecast live from Cuba. Allen took his staff and well-known guests: Skitch Henderson led the orchestra; Steve Lawrence sang; Lou Costello clowned; and Mamie Van Doren cavorted in the hotel's swimming pool. Some three hundred Cuban dignitaries watched the show from seats in the Copa Room, the casino, or by the pool. Gamblers continued to place their bets while cameras caught the casino action, and millions of people all over the United States saw Cuba for the first time and watched other North Americans having fun there.[25]

Time magazine noted Havana's lavish new casinos and credited Meyer Lansky with transforming the city into a gamblers' paradise.

The same week that Mamie Van Doren splashed in the Riviera's pool, *Time* described Cuba's capital as a "fleshpot city . . . where gambling has always been one of the more reputable vices," and *Life* magazine noted that Batista and his friends shared gambling profits with the U.S. mob, "survivors of the era of bootlegging gangs and Tommy guns." Lansky's underworld connections probably deterred no readers accustomed to 1950s gangster films. Moreover, James Cagney, Humphrey Bogart, and Edward G. Robinson filled movie screens with considerably more violence than mobsters brought to Havana. Revealingly, *Life* also characterized the casino boom as the one bright spot in an increasingly dark political picture.[26]

GOOD TIMES TURN BAD

In spite of thriving casinos, Steve Allen's telecast, golf championships, and influential articles in *Time* and *Life*, Cuban tourism already had reached its peak. While gamblers-turned-businessmen sat around the pool at the Hotel Nacional, crowing over their good fortune, the Nevada Gambling Commission tossed a grenade in their laps. A newly elected reformist governor set out to cleanse the state's gaming industry. In his view, if organized crime figures operated Havana's casinos, sometimes in partnerships with Las Vegas casino operators, the notoriety might discredit Nevada's thriving industry. The tie had to be broken, and commission members ordered Nevada gaming licensees to either divest themselves of their Havana holdings or else sell their casino interests in Las Vegas. The commission specifically named Moe Dalitz, Tom McGinty, Morris Kleinman, and Wilbur Clark as casino leaseholders at the Hotel Nacional, and Hyman Abrams of the Las Vegas Sands as an investor in the Havana Riviera. The commission also correctly reported that Edward Levinson of Las Vegas's Fremont Hotel had set up Lansky's casino at the Riviera.[27]

Lawyers for the Las Vegas investors vigorously protested the violation of their clients' constitutional rights, but those who sold their Havana shares were, in fact, fortunate. Scarcely two months after the Havana Hilton's splashy, celebrity-filled April 1958 inaugural, the number of tourists plummeted. A seasonal dip in patronage might have been expected, but a chasm opened instead. The Gastronómico's monthly rental earnings fell by almost two-thirds, from $87,000 to

$30,000. After a profitable first quarter of operation from December to March, in June the Hotel Capri's management asked Bandes to guarantee a $210,000 loan from the privately owned Banco Financiero to cover operating expenses. The hotel was $400,000 in arrears by December 1958 and trying to stretch out payments, with worse yet to come.[28]

Neither foreigners nor investors had the opportunity to enjoy the resort planned for Soroa. The Banco Nacional tried to halt construction to minimize anticipated losses, but appeals from unions and the small merchants who depended on workers' wages turned the bank officials around.[29] Soroa later became a popular vacation spot for beneficiaries of the revolution.

The murky political scene in 1958 did cancel at least one hotel and casino project. Among the Miami residents of Cuban extraction who made up the project's investor group, one was married to the granddaughter of Gerardo Machado. Endowed with a heightened sensibility to Cuban history, perhaps, he proved more skittish than his partners and pulled out.[30] His hesitation saved their money. Batista's show was nearing its final curtain.

Chapter 11

The Tourist Stage as
Rebel Battleground

Revolution and relaxation are inherently incompatible. Politics may make strange bedfellows, but political terrorists and tourists rarely rest their heads on the same pillow. The likelihood that tourists will die in a terrorist attack admittedly is remote, but having saved money for a one- or two-week vacation, tourists have little desire to chance bodily harm or confront political aggression and violence. Most holiday travelers are prepared to take limited risks but avoid real danger. The world, after all, is full of interesting places to visit. Conjure an image of pleasure—romantic, sensual, aesthetic, or intellectual—and the vision rarely includes dodging bullets.

For dissidents and rebels, on the other hand, tourists and tourism make excellent targets. Murdered or wounded tourists are newsworthy, and media coverage casts doubt on the government's ability to protect life and, by extension, property. Because terrorism discourages investors as well as visitors, fear inflicts substantial economic hardship on a tourism-dependent country. Moreover, when perceived as a threat to traditional ways of life and a drain on scarce government resources, tourism serves as a focus for nationalist rhetoric and a catalyst for mobilizing local populations.[1]

165
The
Tourist
Stage as
Rebel
Background

Several recent spectacular incidents demonstrate the economic effectiveness of intimidation and terror, as both tourism and the media have achieved global proportions. In 1985 hijackers gained control of TWA's flight 814 out of Athens. One passenger died and the others suffered through long hours as hostages. The next year, only half the usual summer influx of U.S. visitors went to Greece, and many avoided Europe altogether. Politically motivated attacks on cruise ships that same year left such a lasting impression of vulnerability that six years later, when armed forces moved against Iraq in the Persian Gulf, cruise business suffered as far away as the Caribbean. The Gulf War also took its toll on tourist industries in neighboring Turkey, Israel, Jordan, and Egypt.[2]

At about the same time, Maoist revolutionaries almost eradicated tourism in Peru, a nation that spends millions of dollars to publicize its indigenous cultures and unique Inca ruins. Shining Path guerrillas, operating primarily in rural areas, left the corpses of uncooperative villagers strewn on mountain paths. Their activities gained widespread media coverage, and the number of foreign tourists plunged from 350,000 to 30,000 between 1989 and 1991. After the government imprisoned Shining Path's top leaders in 1994 and appeared to regain control, tourism surged.[3]

As Peru's industry recovered, the focus shifted once again to the Middle East. Religious opponents of the secular Egyptian government attacked tour buses and tourist sites, trying to limit the industry's contribution to the nation's economic well-being. Meanwhile, Algeria's Islamic militants issued an ultimatum to all foreigners to leave the country or risk death. Both Islamic fundamentalists and Kurdish nationalists threatened Turkey's nascent industry by placing bombs in several of Istanbul's most popular tourist sites. As a result of actual attacks and terrorist threats, those countries experienced significant declines in badly needed tourism revenues.[4]

On the other hand, terrorists must guard against alienating the very supporters they hope to attract to their cause. That is, they must weigh the political gains of media exposure against possible loss of public support. In Spain, for example, where tourism generates the major portion of the country's hard currency and provides an income for thousands of citizens, Basque separatists have adjusted their actions to acceptable levels of disruption. They have avoided killing tourists, in hopes of gaining or retaining the sympathy of those who make a living from tourism while still striking a blow at the government. Thus, when they detonated bombs in coastal tourist areas, they generally used small amounts of explosives, set them off early in the morning, and warned the police in advance. Such acts conveyed an ability and willingness to inflict economic and personal injury, while projecting the image of reasonable people forced to use violence when denied alternatives for redressing justifiable grievances.[5]

Even in the early years of mass tourism, before antigovernment groups specifically targeted tourists and tourism, domestic unrest had warranted disclaimers and cautionary statements. For example, travel writers advised North Americans to avoid Bogotá, Colombia, after the April 1948 assassination of the popular political leader Jorge Gaitán. The potential for further confrontation outweighed the attractiveness of the city's notable history. The experts similarly discouraged holidays in Peru because government repression of dissidents made the situation unpleasant, "no matter how charming the dictatorship may be." Warnings on Bolivia also equivocated: "Despite . . . the state of siege — Bolivia's setting is spectacular and there is no cheaper place in the hemisphere."[6]

By contrast, the March 1952 Batista coup, accomplished with remarkably little disruption, minimally affected the tourist season. Guests at the Sevilla-Biltmore Hotel, awakened by the rattle of machine guns and crack of rifles at six-thirty in the morning, crowded into the lobby while combatants exchanged shots nearby. One blasé New Yorker who had arrived the day before viewed the action from her hotel room and later compared the experience to watching a movie. Less sanguine vacationers fled to the airport, where they found airline employees on strike and the army in charge. They returned to their hotels and, because the fighting ended quickly, remained in Cuba and completed their scheduled vacations. In a matter of days the casinos, bars, and nightclubs operated as usual. Batista suspended constitutional guarantees for forty-five days but allowed carnival celebrations to proceed.[7] Once firmly in command, he reorganized the tourist commission, backed its efforts with public financing, and positioned the island to compete in the era of mass tourism.

167
The
Tourist
Stage as
Rebel
Background

REVELRY AND REVOLUTION

Batista's strategies worked, but at the high point of the tourist boom, Cuba became a holiday paradise in the midst of a political hell. Rebels challenged his legitimacy, battling on the ground and in the media, and tourism itself became a character in the drama.

Batista had thwarted Cuba's electoral process. Resistance to the coup came primarily from university students and frustrated political opponents. Many Cubans, long accustomed to graft and political violence, regarded the new regime with cynicism or disinterest. When Batista's enemies failed to mobilize sufficient mass support to oust the usurper, many of them went into exile. They stockpiled weapons and prepared for a comeback. Meanwhile, Batista fed hopes of material gain with proposals for economic expansion and pursued political loyalty with promises of profits and jobs. Tourism, for example, affected Cubans across the social spectrum, from the investor in hotel development to the urban migrant employed in the restaurant kitchen or peddling postcards and sunglasses on the street.

To its beneficiaries, the tourism policy represented economic diversity and a source of revenue. To political dissidents, it opened a battleground. Faced with Batista's control of the military and police forces, antigovernment groups relied on unconventional warfare. That is, urban guerrillas need not attack tourists personally to gain their objective but could make the island appear hazardous—or merely inconvenient—by disrupting daily life. The rebels began to compete with Batista for media attention with contrasting images of Cuba. Between 1955 and 1959, bombings, assassinations, and government reprisals shared newspaper space with yacht races, carnival festivities, golf championships, and hotel openings. Each side manipulated news outlets and used public relations to disseminate messages favorable to its cause. Tourist officials entertained travel writers and travel agents who wrote enthusiastic pieces or told clients about Cuba's attractions. They

168
The
Tourist
Stage as
Rebel
Background

published brochures that pictured an inviting tropical retreat. Meanwhile, rebels aired their charges, voiced complaints, and expressed their ideals to sympathetic journalists.

Tourism and insurrection chugged along on separate tracks for a time before they crashed head on. Visitors to the island spent some thirty million dollars in 1956, a figure barely 10 percent of the value of that year's sugar crop but considered promising. Hotel construction and operation offered steady jobs at good pay. Financially comfortable *habaneros* enjoyed the restaurants, bars, and shows patronized by tourists. Some of them attended the horse races in season and applauded the showgirls at the Tropicana. On Sundays families went to the Coney Island Park in Marianao or packed a picnic basket and rode the bus to newly developed beaches. Middle-class families vacationed at Varadero or took the ferry to Key West and the Greyhound bus from Key West to Miami for a holiday.[8]

Thus tourism presented the rebels a strategic but tricky target. Terrorism scared away tourists but also struck a blow at an industry that created jobs. Would people co-opted by economic opportunities and diversions turn against the government? If Batista's responses reached a level of intolerable ruthlessness, a morally outraged citizenry might join the rebel ranks. Repression and escalation of police violence could make it more difficult to legitimate the regime through favorable press coverage and the sympathetic reminiscences of tourists.

Few vacationers who made plans to flee the snow or sample Cuba's temptations were deterred by its politics before 1958. To most readers of magazine articles and newspaper travel sections, the island beckoned with new and improved gambling facilities, nightclubs, and beaches. Cabaret owners competed for customers with ever more elaborate productions and the reigning stars of show business: Maurice Chevalier, Nat "King" Cole, Tony Martin, Billy Daniels, Diahann Carroll, Liberace. Casinos gave away thousands of dollars in cash prizes and installed huge screens to accommodate bingo aficionados.

Batista's opponents appeared less than forbidding. Lacking organization and effective leadership, they often agreed only on their dissatisfaction with the status quo. Even the most radical opposition did not conform to a single ideology or strategy for victory. Batista skillfully manipulated the situation, offering material rewards to friends and inflicting severe punishment on enemies. Little noted by most Cubans, however, and certainly beyond the ken of tourists, two groups of opponents joined together just as Batista's hotel/casino policy began to bear fruit. Work had started on the Hilton and Caprí hotels and was about to begin on the Riviera in August 1956 when Fidel Castro met with ex-president Prío Socarrás in McAllen, Texas. They discussed an invasion by Castro's forces, then training in Mexico, timed to coincide with an uprising inside Cuba. In September Castro and José Antonio Echevarría signed an agreement that committed their followers—Castro's Twenty-sixth of July Movement and Echevarría's Revolutionary Directorate (the militant arm of the University of Havana's student federation)—to armed struggle against the government.

The revolutionary coalition agreed on ends but diverged on means. Castro opposed violent actions in cities where Batista concentrated his intelligence apparatus and military power, opting instead for an operational base in rural, eastern Oriente province, where the regime was weak and the tradition of rebellion strong. From there he would organize mass support and build toward a general strike to bring down the government. Conversely, the Revolutionary Directorate regarded Havana as the critical economic, military, and political nerve center of revolutionary struggle and the preferred target for action. Castro and Echevarría granted each other the freedom to carry out plans as they saw fit. Once Castro arrived in Oriente, he would open a guerrilla front in the eastern mountains while other members of his movement staged actions throughout the country. The directorate would work toward a definitive armed insurrection centered in the capital, preceded by the disruptive actions deemed necessary to engender public anger and ferment.[9]

The Havana contingent fired the first shots. Rebel gunmen targeted a cabinet minister, set his assassination date, and carefully selected the site—outside Meyer Lansky's popular Montmartre nightclub in the heavily trafficked Vedado tourist section. When the minister failed to appear, the determined killers fatally shot the head of the military intelligence service (SIM) instead and wounded the son of the army chief of staff, his wife, and another woman as the foursome waited for the Montmartre's elevator. The assassins fled down an auto ramp to the ground floor and escaped. During the massive police hunt that followed, the killers sought refuge in the Haitian Embassy. When the army assaulted the embassy—in violation of the right of asylum—the rebels shot the leader of the assault team and then lost their own lives, gunned down on the embassy grounds.

170

*The
Tourist
Stage as
Rebel
Background*

THE IMAGE WAR

Whether or not the rebels had timed the action to coincide with the Inter-American Press Association's October meeting in Havana, dozens of journalists were in the city at the time of the shooting. Both the government and the rebels pled their cases before the influential visitors. Batista accused Prío Socarrás of ordering the Montmartre murder and charged that the former president wanted to convince foreign newsmen that no personal security existed in Cuba. The Revolutionary Directorate condemned Batista, alleged police brutality, and charged the government with torture, rape, and murder. While policemen retaliated against known dissidents, militants of both the directorate and Castro's Twenty-sixth of July Movement placed phosphorous bombs in highly visible and well-used locations: moviehouses, buses, nightclubs, theaters, and parks. The confrontation escalated, and Batista closed the university in November—just as Castro left Mexico for Cuba. Journalists reported the stories, and some tourists undoubtedly rearranged travel plans.

Although the rebels had prepared to lead an insurrection, no mass uprising accompanied Castro's December arrival. The handful of *fidelistas* who survived the rough trip by sea and the equally perilous landing made their way cautiously and painfully to the Sierra Maestra, in no condition to foment revolution.[10] Batista proclaimed Castro dead, declared the movement aborted, and announced plans for a rousing Havana carnival season. The publicity blitz also heralded the premier event of the winter tourist season: Cuba's first Gran Premio (Grand Prize) automobile race, set for 24 February 1957 to coincide with the anniversary celebration of Cuba's 1895 independence uprising.

Sports festivals have become politically significant tourist events. The Olympic games, for example, attract visitors with money to spend. Countries compete to host the games and invest public funds to make the venue appear unique and interesting to those who read about or watch the pageantry. The games also showcase the government's ability to maintain order and meet the logistical and infrastructure requirements of such a large undertaking.

Similarly, Batista expected to gain stature from his Gran Premio event. If journalists of the Inter-American Press Association had left Havana in October with an impression of political conflict and government repression, February's international cadre of sports writers would experience effective, benign leadership. Thirty high-powered cars racing down the Malecón, steered by the world's ace drivers and cheered by an international multitude, would thrust Cuba into the center of the racing world. Millions of fans would follow racers from Spain, Belgium, Germany, Venezuela, Brazil, France, the Dominican Republic, and the United States. Britain's Stirling Moss and Italy's Eugenio Castellotti would compete. But most eyes would follow Argentina's Juan Manuel Fangio, world champion in four of the previous five years, speed demon in Maseratis and Ferraris. Fangio could bring chills to a crowd of one hundred thousand eager spectators. What an opportunity to acquire favorable media coverage!

The tourist commission had worked on the race for three years and had spent $150,000 to promote it. Batista subjected the Cuban press to six weeks of rigid censorship, a muzzling that muted an audacious, though unsuccessful, attempt to blow up the Ambar Motors Building in Vedado and the nearby Telemundo television tower. More than twenty other bombs that exploded around Havana between 15 January and 21 February 1957 also went unreported. Even though he claimed to have overcome Castro's threat to his government, Batista clearly feared rebel activities that could frighten away potential visitors. As the event approached, he assigned one thousand policemen, soldiers, and sailors to patrol the race course and the adjoining streets in order to ensure the safety of drivers, newsmen, and tourists.[11] With Havana's nightlife in full gear and the frameworks of three new hotels climbing toward the blue Cuban sky, the race could be no less than a public relations blow-out.

Unfortunately for Batista's carefully constructed publicity barrage, reports of Fangio's victory coincided with the *New York Times* correspondent Herbert Matthews's explosive interview with Fidel Castro. Castro lived, Batista's assertions to the contrary notwithstanding. Moreover, during the interview, the rebel leader urged Cubans to get rid of the president. The Matthews interview endowed Castro with a heroic aura that his achievements as a guerrilla fighter had yet to earn. In those first two months of 1957 he had worked desperately just to gather his forces together and establish his base of operations. Nevertheless, Batista not only lost the public relations momentum of the Gran Premio but was forced to acknowledge the guerrilla movement entrenched in the eastern mountains.

172

*The
Tourist
Stage as
Rebel
Background*

While Castro pulled his followers together, the Havana rebels assumed the lead. Within a month of the Gran Premio race, tourists confronted the risks inherent in an insurrection. Because communication between the Revolutionary Directorate in the capital and Castro in the Sierra was sporadic at best, the isolated rural forces apparently knew nothing about the directorate's imminent attempt on Batista's life. They planned a daring exploit to eliminate a tyrant and unite Batista's opponents behind the revolutionaries.

The assault came on 13 March, halfway between carnival celebrations and Easter Sunday, a time when the town overflowed with visitors. Between eighty and one hundred young men left Vedado at about three in the afternoon, headed for downtown Havana in a caravan of vehicles. They made their way through the afternoon traffic, focused on their mission. The rebels' various cars and trucks converged on the presidential palace, and eager young assassins spilled out onto the sidewalk. They began firing their weapons as soon as they reached the gates, fighting their way through and onto the grounds. Unlike the remote guerrillas, however, Batista had sufficient intelligence resources. Telephone taps had provided advance notice. Aware of the plot, though uncertain of the date, he had prepared his defense. Alerted guards killed some three dozen attackers around and inside the structure, while other rebels suffered wounds inflicted by military forces stationed along the streets. Some captured participants were later tortured and murdered.[12]

The first shots rose above the usual afternoon din of car horns and bar music as hundreds of people strolled along the Prado or through Central Park, unaware of the impending danger. Suddenly soldiers filled nearby streets, spraying bullets. In an instant, tanks moved in; gunners fired upward to stop rebel snipers assumed to occupy building tops. Attackers fleeing the blood-soaked palace shot their way out. Bullets flew in every direction. Even after the rebels retreated or were captured, military and police personnel near the palace continued to blaze away, shattering the upper-story windows and walls of many surrounding buildings.

The Sevilla-Biltmore Hotel lobby became a center of refuge for tourists who fled the bullet-riddled streets. A woman caught near a burst of gunfire on the Prado raced for the hotel and rushed in, gasping for breath and nearly hysterical. A few daring souls ventured to observe the action from the hotel's doorways, but most bystanders stood well back. One hotel guest acquired two unexpected souvenirs: a twenty-millimeter shell that tore out a wall in his room and another that landed on the floor but fortunately failed to explode.

When the shooting finally ended around six o'clock, people poured into the streets for a better look. Pools of blood remained on the sidewalks, and most tourists agreed they would have plenty to tell the folks back home. However, with flights out of the country canceled to prevent conspirators from escaping, they would have to wait several days. While they waited, military intelligence officers rounded up suspects and murdered the head of the opposition Ortodoxo Party. They dumped his body beside the lake at the Havana Country Club, an indisputable message that Batista's government would not wait for the courts to determine guilt or innocence.

The Revolutionary Directorate had intended to change the course of Cuban history that afternoon, but two young men from New Jersey, Peter Korenda and Edward Butts, did not know that. They had gone to Havana like thousands of others, to enjoy the revelry and a reprieve from chilly East Coast weather. Korenda certainly never intended to be felled by a bullet as he stood in the doorway of his hotel on the Prado. He died en route to a hospital, his ambulance unable to break through the street battle. Butts, less seriously wounded, survived the wild ride.[13]

Although the rebels failed in their primary objective, that is, to kill Batista and topple his government, they struck a costly blow at Batista's image. Newspapers carried stories of the bloody assassination attempt and, of course, the death of Korenda. The tourist commission's worst nightmare came true when the *New York Times* warned visitors to take cover in any handy building at the first sound of shots. Stay there, the *Times* advised, and do not look out. The most damaging accounts, however, probably came from stories told to friends by returning tourists. A Havana newspaper lamented that some tourists considered revolution a "romantic adventure," and those who did not even witness the shooting simply exaggerated for effect, recounting their close calls "caught in the middle of the revolution with bullets flying all around."[14]

The assassination attempt scarcely had left the front pages when the CBS news reporter Bud Taber and the photographer Wendell Hoffman broke another hot Cuban story. Three U.S. teenagers, sons of military personnel stationed at the Guantánamo Naval Base, had left home to join Castro's forces in the Sierra Maestra. Despite parental pleas sent by way of revolutionary couriers, the boys had chosen to remain in the rebels' mountain hideout. They had been gone two months when Taber and Hoffman made their way to the guerrilla camp and convinced Castro that he should send the two younger, underage boys home. When Taber brought Michael Garvey and Victor Buehlman back to their parents in mid-May, the still-enthusiastic young fighters declared Castro's victory a certainty. Their understandably nervous fathers tried to keep the boys away from the media, but photos, interviews, and newsreels bombarded audiences in the United States.[15] How could their prediction not discourage all but the most intrepid, or foolish, travelers?

Batista countered with a damage-control publicity blitz. First, he oversaw the inauguration of Shell Oil Company's new twenty-five-million-dollar oil refinery and then laid the cornerstone for a sixteen-million-dollar steel processing plant on the outskirts of Havana. He kept the newspapers filled with favorable economic statistics. An expansion program at the Nicaro nickel works stepped up capacity by 75 percent. Construction continued at record levels. The president took personal credit for record-level wages for four hundred thousand sugar workers, although the elevated rates in fact reflected a rebounding sugar market. The government also granted a 5 percent wage increase to public employees. When Batista addressed a huge rally three weeks after the foiled assassination attempt, he promised the boisterous throng that he would allow no terrorist to deter Cuba's progress. The speakers assembled for the occasion applauded the president's message and praised his courage under fire. Leaders of industry and commerce rallied behind a president who promoted business interests, and they mobilized a substantial segment of their employees in support of the government.[16]

The image pendulum continued to swing between government-sponsored events and rebel actions. Even as confident pronouncements rolled across the heads of the multitude, to be reiterated in newspaper headlines and accounts, a well-timed and adroitly executed rebel action challenged Batista's vow to put an end to violence and sabotage. At seven downtown hotels within shouting distance of the rally, mattresses exploded and rooms caught fire. A handful of guests, whom desk clerks later described as rural in appearance, had rented those rooms and had placed antiaircraft shells inside the mattresses, set the bedding on fire, and casually left the hotel. Police and firemen found three more mattresses with unexploded shells and a bottle of gasoline in one of the rooms.[17]

175
*The
Tourist
Stage as
Rebel
Background*

Clearly the insurgents had meant for the hotel explosions to embarrass Batista and to derail tourism. But scarcely two weeks later, Ernest Hemingway presided over the eighth annual International Marlin Fishing Tournament, unofficially—and affectionately—known as the Hemingway tournament. Some two hundred deep-sea fishermen competed alongside the celebrated novelist and Cuba booster, and the trophy-awarding ceremony at the end of the event merited space in newspapers and sports magazines all over the United States.

The momentum shifted again when a bomb exploded in Havana's Central Park area and cut electric power to the entire old colonial section of the city. Youthful rebels, including employees of the Cuban Electric Company, had rented a house, tunneled down from the kitchen to reach a central transformer, and precisely placed their bomb so as to guarantee maximum impact. The early-morning explosion caught most newspapers ready to go to press. Without electricity, they could not publish. Tourists and residents, however, needed no outside source to tell them that something serious had occurred. Elevators in hotels and apartment buildings did not operate, nor did the electric pumps that lifted water from underground pipes to rooftop tanks. The central section of town remained without water for three days.[18]

Batista accelerated the arrest, torture, and murder of suspected rebels. At the same time, he issued weekly newsletters extolling Cuban prosperity. He brought feature writers and newsmen to Cuba on junkets, assuring them that the rebels exaggerated the level of government repression. Pushed by foreign and domestic critics, he also set elections for the following year. Statements issued for public consumption tried to mask the growing tension but failed to assuage jangled nerves. When a guard in front of Batista's summer home in Varadero clubbed a suspicious character, the man turned out to be a Wyoming rancher looking at investment possibilities. He and his wife were driving through the resort town, accompanied by the son and daughter of the Brazilian ambassador to Cuba. With Batista and his family in the house at the time, however, the guard had reacted to the cattleman's slow-moving vehicle, distrustful of its unknown occupants.[19]

The summer months of 1957 ushered in the customary seasonal downturn in tourist traffic. Rebel actions slowed, too, but not before

176
The
Tourist
Stage as
Rebel
Background

a significant victory. The military had failed to dislodge the Sierra Maestra guerrillas during the months in which physical survival had absorbed a considerable portion of their energy. Then, late in May, eighty of Castro's followers had delivered a crucial political and psychological blow with a successful attack on the military post at El Uvero. Heavy battle casualties diminished their capacity to strike again soon, however, and they used the summer months to recuperate, consolidate control of territory, and establish rebel strongholds in preparation for the next offensive.

In Havana, sporadic bombings kept the rebel-versus-police, cat-and-mouse game going, although the disastrous and disappointing attack on the presidential palace and the government's deadly response had decimated their leadership ranks. In August a bomb exploded in a Havana Woolworth store. When a worried New Yorker queried the U.S. State Department about safety, he was advised to consult U.S. officials in Havana "if local disturbances occur." What they would do remained unclear, but the uncertainty spread. One late-summer morning a correspondent on Dave Garroway's popular *Today* show told millions of Americans that the tense political situation should make tourists think twice before visiting Cuba, since neither the U.S. nor the Cuban government could guarantee their protection. Forced to respond quickly, the privately funded Cuban Tourist Development Board hired a public relations firm to keep the winter season's tourist dollars from deserting Cuba for Jamaica or some other island.[20]

WINTER HOLIDAYS AND A PEACE OFFENSIVE

Before the end of 1957 Batista seemed to regain some balance in the image war. The winter months held bright economic prospects. Syndicates of investors proposed new hotel complexes and resorts, a clear indication that they discounted threats of revolution. Thousands of North Americans took responsibility for their own safety and good times, unable to resist the pull of sensational new hotels, casinos, and cabarets. Nightclubs pulled out all the stops to fill Havana with gaiety. Rebel attacks on soldiers and the burning of sugarcane fields in Oriente did not interfere with the holidays. In addition to tourist revenue, the government had ordered a bonus totaling seventeen million dollars for sugar workers, and they spent a substantial portion of the windfall on toys and other presents for Three Kings' Day (6 January). A year after Castro's arrival on the coast of Oriente, souvenir-hunting tourists and gift-buying Cubans filled the stores.[21]

The plush five-million-dollar, 250-room Hotel Caprí and casino, with its red damask walls and crystal chandeliers, had opened with great fanfare for the Thanksgiving holiday, and George Raft had welcomed a multitude of gamblers. Guests and scribes marveled at the Caprí's rooftop swimming pool and watched the underwater show through its specially constructed windows. Or they clapped their hands rhythmically to accompany José Greco and his troupe of flamenco dancers in the cabaret. On 10 December the owners of the even bigger and more lavish Havana Riviera celebrated its inaugural. Turquoise and gold where the Caprí blazed red, the Riviera's casino filled with high-rolling gamblers who hardly blinked when they covered a night's losses with five-figure checks. The Riviera publicity team had put together a guest list worthy of media attention.

Both hotels inundated Havana with dignitaries and celebrities from the United States who willingly posed before every camera. Newspeople and feature writers arrived with each planeload of junketeers that left Los Angeles, New York, or Miami, guests of the Caprí or Riviera management. Hotel owners gladly paid the bill for appropriately praise-filled articles in *Holiday, Variety, Look* magazine, and the mass-circulation *New York Daily News*.[22] The hundreds of invited celebrities and journalists enjoyed themselves and then spread the word to friends and readers.

For the flood of tourists generated by the hotel openings, the Tropicana offered two new musical fantasies: "An Asian Paradise" portrayed the exotic Orient, while "Chinatown" interpreted the "typical" Chinese way of life in a large North American city. In the Tropicana casino, Lefty Clark added a daily ten-thousand-dollar bingo jackpot and free raffle tickets for new automobiles, one given away every Sunday. In other clubs, girlie shows and sex spectaculars titillated late-night gawkers.[23]

From the presidential palace, where he had repelled the March assassination attempt, Batista could look out at thousands of tourists and anticipate a profitable, pivotal season. Steve Allen's telecast from the Hotel Riviera would project the new hotel and its glamour into thousands of North American living rooms in wintry January, when many families huddled in front of their television sets. They would watch

178

The
Tourist
Stage as
Rebel
Background

bathing beauties frolic in the hotel's swimming pool while snow piled up in front of their doors. Television would make Cuba seem as familiar and safe as any place in the United States. On 24 February 1958 millions more would see Cuba's second thrilling Gran Premio sports car race along Havana's beautiful Malecón. Two days later, world lightweight boxing champion Joe Brown would fight Cuba's own Orlando Echevarría, to be broadcast to the United States from Havana's new two-million-dollar sports arena.

If those events did not sufficiently propel Cuba to the forefront of Caribbean tourist destinations, Hilton Hotels International was already cranking out publicity for the Havana Hilton's grand opening in March. The towering structure overlooked a whole complex of new hotels, souvenir shops, bars, and restaurants clustered in Vedado. The refurbished Hotel Nacional, with its casino and showroom, sat poised on its seafront vantage point. La Rampa, five commercial blocks of Twenty-third Street, angled up the hill away from the shore, but not too steeply for tourists to stroll, and met the Hilton at the top. The Caprí stood a block to the west and the smaller, less expensive Vedado, St. John's, Flamingo, and Colina surrounded the Hilton site on the east. The congeries of tourist enterprises represented thousands of new jobs, millions of dollars in investment and revenue, and countless pleasure-bent goodwill ambassadors.

Batista had every reason to gloat over Cuba's fortunes. The Hilton name, electrically lit in capital letters high above the skyline, sent an unmistakable, politically advantageous message. Repeated endlessly in its propaganda, the Hilton name imparted a stature to Cuba and to its tourist industry that Batista had labored hard to acquire. Foreigners hesitant to invest would see that Hilton had confidence in Cuba. The name signaled both the tangibles and intangibles of stability and safety. Even timid tourists would recognize the distinctive logo and know that modern comforts and familiar amenities (such as chambermaids) would put them at ease.

Moreover, the influential U.S. Commerce Department published a bullish prediction for Cuba in *Foreign Commerce Weekly*, citing increased economic activity and renewed consumer confidence. The sugar harvest proceeded, harassed but not unduly impeded when rebels burned a number of cane fields. When the millionaire sugar broker Julio Lobo acquired Hershey Corporation's three sugar mills, Cuban nationals dominated the island's sugar industry for the first time in twenty years, a psychological boost even if nothing changed in Cuba's hazardous reliance on sugar.[24]

Perhaps buoyed by his successes, Batista opened 1958 with a peace offensive. He restored constitutional guarantees in anticipation of scheduled midyear elections, ended press censorship, and encouraged political parties to reorganize. The Cuban Council of Bishops urged the rebels to lay down their guns and participate in the elections. They refused. Increasingly sophisticated in the use of media, Castro hammered away at Batista instead. With the jails full and law enforcement on the lookout for more inmates, young people fled to the Sierra. Batista's reprisals and arbitrary murders had increased rebel ranks, which facilitated the expansion of guerrilla-held territory into the Escambray Mountains of central Cuba.[25]

Cuba's tourist expansion peaked that winter of 1957, earlier than most people realize. Reports of shootouts, bomb threats, explosions, and power failures in the capital and guerrilla activities in the mountains stalled its growth. Sufficiently publicized, distant warfare in the Sierra Maestra worked as effectively as nearby explosives to discourage travelers. Photos of rebels executing traitors in guerrilla camps probably diverted more than one vacationer to Puerto Rico, Haiti, or the Bahamas for beaches and gambling. While revolution might attract a few adventurers, Cuba counted on masses of travelers. For most tourists, excitement took a different form.

While Batista struggled to sustain the nascent industry, rebels cited tourism as proof of government corruption and complicity with scurrilous foreigners. Gambling soaked up money that should be turned into more constructive investments, critics charged. *Traganiqueles* (slot machines) had proliferated beyond the casinos. They jangled in many cafés and public places where young people congregated. The ubiquitous "mechanical thieves" became the object of a moral crusade to save Cuba's youth from temptation.[26] In the unpredictable contest for media attention, tourism helped to erode Batista's power. Havana tempted the tourists, but Cuba's casinos increasingly served the rebels as a symbol and a catalyst to mobilize dissidents.

Chapter 12

No Peace, No Pleasure, No Tourists

Tourism did not unseat Batista but rather acted as a catalyst in the political conflict, an accelerant to the action. Tourist industry requirements—positive image, favorable publicity, and personal safety—afforded anti-Batista elements opportunities to embarrass and discredit the regime. Media exposure increased the government's vulnerability, and the insurrectionists used high-visibility tourist events as opportunities to inflict economic and political wounds. Moreover, they used Batista's involvement with organized crime figures as evidence of government corruption. Once victorious, however, the new leadership found tourism a capricious benefactor. First of all, its complex underlying financial structure and job production compelled the rebels to reconsider their condemnations. Then, just when they decided to embrace the industry for its economic value, it slipped away.

In the surprising and ironic twists of the 1958 media battles, New York's crime families inadvertently handed Batista's enemies a propaganda weapon. A decade-long history of Mafia squabbles led to the death of the mobster Albert Anastasia late in 1957. Although it had virtually nothing to do with Cuba, the mob killing cast a sinister, and highly newsworthy, shadow over Havana's casino business.

When the U.S. government had arranged Lucky Luciano's deportation from Havana to Italy, it had instigated a leadership vacuum that sucked in a number of highly ambitious young men. Heads of various crime families quarreled over both the leadership hierarchy and mob policy. For one thing, they disagreed on the advisability of involvement in the lucrative narcotics trade and, for another, on association with Meyer Lansky and other Jewish mobsters. Frank Costello, the influential heir to Luciano's power in New York, opposed trafficking in narcotics and any split with Jewish organized crime figures. Albert Anastasia, nicknamed "The Executioner," belonged to an anti-Costello, anti-Lansky faction. In May 1957 a hired gunman failed in an attempt on Costello's life. Anastasia feared retribution for his involvement in the assassination attempt and initiated a bloodbath, murdering whomever he suspected might get to him first. Personal enemies within the various families arranged Anastasia's assassination. Police found his bullet-riddled body in New York's Park Sheraton Hotel barbershop on 25 October. Several people had witnessed the shooting, but their fear of an equally swift and bloody death protected the killers.[1]

Denied an easy resolution to the murder, detectives hunted for evidence to tie someone to the crime. Only a speculative trail pointed toward Havana, but tenacious sleuths and media bloodhounds pursued the scent of slaughter and scandal. Among the various items found in the victim's pockets, an unmarked hotel key led to the room in the Warwick Hotel that Anastasia had kept as his base of operations. A check of the hotel register for the days preceding the murder turned up several interesting names, among them Roberto Mendoza, a well-known and highly respected member of the socially prominent Havana family and a friend of Fulgencia Batista. At the time of Anastasia's death, Mendoza's construction company was completing work on the Havana Hilton Hotel. Also registered was Santo Trafficante Jr., who listed his address as the Sans Soucí nightclub in Havana. Detectives determined that Anastasia had met with Mendoza but remained uncertain about Trafficante.

Rain plagued Cuba in January 1958, a gloomy harbinger of tourist woes to come, as the harsh light of the media focused on the underside of Cuban tourism. Attention swung from swimming pools, rumba bands, celebrities, and roulette to Batista's decades-long Mafia connections. With little else to go on, police theorized that Anastasia had tried to muscle in on Havana's casino action and that Meyer Lansky had arranged the assassination. They pursued known gamblers with connections to both Cuba and the New York Mafia and found Lansky and Trafficante in Havana. New York authorities issued a forty-eight-state alarm for information regarding Santo Trafficante and Joseph Silesi (a.k.a. Joe Rivers), wanted for questioning in connection with the Anastasia murder, specifically to clarify reports that the victim died while trying to break into Cuban gambling circles. Newspapers across the U.S. and in Havana carried the provocative stories.[2]

While *New York Times* headlines proclaimed, "Gambling in Cuba Tied to U.S. Gangs," New York District Attorney Frank S. Hogan questioned Hilton personnel about Anastasia's connections to their Havana casino. Anxious executives, set to open the new hotel in two months, repeatedly denied having had any contact with Anastasia or any ties to underworld figures. Although thirteen groups had applied to lease the new casino, only one had passed the rigid screening conducted by a former Chicago F B I agent. The favored Hilton casino lessees included Roberto and Mario Mendoza; Clifford Jones, a former lieutenant governor of Nevada; Kenneth F. Johnson, a Nevada state senator; and Sidney Orseck, a New York lawyer.[3]

Although the inquiry failed to tie Anastasia or any other mob figure to the Hilton's casino operators, some skepticism remained; the story would not die. Santo Trafficante Jr. and Joseph Silesi were well known in Havana's gambling world. Trafficante, a legal resident in Cuba, complained to anyone who would listen that the publicity hurt his legitimate interests in the Sans Soucí nightclub and the Caprí and Comodoro hotel casinos. Silesi, Trafficante's less visible right-hand man, had shuttled between Cuban and U.S. gambling operations for twenty years or more.[4]

Both Trafficante and Silesi indeed had been in New York at the time of Anastasia's death and were there on business that involved the Hilton casino. The Mendoza family owned Havana's leading baseball team; according to Silesi's story, he had suggested that Roberto Mendoza might hire the baseball hero Joe DiMaggio as a greeter in the Hilton casino, a position similar to that held by George Raft at the Caprí. A meeting between Mendoza and DiMaggio took place at the Hotel Warwick in October 1957, shortly before Anastasia's murder. DiMaggio declined the offer, Silesi maintained, after which he and Mendoza discussed baseball with the Yankee center fielder for a while. Silesi acknowledged that he also had arranged a meeting between Mendoza and Albert Anastasia. Anastasia had indeed wanted to participate in the hotel casino and argued in his own behalf that his brother Tony's position as head of Longshoremen's Local 1814 should pull some weight in the union-owned Havana Hilton.[5]

Although mobsters in Cuba most likely knew that the killing had been ordered and who had ordered it, no credible evidence pointed to Cuban gambling interests as directly responsible for the death. New York police officials eventually concluded that internal gang rivalries had led to the slaying. Nonetheless, the widely reported accusations sufficiently tainted the Cuban casino industry to be of use against Batista.

SINISTER SIGNALS

Time magazine's January 1958 article on the Mafia connection described Havana's gambling industry as sordid but one of the more reputable vices in "the fleshpot city." *Time* referred to Batista as Lansky's benefactor and alluded to favors for Lansky from Cuba's labor minister that earned the minister's brother a partnership in one of the new casinos.[6] Only a few years had passed since Kefauver's committee had grilled Lansky, and people still connected the name with vice and political corruption. He had carried out his illegal operations in the United States with the well-paid cooperation of local officials. Although Cuban gambling was legal, the suggestion of unsavory dealings between Batista and Lansky bore the weight of precedent.

Life magazine photographed the identified suspects for its March 1958 story—Meyer Lansky at the recently opened Riviera, brother Jake at the Hotel Nacional, Santo Trafficante and Joe Silesi at Sans Souci—

and connected them to U.S. crime syndicates. Most Cubans already believed that nothing sponsored by their government could be honest, *Life* editorialized, so the talk of American gangsters only increased their cynicism. "Who did you expect to find running the games down here? John Foster Dulles?" quipped a Havana gambler, referring to the U.S. secretary of state.

Life told North Americans what most Cubans suspected: Batista had built a considerable personal pension from the graft involved in his new gambling enterprises. Moreover, Batista's brother-in-law, the army general and government sports director Roberto Fernández y Miranda, controlled Havana's slot machines and took a cut from every machine in Cuba. The magazine also linked Fernández y Miranda to Havana's hated parking meters and claimed that he shared in the reported five million to ten million dollars that they brought in every year.[7] Thousands of automobiles, which *habaneros* parked for hours and sometimes days on streets that had been built for carriages and pedestrians, choked central Havana, but understandably cynical citizens regarded the meters less as a way to restrain urban congestion than as another method for corrupt officials to steal their money.

Before the glow had had a chance to fade from Steve Allen's favorable glimpse of Cuba, with its plugs for Havana's hotels and casinos, the *New York Times* reported that the American Federation of Television and Radio Artists (AFTRA) had demanded life insurance policies valued at three hundred thousand dollars for television performers who traveled to Havana to appear on American programs originating there. AFTRA labeled Cuba a hazardous area and demanded additional coverage to compensate for loss of vision, limbs, and other injuries and salary replacement in case of violence-related physical incapacity. As if to prove AFTRA's point, a photo of the actress Mamie Van Doren swimming in the Havana Riviera's pool, a scene featured prominently on Allen's television show, shared space in a Havana newspaper with news of a bomb blast in Vedado.

Insistent media coverage of gangster connections and domestic violence locked Batista in a vise, squeezed from one side by pressure to maintain press freedom in advance of upcoming elections and from the other by published reports of rebel activity. The exasperated minister of the interior accused the Associated Press and United Press of greatly exaggerating the confrontations between rebels and the army, which he belittled as military patrols surprising bandits, not actual combat.[8]

Castro's supporters were not outlaws, of course, but they could work the association to their advantage. Cuba's legendary independence hero, the "bandit" Manuel García, had dominated the Havana countryside in the 1880s. He had extorted money and had kidnapped wealthy landowners to raise needed funds for the patriots' cause. He had crowned himself "King of the Cuban Countryside" and had kept his name in front of the people with a steady barrage of letters to Havana's newspapers extolling his own exploits and taunting the Spanish governors general. Not unlike the 1958 contest, embarrassed authorities, unable to end García's activities, had denied his political importance and had dismissed him as merely an outlaw. The rebels of the 1950s certainly knew about García. They probably had mimicked his exploits in childhood games based on the Cuban radio serial that idealized an often-violent gunman. Courageous, patriotic, virile, and enduring, the fictional García overcame forces that betrayed Cuban ideals. When the film *Manuel García, el rey de los campos de Cuba* opened in Havana in 1940, many of the rebel leaders had been impressionable preadolescents.[9] If Batista saw banditry in their antigovernment actions, he soon would learn what "bandits" could do.

Journalists did impart an aura of romantic daring to rebel exploits. When the Castro aides Armando Hart and Felipe Javier Pazos escaped from jail while nine inmates maintained a running gunfight with prison guards and soldiers, some newspaper accounts read like an adventure novel. A sense of rebel invincibility grew with each embellished story. Three days after the well-publicized prison break, a spectacular fire erupted at the Esso petroleum refinery in the Havana suburb of Regla, and the uncertain origins of the blaze translated as rebel sabotage in the minds of many Cubans.[10]

Stories of violence and death filled Havana papers and frightened citizen and tourist alike. Published accounts of violence could be as damaging to the regime as the events themselves. For example, soldiers killed a young mother by shooting her through the head as her car pulled away from a military check point. The government called it an accident, but the storm of protest and angry responses kept the story alive for days and suggested that the official version had failed to convince most people. Before the furor subsided, a soldier and a civilian died in a shooting match alongside a Havana bus. Two gunmen had halted the vehicle, forced the passengers to disembark, and set fire to the bus. Later that day, arsonists burned an elementary school in sub-urban Marianao. Were the incidents related? Even if they were not, the headline "Fire and Terror Campaign Continued by Rebels" linked them in the public mind.[11]

During a period marked by mayhem, suspicion, and denial, the *New York Times* blamed Castro's rebels for discouraging tourists and as-serted that the "wailing and crying" about racketeers operating Cuba's casinos did not help either. At the same time, *Look* magazine pro-nounced Cuba's struggle a "savage civil war" in which Fidel Castro and a thousand rebels fought "Cuba's rifle rule." *Look* captivated its readers with vividly graphic documentation of guerrilla life. They had photographed Castro plotting strategy with top lieutenants and rebels setting fire to cane fields and skinning a snake for supper. For a lesson in revolutionary justice, photographers recorded the execution of law breakers by firing squad and an officer delivering the coup de grâce to a blindfolded dying man.[12] Those fighters could not be dismissed as mere bandits; they were rebels engaged in a desperate battle, using whatever weapons they had.

SPOILERS AT BATISTA'S PARTY

Pedestrians hunched their bodies against the cold and snow as a blizzard walloped the east coast of the United States in mid-February. The cold wave bludgeoned northern and central Florida with the tenth freeze of a bitter winter. As North Americans dug their way out from under the latest snow blanket, the Tropicana nightclub turned up the heat, replacing its Asian floor show with the sensuous drumming and torrid dance of choreographed Haitian voodoo rituals. Despite the political tension and the mobsters, Cuba began to seem inviting to some shivering snowbirds.

In the tourist commission's ambitious strategy for 1958, sporting events would surpass carnival season as celebrity attractions. Race car drivers began to arrive in Havana for the second annual Gran Premio. The previous year's top drivers, Juan Manuel Fangio, Stirling Moss, and Jean Behrs, would return to pit their sleek and shiny cars against each other and against the Dominican playboy-racer and tabloid favorite Porfirio Rubirosa. Two days later the lightweight champion boxer Joe Brown would arrive for his match. Golfers Ben Hogan and Sam Snead would open a new course in March. The high-powered lineup would reaffirm Cuba's stature in the tourist world and recapture Batista's momentum.

All through the week preceding the race car competition, twenty-eight veteran drivers studied the course along the Malecón. Each day they tested and fine-tuned their cars. Some 150,000 eager fans (50,000 more than the previous year) began to gather for the contest, anticipating a thriller. Argentina's Fangio, once more the favorite, captured everyone's attention as he took trial runs on the coastal avenue in a Maserati 450S. He had been racing for twenty-three of his forty-six years and had won numerous championships in Europe and the United States. He also had hinted that he might enter the Indianapolis 500 in May, a race passed up by most foreign drivers.

Tension built day by day as 24 February drew closer, particularly among the small circle of drivers and mechanics around Fangio: something about the car disturbed him. He knew the Maserati line, and this car did not feel right. The night before the race Fangio stood near the reception desk in the lobby of the Hotel Lincoln with Guerino Bertocchi, chief of mechanics for the Maserati team; Nello Ugolini, team manager; and Alejandro de Tomaso. They had rested briefly after the day's test runs, then changed clothes for the evening and were discussing the car's problems, their attention focused, as might be expected, on how to handle the next day's race.

The hotel lobby filled with people about to set out on the evening rounds of restaurants, bars, and nightclubs. A number of race car drivers stood or sat in groups with colleagues and admirers; other guests chatted casually. They scarcely noticed as two young men entered the lobby. One stood by the door; the other, undistinguished in slacks and windbreaker, perhaps twenty-five years old, asked for Fangio and casually crossed the lobby toward the registration desk.

Fangio, absorbed in his conversation, scarcely noticed the young man until he stopped a few feet away, displayed a pistol, and asked, "Which one of you is Fangio?"

"I am, what do you want?" the racer responded.

"I'm from the Twenty-sixth of July Movement. I want you to come with me. Don't resist and you won't be hurt." The assailant grabbed Fangio, pushed the pistol into his side, and moved toward the door.

When they approached the exit, the kidnapper turned to the startled and speechless crowd. "Don't anyone leave the hotel until five minutes have passed. There are four men outside with machine guns pointed at the door." The rebels left the hotel with their prisoner and walked some hundred feet to the corner, where they shoved Fangio into a black sedan and took off. Within minutes telephones rang in every news agency: revolutionaries held the champion racer and refused to say what would be done with him. The next day, headlines blared the news to the world.

Havana's police had plunged into action after the rebels' telephone call. First, they assigned squads to guard the other race car drivers and Joe Brown. Then they unleashed an intensive manhunt, searching all known rebel haunts, desperate to find Fangio before the next day's race. Officials delayed the start of the race, hoping the rebels might release Fangio; they did not. The competition began, only to end in tragedy half an hour later, when a Cuban driver, Armando García Cifuentes, skidded on a patch of oil leaked onto the race course from the burst oil line of another car. García Cifuentes's car slammed into one of the supports of a grandstand section and spilled dozens of spectators onto the pavement. Authorities at first charged sabotage, but further investigation confirmed the original explanation: an unfortunate, accidental chain reaction. The crash killed four people and injured close to fifty.[13]

Shortly after officials called off the race, a well-groomed and fresh-looking Fangio reappeared and related the details of his abduction to the press. To avoid the police dragnet, the rebels had transferred Fangio three times to three different houses, all well-furnished residences. They had treated him with care and concern, he reported, and had explained their reasons for his kidnapping and the aims of their organization. A young woman had brought his meals, and he had been well looked after. When it was time to release him, the rebels had called the Argentine Embassy, and someone there had picked him up from a house on the edge of town.

Fangio had only praise for his captors; in fact, given the tragedy of the race, he told reporters, they may have saved his life. Major media outlets in Europe and the Americas repeated his appreciative words. Joe Brown's televised first-round knockout became a footnote to the amazing and tragic Gran Premio story.

The audacious kidnapping had even more power than explosives;

Manuel García could not have done better. Castro and his supporters already had denounced the government for wasting money on big sports events instead of aiding the unemployed. They had openly threatened to cripple Cuba's most important sports contest in order to embarrass Batista and force him to call off the race. They had circulated bulletins for three days, warning Cubans to stay off the streets and away from public spectacles. To reinforce their point, they had hurled phosphorus bombs into seats and aisles of Radio Centro Theater in the heart of Havana.

Twenty-five years later, on 24 February 1983, Fangio received a cable in his office at Mercedes Benz headquarters in Buenos Aires: "On the occasion of the twenty-fifth anniversary of your historic encounter with the Twenty-sixth of July Movement, we remember you fondly and wish you health and well-being. That episode, more than a kidnapping and patriotic detention, together with your noble attitude and fair understanding, served the cause of our people, who feel great kindness for you and in whose name we salute you at the end of a quarter of a century. In hopes of seeing you again in Cuba, your friendly kidnappers."[14]

Faustino Pérez Hernández, the Cuban official who signed the cable, had headed the successful 1958 kidnapping operation. He had accompanied Castro on the *Granma*, the boat that had carried the rebels from Mexico to Cuba in December 1956. They had hidden together for days, almost afraid to breathe for fear of discovery by the soldiers who hunted them. They had made their way to the Sierra Maestra, and when Castro stayed to build the guerrilla movement in the mountains, Pérez had returned to Havana as a member of the Twenty-sixth of July Movement's national directorate.

Two days after Fangio's release, Fidel Castro announced that victory was not far away. Guerrilla leaders considered the morale-building, high-profile caper a turning point in their battle. They had challenged authority, displayed fearless commitment to their cause, fostered a perception of rebel invincibility, and reaffirmed humanitarian principles. And Batista's tourist ambitions had made it all possible. Stepping into the media spotlight, Castro condemned the president as an ineffectual leader, unable to protect his people against a handful of rebels, a man whom the Twenty-sixth of July Movement intended to overthrow very soon in order to return Cuba to constitutional authority. He scorned Batista as a lackey of Washington, an obedient man who followed orders, and a corrupt tyrant in league with mobsters. What soldier would fight, he asked rhetorically, knowing that his chiefs lived comfortably in Havana and enriched themselves at the cost of his blood and sacrifice?[15]

The media pendulum continued to shift in the rebels' direction. During "Unhappy Cuba's Cockeyed Week," *Life* magazine commented, behind Batista's smiling face (referring to a photo of the president), loomed an abduction, violence, and tragedy. A "beefy and bellowing guard" had to clear the way for Batista when the "dictator" arrived for the Joe Brown fight. In the same article, *Life* repeated Fangio's favorable comments about the rebels and paired the popular Fangio with Castro, shown instructing a recruit in the use of a rifle and claiming he could enlist ten thousand more, given enough weapons.[16]

When the rebels held up a branch of the Banco Nacional and burned a pile of checks instead of taking cash, they demonstrated both their capacity to disrupt daily life and their disinterest in personal gain. Meanwhile, Oriente insurgents burned a sugar warehouse, wrecked a railway station, grenaded an army patrol car, raided a passenger train, and bombed an aqueduct. The *New York Times* reported that many Cubans believed Castro could succeed with the help of a paralyzing general strike and the sabotage of utilities by urban underground forces.[17]

The rebels stepped up their verbal and military pressure on the government. While spectators cheered Ben Hogan and Sam Snead at the new golf course east of Havana, a bomb exploded in a vacant lot in Cárdenas and injured two nine-year-olds; another exploded in Santa Clara; a railroad coach burned in Los Pinos; a young man was burned with live phosphorus in a Cienfuegos theater; and twenty-two persons faced charges of terrorism in a Havana court. Raul Castro, Fidel's brother and fellow guerrilla, opened another front in the Sierra. When an exhilarated Faustino Pérez Hernández, buoyed by February's events, conveyed a positive assessment of Havana support levels to the eastern headquarters, confident rebel leaders set 9 April 1958 for the long-threatened general strike.

At the height of the tourist season, a defiant manifesto from the Sierra Maestra called for all-out war against Batista, starting with the April general strike and then unrelenting armed struggle until victory. The scene in Havana tended toward the surreal as Batista proclaimed a holiday to celebrate his six years in power. Residents and tourists alike hesitated to ride public transportation for fear that rebel terrorists would board the buses and set them on fire. They avoided busy shopping districts and motion picture theaters because of bomb threats. Only the nightclubs adjacent to casinos in the large hotels operated safely. Many Cubans gave up and just stayed away; so did the tourists. As the rebels escalated the propaganda and violence, tourist revenue declined. Batista once more suspended constitutional guarantees and reestablished press censorship.[18]

Meanwhile, at the corner of Twenty-third and L Streets an understandably jittery Hilton Hotel team agonized through the final days of preparations for its inaugural gala, capping two years of planning and construction. Casino, restaurant, and cabaret managers consulted with officers of the culinary workers union; executives conferred with bankers. HHI had worked for months on publicity and arrangements. Hotel officials had withstood January's negative association with Albert Anastasia's murder in New York and February's high-visibility kidnapping. Now, nervous and exasperated, they all watched and listened as sinister escalations of violence and threats of strikes and armed confrontation bubbled all around them. The call to arms and timing of the general strike could not have been worse for HHI and Cuba's tourist image.

With rumors flying across the city, Hilton employees prepared to welcome an exceptional assemblage of guests to the hotel's domed lobby, to show off the glass-bubbled ceiling that threw sunbeams of light on the marble floors, and to escort a host of celebrities up the staircase that seemed to float from the lobby to the casino and bar above. Chartered planes carried large contingents of guests, including union officials (because the Gastronómico owned the hotel), bankers and businessmen, big names from Hollywood, Washington, and Broadway, and of course, several dozen members of the press.

Circumstances forced the Hilton management to hire a hundred or so plainclothes security officers to circulate among the guests, while uniformed policemen with billy clubs and guns stood conspicuously inside the lobby. Squad cars stood at each corner of the hotel. The heavy police presence certainly altered the intended mood of a lighthearted, carefree celebration. Conrad Hilton brought his own bodyguard, as did Virginia Warren, daughter of the U.S. chief justice. A trio of uniformed guards accompanied the Hollywood gossip columnist Hedda Hopper when she insisted on wearing a huge diamond to the formal ball.[19] What a headline her abduction would have made!

Did Batista realize that his painstakingly built tourist industry was in crisis? He did not attend the Hilton's opening ceremony even though he had been instrumental in putting the hotel deal together and had taken great pride in adding Havana to the chain of Hilton hotels. He sent his wife instead.

Despite the attention paid to the Hilton inaugural, the rebels maintained a publicity advantage. A host of respected, top-level newspaper and radio-TV correspondents, assigned to cover the announced general strike, roamed Havana's streets in search of good stories while they waited. *Paris Match* had sent an experienced reporter-camera team. The *New York Times'* reporter had covered civil conflicts and revolutions. The Chicago *Tribune* and *Sun Times* were represented, and United Press sent a crew of first-line reporters. *Time*, *Newsweek*, and *Life* fielded teams. Hearst-Movietone photographers covered events for the newsreels.

Violence made good copy, and journalists filled the papers, airwaves, and movie screens with evidence of the danger in Cuba: gun battles in the streets, power failures that paralyzed restaurant and nightlife along the Prado, attacks on city buses. The story out of Cuba focused on Castro and revolution, not casinos and romance. Some correspondents had to send their stories out of the country with returning tourists when the government increased its vigilance over outgoing dispatches and long-distance telephone calls, which added to the sense of tension. Rebel actions made exciting news copy and photos but terrible postcards.[20]

To Batista's satisfaction and the rebels' chagrin, their widely proclaimed general strike failed. Most workers stayed on the job. Poor planning and lack of coordination, as well as Batista's advance preparations, doomed it. Faustino Pérez Hernández had overestimated the *habaneros'* commitment.

After the April disappointment, the center of revolutionary activity shifted back to the Sierra. By then, the winter tourist season had ended anyway. As with the failed 1957 assassination attempt, the strike threat had damaged tourism even though it did not bring down the government. Tourism backers and businessmen worried about the big "if" — what if organizations canceled the conventions that brought thousands of free-spending visitors to Havana, people who contributed substantially to the local economy. If cautious arrangements committees altered their plans, and then suddenly the political situation brightened, it would be be too late—a lucrative opportunity would have been lost.

Tourist revenues for 1958 not only fell far behind expectations of growth but even lagged behind 1957 levels. The major culprit was rebel activity and the accompanying publicity. Prospects were downright bleak. New hotels, encumbered by multimillion-dollar mortgages, baited the casino hook with inexpensive dinner prices that included the floor show and dancing. The lowered cost reeled in more Cubans but did not appreciably increase the number of foreign tourists. The Hilton found a market for its banquet and meeting rooms among the local population, but that clientele did not patronize the gaming rooms sufficiently to produce profits.

Desperate to counteract newspaper and magazine accounts of political unrest, civic leaders formed a "New Cuba" committee. They prepared an advertising campaign that flooded major U.S. cities with their slogan, "NEW, all NEW." Havana officials even sent peace offerings to Miami after a winter of competitive mudslinging. The Cubans claimed that Miamians had gone out of their way to play up horrors that might befall tourists in revolution-riddled Cuba. On the other hand, Floridians charged that Havana's newspapers exaggerated a Miami polio outbreak to keep Cubans at home. Cuba needed an end to the sniping, and Batista personally bestowed warm words of encouragement on a group of Miami businessmen who flew to Havana. They shook hands and called the goodwill visit a great success. In fact, the downward slide continued. Promotional campaigns, new committees, fence mending, and intensive public relations campaigns all failed. The Fangio kidnapping, talk of strike, and fear of civil war had halted the tourist momentum.[21]

Meanwhile, the conflict intensified. The military high command interpreted the general strike's failure as a measure of Batista's strength. Even though the army had not eliminated the guerrillas in more than a year of fighting, Castro's call for total war required a showdown, and the officer corps urged the president to take the initiative and destroy the insurrection. Batista agreed. The army prepared through May and launched its big offensive in June. Rebel forces, clearly outnumbered, let Batista's troops move forward, then hit the advance platoons and units and fell back again. For guerrillas, the ability to outlast a numerically superior force counts as a victory; thus they ambushed and retreated and protected their limited resources. The struggle continued through the summer, and Batista failed to achieve his objective. A censored press downplayed the government's peril, but Castro broadcast the details of his successes on Radio Rebelde, heard by Cubans all over the island.

In the face of a prolonged, bitter, bloody, and well-publicized armed struggle, the 1958–59 winter tourist season hadn't a prayer. The guerrillas went on the offensive and moved west, as Cuban patriots had done in 1895–96. The army pulled back, and new volunteers joined rebel veterans. Late in the year insurrectionists in the Escambray Mountains battled for control of the city of Santa Clara. Castro set out to take Santiago. More new supporters fought alongside the guerrillas as Batista's soldiers deserted. By early December U.S. authorities tried to obtain Batista's resignation in favor of a military junta.

A glum Christmas season was made more so by airline strikes in the United States that kept even the most stalwart visitors away. The rebel advance continued. Castro's forces could claim control of 80 percent of central Cuba's Las Villas province by 20 December. Insurgent columns advanced on Santiago de Cuba, and Radio Rebelde announced control of the Central Highway in Oriente. Travelers reported that a beach near Santiago was in rebel hands and that they saw a red-and-black rebel flag flying from an army radio station just outside Santiago. The nearby town of Palma Soriano had fallen after a five-day seige. Still, government press releases trumpeted army victories.[22]

THE REBELS' NEW YEAR GREETING

Several thousand tourists did come to Cuba during the holiday season, and the rebel victory took those daring—or foolish—revelers by surprise. Batista had maintained the public charade right up to the time of his departure, just after midnight, 1 January 1959. Before he left, the fleeing president placed the reins of power in the hands of one of his generals; but both the government and the army collapsed as rebels swept into Havana. Banner headlines and radio announcements proclaimed the victory, and Cubans poured into the streets. Carloads of people raced through Havana with horns blaring, cheered on by fellow citizens who jammed windows and balconies. By 9 A.M. the mood turned destructive; vandals and looters attacked shops, restaurants, hotels, casinos, and the odious parking meters. They set bonfires and piled stolen goods on the fires. Roving bands smashed the windows at El Encanto department store. Mobs swarmed into Vedado and Miramar and looted the homes of Batista's relatives and friends. By nightfall most of the city fell quiet as residents shuttered themselves in their homes.[23]

For the chastened North Americans, New Year's Day was a night-mare of uncertainty. Early risers flooded U.S. Embassy phone lines and were told to board the regular Thursday morning (1 January) sailing of the Key West ferry. Some thirty anxious refugees rushed to the docks. A state of general alarm set in as the destruction and looting began. Embassy personnel moved to round up U.S. travelers, assembled them at centrally located hotels, and transported them to the ferry pier and airport to begin evacuation. The embassy had anticipated Batista's fall and, although unsure of the date, had prepared for the eventuality.

The evacuation was a formidable task, with tourists conveyed to de-parture points by car and truck convoys. Planes left for Varadero and the Isle of Pines (later renamed the Isle of Youth) to pick up other New Year's celebrants, before a general strike grounded all departing flights and hampered evacuation plans. Embassy officials had to negotiate for exit permits with rebels concerned that some of Batista's hench-men might slip out with the tourists. Meanwhile, the airport filled with people anxious to leave a city in the throes of revolution. The Key West ferry returned to Havana on Friday, loaded some five hun-dred American tourists and businessmen on board, departed around nine in the evening, and disembarked the tired and hungry lot at Key West the next morning, 3 January. Many in the frazzled group had been forced by events to stay in Havana longer than they had planned and had no money left.

By Saturday evacuation flights started from Rancho Boyeros air-port, and almost 700 vacationers left the island. Airplanes actually exchanged returning Cuban exiles for fleeing tourists. On Sunday another 550 left by plane and ferry. Guests at the Plaza and Sevilla-Biltmore hotels, where a great deal of destruction had taken place, openly displayed their fear and anger. Resentful of the inconvenience, or covering for their poor judgment, some of them turned surly. They threatened to write their senators or to call Secretary of State John Foster Dulles, or to tell the press of their travail at the hands of em-bassy employees.

Within days, however, the Twenty-sixth of July Movement militia controlled Havana, and regular air service returned almost to normal. Some two hundred remaining tourists decided to take their chances and see whether the shooting indeed had ended. A few of the more brazen stragglers even plopped themselves down among groups of rebel fighters encamped in the hotels while their friends took the ultimate in souvenir photos. By Tuesday, less than a week after the rebel victory, the city had settled down.[24]

REVOLUTIONARIES IN THE CASINO BUSINESS

On New Year's Eve Havana counted thirteen casinos. Rebel bulletins had warned that victory would bring an end to the gambling enterprises. Any business so closely associated with Batista could not withstand the wrath of his enemies or the rebels' commitment to cleanse Cuban society of corruption. In a televised interview, Castro promised to protect legitimate U.S. business interests in Cuba, but not "those gangsters" who owned casinos. Triumphant rebels arrested the president of Casino Caprí Corporation and questioned him for nearly nine hours before they set him free. They also seized the Caprí's daily receipts and sealed the hotel's safety deposit boxes. Interrogation of casino officials and owners prompted some gaming room employees to inquire about jobs in Las Vegas. Casino operators desperately sought to save investments with a total estimated at twenty million dollars or more, including hotels and gaming rooms. Meyer Lansky, determined to hold on to his hotel, publicly expressed his willingness to cooperate with the new government.[25]

The rebel leadership ordered the casinos closed, arguing that they destroyed morals, took money out of Cuban hands, and put it into the pockets of rich American racketeers. However, Cuban workers quickly joined forces with gambling interests to oppose the drastic action. Their swift and angry response confounded an inexperienced leadership with little understanding of the tourist industry. Gambling had become a key factor in the tourist boom, and thousands of Cubans faced unemployment if the casinos shut down. The biggest loss of jobs would be felt in the hotels that operated casinos. The Riviera, Hilton, Caprí, and Nacional alone employed close to four thousand workers during peak tourist periods. Most of them were not casino workers, but casino revenues helped to pay their wages. Gambling paid for the entertainment at the Hotel Nacional, for example, a weekly average of $8,000 for show talent, plus another $2,500 for musicians. Because of gambling, the Tropicana nightclub could spend an estimated $12,000 for its shows, which employed seventy showgirls, singers, and dancers, plus some forty musicians in the orchestra. Between the Riviera, Nacional, and Caprí hotels and the Tropicana nightclub, an estimated $50,000 weekly flowed through the cabaret talent into the Cuban economy. (The Hilton's late arrival on the scene precluded typical payrolls.) Moreover, the government collected $2,000 per month and 20 percent of the net profits from each casino, revenue that could be used by the new government in the best interests of Cuban citizens.

While some officials proclaimed a willingness to sacrifice tourism if it meant an end to gambling, Castro quickly reversed his stance and conceded that total suppression of gambling would be detrimental to the economy. The protesters had won him to their side, and he justified his retreat in utilitarian and humanitarian terms that reiterated their arguments: rich tourists and wealthy Cubans who gambled supported enterprises that employed thousands of Cuban workers. Moreover, the government could use casino revenue to establish a rehabilitation agency to create jobs that eventually would replace gambling-dependent employment and prostitution. The casinos could reopen, he proclaimed, as long as honest men, and not card sharks "who try to trick people out of their money," operated the games.[26]

When the rebels gained control of the government, they not only became responsible for gambling policies but also took charge of the highly sophisticated financial apparatus that gave them a stake in many Cuban industries, including tourism. Presidents Prío and Batista had established the various lending institutions to compensate for the reluctance of domestic and foreign capitalists to invest in Cuba. Banfaic, Bandes, the Financiera, and so on, had issued bonds guaranteed by the government. Private banks, insurance companies, and pension funds had purchased the bonds, and enterprises had borrowed the proceeds, including the Gastronómico and other hotel corporations whose casinos Castro had tried to close.

Almost overnight, guerrilla fighters who had struggled to stay alive during two years in mountain encampments had to think like seasoned bankers. Alberto Guevara, who had attended Havana University with Castro and had joined his revolutionary forces, later recalled planning sessions held immediately after the rebel victory. "Castro wanted us to start going to the bank, and we were there once a week. Fidel kept saying, 'We don't know what a bank is, and we must know what a bank is.'"[27]

Batista had left an ironic legacy, for the governing rebels quickly realized that their financial involvement in tourism created a classic catch-22. Hotel profits repaid government lending institutions, funds intended to redeem bonds issued with government backing. To earn that profit, hotels needed casinos and tourists. Suppression of gambling, a crippling blow to tourism, also would preclude an estimated $110 million in hotel construction predicated on casino earnings to repay negotiated loans. Lack of expertise required the rebels to retain Joaquín Martínez Sáenz as head of the Banco Nacional because, among his other duties for Batista, Martínez Sáenz had authorized most of Bandes's hotel loans. So they kept him and other financial experts under surveillance at their desks, without authority to make loans but with a mandate to untangle the financial situation and stabilize the economy.

Furthermore, the former guerrillas knew as much about hotel operations as they did about banking. Ideology and morality notwithstanding, the new government needed knowledgeable hotel managers and casino operators. Thus revolutionaries became reluctant partners with some of the very mobsters they had vowed to expel from the island. Within two weeks they reorganized the tourist commission and inaugurated a vigorous campaign to bring the tourists back.[28]

The new tourist commission pledged to attract even greater numbers of visitors to a new, democratic Cuba. Less a morale builder than a pragmatist, the tourist chief weighed Cuba's precarious finances against potential revenues. Batista had left a treasury depleted by both looters and the costs of war. Cuba desperately needed foreign exchange reserves and money to circulate domestically. The contribution of American tourists, projected to reach six billion dollars a year by 1964, appeared as economic redemption to revolutionaries in need.[29] Reminiscent of the cross-sector tourist board that operated in the 1930s, representatives of Cuba's hotels, restaurants, nightclubs, harbor commerce, tourist agencies, alcoholic beverage distributor, tourist shops, airline transportation, transport workers, labor federation, and New Cuba Association worked together to breathe life into an expiring industry. First they tried to salvage the winter season and then moved to recapture the American Society of Travel Agents convention scheduled for October 1959. ASTA had dropped Havana from its plans because of the political crisis evident by late 1958, and the association's renewed commitment signaled a welcomed vote of approval.

Tourist interest reappeared. By mid-January some Miami–Havana flights filled with curiosity seekers. A few tourists grumbled about thorough searches on arrival, as though the revolutionaries need not take precautions against enemies. Most visitors quickly forgot their irritation, overwhelmed by their proximity to real-life rebels. They thrilled at the opportunity to survey a freshly enshrined battleground. They poked their noses into the wreckage of once-elegant casinos, looking for war souvenirs, and clicked their camera shutters at bearded revolutionaries incongruously camped in luxurious hotel lobbies.

Unfortunately, even government goodwill could not salvage the season. Frustrated casino operators lamented the month or two required to repair and reequip the gaming rooms, a delay that sacrificed critical January–March earnings. The Havana Hilton had yet to enjoy the profits of even one winter season, and the Caprí's steadily increasing credit line, opened the previous summer, understandably worried the revolutionaries-turned-bankers. Even the inexperienced financiers recognized the necessity to maintain constant vigilance over their new partners to ensure that hotel managers applied profits to the amortization of bank loans and did not divert profits to stockholders through payment of excessive dividends.

Bank employees kept an especially close watch on the Havana Riviera, where reported losses rather quickly began to threaten repayment of outstanding debts. Lansky's accountants listed operating losses of $750,000 for the period December 1958 through April 1959, and the next big tourist season would not begin until November. Gross income for March 1959, after the casino reopened, totaled $600,000, barely more than one-third the March 1958 figure ($1.7 million) and a sum clearly insufficient to cover expenses, much less pay debts. In July the bank expressed concern over possible skimming of the Riviera's casino revenues and assumed responsibility for counting the casino take. An angry corporate treasurer, Julius Rosengard, accompanied by Jake Lansky, went to Miami to consult with stockholders. The government intervened in the money-losing hotel operation the following month, although the Riviera Hotel Corporation remained the nominal owner, with many of the original investors still on the board of directors.

As the hotel continued to bleed money, Cuban officials charged that hotel personnel illegally shipped U.S. dollars out of the country and extended credit to questionable casino customers. They also decried the women of "doubtful morality" who hung around the casino as an attraction to gamblers. Exasperated, they fired the publicity director, stage manager, social manager, and assistant purchasing manager and put a Bandes delegate on the premises with the power to make administrative decisions. When company stockholders ordered Rosengard to abandon the position of treasurer and return to the United States, Bandes managed the hotel directly.[30]

Hotels continued to operate well under capacity. Nightclub ads, notable by their absence in January, had reappeared in the local press late in February. Package tours attracted hundreds, but not thousands, of visitors. The Tropicana mounted two brand-new shows and in a burst of patriotism dedicated the proceeds of its premiere (at an eight-dollar minimum charge), along with the contribution of a day's salary from all personnel, to reconstruct war-torn towns.

Did tourists object to the summary trials of Batista supporters and the subsequent execution of war criminals? If they paid attention to the revolutionary justice meted out to *batistianos* accused of torture and killing, they apparently offered few opinions as they made the rounds of bars and nightclubs. The skittish travel agents' association wavered again, hesitant to favor a location pilloried by the U.S. media for revolutionary excesses. Hard-pressed Cubans endured many anxious hours before ASTA reaffirmed its commitment.[31]

By June a tourism development board announced hotel and motel construction projects in the island's interior and the embellishment of the old colonial city of Trinidad. The Ministry of Commerce made sure that tourist establishments received all the food, beverages, linens, and other supplies that they required. After all, the recommendation of a homeward-bound visitor carried more clout than any brochure. The Instituto Nacional de Industriales Turísticas (INIT) committed $200 million to a four-year development program, with $400,000 set aside for advertising. Airport expansion to accommodate jet aircraft would bring more people from farther away in shorter times. Castro opened formerly private beaches to the public for wholesome family vacations, and INIT took over responsibility for their administration, along with forty-three centers dedicated to hunting, fishing, and boating. Santiago de Cuba would anchor tourist plans for the eastern end of the island.[32]

Whatever promoted tourism helped Cuba, Castro declared, and he personally fostered its success. Promising to make tourism Cuba's biggest business, his smiling, bearded countenance graced the pages of *Cuba, 1959: Land of Opportunity, Playland of the Americas,* the one-hundred-page slick magazine published for the October travel agents' convention. The promotional piece overflowed with flattering articles, attractive photographs, useful information, and hundreds of advertisements for hotels, restaurants, airlines, car rental agencies—everything a vacationer might need or want.

When Fidel welcomed the two thousand ASTA delegates and family members, he openly and unapologetically acclaimed tourism as Cuba's salvation. He treated the travel agents like visiting royalty and implored them to bring back the tourists. The agents applauded wildly and, like teenagers, fought to have pictures taken with the famous revolutionary, or at least to get his autograph. ASTA's president, Max Allen, avoided political controversy. "We are not here to give praise to the government," he said. "Travel . . . provides the broadest and shortest road to understanding between nations. . . . next week Cuba will have 2,000 super salesmen dotted all over the earth." Castro, obviously pleased with that prospect, unhooked his gunbelt in a symbolic gesture of friendship, laid it on the floor, and responded, "Never mind political propaganda . . . help your friends to the happiness which travel to Cuba can give them."[33]

The ASTA convention turned into a surprising love fest. The association made Castro an honorary member, the first time they had ever done so with any political figure. Delegates appeared ready to send as many tourists to Cuba as possible. They seemed willing to disregard the armed terrorists who tossed bombs and grenades from moving cars and the leaflets dropped from airplanes that urged Castro to throw the communists out of his government. Most of the ASTA delegates had been in their rooms dressing for a lavish champagne party at the Havana Riviera when the bombs went off, and they dismissed the leaflets as the work of Castro's enemies trying to sabotage the tourist effort. At the final banquet Castro praised the delegates and told them, "Just tell us what you want, and we will give it to you."[34]

Disappointingly, the tourists did not return, but not because of any lack of will or enthusiasm on the part of the travel agents or the Cuban government. Castro had kept the casinos going and had spent a million dollars to entertain the ASTA delegates. The travel agents expressed great enthusiasm and willingness to recommend the island to their clients, particularly after they heard U.S. Ambassador Philip Bonsal praise Cuba as "one of the finest countries in the world from the standpoint of the American tourist."[35]

Despite good intentions, the ASTA convention proved a last hurrah. Even as the delegates departed, five major steamship lines canceled their stops in Havana. Revenue in November fell to just 20 percent of the previous year's already declining levels. The tourist board campaigned hard to lure visitors for a combined Christmas holiday and first anniversary celebration. Thirty hotels offered plane fare rebates. Foreign dignitaries and celebrities, invited by the government for the occasion, stayed at the Hilton, Riviera, and Caprí hotels as guests of INIT, including the former world heavyweight boxing champion Joe Louis. Cuba apparently intended to extend its hospitality to a previously ignored segment of the North American market, and representatives of the African American press followed Louis closely, taking lots of pictures when Castro singled him out for praise at a star-studded luncheon.[36]

As in prerevolutionary times, Oriental Park opened the racing season with a big media splash. The government had spent more than a half-million dollars to refurbish the Jockey Club, and a thousand new rocking chairs lined the club's terrace. INIT had joined forces with the widely known turf figure Dan Chappel, and entries and race results published in the stateside racing form tempted readers to visit Cuba. Everything stood ready, including the track's plush casino.

In spite of prodigious efforts, the tourist business succumbed to uncertainty, inconvenience, and unpleasantness. Even the Tropicana was dead by February 1960. The manager of its famous show, who also had controlled Havana's slot machines in conjunction with Batista's brother-in-law, had long since fled the country. Castro brought Cuba's farmers into Havana for the May Day celebration, and they slept on the Malecón. His anti-Yankee speech to that multitude would have frightened those tourists not already disaffected by street thugs, bullies, and gun-carrying youngsters who had joined the militia. When factionalism and sabotage threatened his reforms, Castro asked the people to inform police of antirevolutionary remarks. In the ensuing atmosphere of suspicion, political denunciations drove some Cubans from the island.

The novelty of revolution wore off quickly. The glamour and the excitement vanished. Lack of tourists doomed Cuba's hotels and casinos and many of its restaurants and bars. Souvenir shops closed; their proprietors faced bankruptcy. A few managed to send some goods or money out of the country. Others fell before the accusatory claims of avid *fidelistas*, lost their businesses to the government, and left the country. Visitors who experienced arbitrary, thorough searches and confiscation of possessions when they arrived were uncertain whether the searchers' motivation was political vigilance or material gain.

Failure to pay its bills, not moral outrage on the part of Castro's minions, caused the demise of Meyer Lansky's Havana Riviera. Overwhelmed with unpaid debts, the hotel became government property. Revolutionaries already controlled its casino operations and managed the hotel. Lansky lost an estimated four million dollars, a considerable sum for someone who had been listed on the payroll as the kitchen manager.[37]

People stopped going to Cuba because the island no longer was pleasurable to visit. Vacationers wanted to relax, and they had their choice of sunny beaches and gambling casinos elsewhere in the Caribbean. Escalating antagonism over issues of sovereignty, property, and ideology threatened, and then ruptured, U.S.–Cuban relations. By the time Castro nationalized U.S. property in October 1960, most North Americans already had scratched Cuba off their lists of desirable travel destinations.[38]

Tourism had brought critical hard currency, as well as gaiety, to Havana during two boom periods. Travelers had introduced ideas, values, and cultural elements and had forged new relationships with Cubans. If corruption and vice flourished alongside tourist enterprises, they sprouted from seeds in well-plowed ground. Cuba changed direction just as the tourist industry enjoyed worldwide expansion. After 1960 its leaders sought a more suitable image than that of a pseudo–Las Vegas. When Castro embarked on a third tourist cycle in the 1980s, diplomatic and trade relations had been broken for more than two decades, and U.S. citizens were forbidden by law to enjoy his pleasure island.

Chapter 13

Act 3

The Phoenix Rises

Cuban tourism ascended for a third cycle in the 1980s, thirty years after the second (1950s) and sixty years after the first (1920s). The current revival has endured longer than either of the others, even without casino gambling, and tourism is viewed—yet again—as the island's economic salvation. Because of its perceived centrality to Cuban well-being and its geographic reach throughout the island, the industry undoubtedly will have a more profound and lasting impact on the society this time than in previous incarnations. The government directs a large proportion of resources toward the tourist sector, trains a considerable cadre of citizens to be tourist employees, and promotes cultural programs of tourist value. The behind-the-scenes action—that is, a socialist leadership under ideological pressures in a changing world—is arguably even more dramatic than in the 1920s or 1950s.

THE LOGIC OF A TOURIST RESURGENCE

205

Act 3:
The
Phoenix
Rises

For more than a decade after the break with the United States, Cuba concentrated on sugar production while other Caribbean islands and neighboring Mexico welcomed vacation travelers. A new generation of working adults, with disposable income and paid holidays, fed a robust resort industry. The region drew five million international tourists in 1972, many of whom might have gone to Cuba had the United States not imposed a travel ban along with its economic embargo. That year Cuba played host to about three thousand sun seekers, mostly from the Soviet Union.

Shortly thereafter, Cuba's economic planners recognized that the worldwide tourist industry had begun to outpace even manufacturing in annual growth rates, and the Castro government reentered the competition for tourists and hard currency. A decade later, in 1982, the island attracted two hundred thousand visitors, a significant increase but far behind neighbors who collectively reached the seven million mark. Two-thirds of Caribbean tourists came from the United States, Cuba's traditional market.

Although Castro disapproves of gambling, he wagered Cuba's future on tourism's success. Since the 1980s the government has dedicated considerable financial and human resources, as well as political capital, to the industry. As his government diverted concrete from housing to hotels, Castro exhorted the people to patience and reminded them, "We are not . . . an oil-producing country. . . . the sea, the climate, the sun, the moon, the palm trees . . . are the natural wealth of our country, and we have to take advantage of them."[1]

Careful cultivation has produced growth. More than half a million visitors arrived annually by the early 1990s, and an ambitious goal was set for two and a half million entries by the year 2000. An end to U.S. travel restrictions might add another million. At its first travel trade show in 1982, the government signed twenty contracts with European and American (other than U.S.) travel agents. At Havana's fifteenth tourism convention, in 1995, more than one thousand delegates attended. European, Canadian, Central and South American, Caribbean, and Japanese tour, airline, and hotel company representatives arrived ready to negotiate agreements. The event also drew some two hundred journalists, an indication of interest in Castro's gamble.

If the tourism effort seemed worthwhile in 1982, it became impera-
tive seven years later, with the breakup of the Soviet Union. In his
annual 26 July speech in 1989, Castro warned the Cubans that they
could anticipate a decline in Soviet economic aid, and he asserted that
tourism would be the country's leading source of foreign exchange
within a few years. That projection proved less farfetched than similar
claims made by leaders in the 1920s and 1950s, but it acknowledged
a grim reality. Cuba's Soviet partners had exchanged their goods for
sugar priced above world market levels, a gesture of socialist solidarity.
When the break came, the end of favorable trade terms left Cuba desperate for hard currency. Then sugar production plummeted, from
8.4 million tons in 1990 to 4.2 million in 1992–93, and even lower in
1994–95. Tourist revenues and tourist jobs became critical.[2]

Tourism's 1994 earnings of $850 million did indeed surpass disap-
pointing sugar revenues of $720 million, and 30 percent of tourist
dollars bought imported food for a hungry population. At that, the
number of visitors fell behind projections because of negative publicity. The August 1995 exodus of rafters fleeing economic hardship
and political pressures probably cost Cuba between $80 million and
$120 million. As in the past, resort tourism's fortunes depend on posi-
tive images and expectations of relaxation and good times.[3]

REWARDS AND RISKS

Ironically, in 1982 Castro confronted the same specter that had
haunted Batista's tourism dreams in 1952: insufficient capital resources
to build or refurbish the hotels needed to accommodate the desired
number of visitors. Not only was construction money a problem in
the 1980s, but Cubans no longer knew how to build or run the kind
of tourist-pleasing hotels and resorts that attracted vacationers to their
Caribbean competition. Batista had been forced by lack of domestic
capital investment and expertise to appeal to foreign interests; Castro
did the same. In 1987 Cubanacán, SA, began to arrange joint ventures
with foreign companies.

Reality and the capitalist nose entered the pragmatic socialists' tent.
By 1994 foreign investment in Cuba's hotels, beach resorts, and other
attractions reached about five hundred million dollars. Since profit

motivated investors, Cuba made adjustments and permitted foreign partners to control the labor force and to repatriate their half of the gain. "Cuba's tourism potential is obvious," explained Abraham Maciques, Cubanacán's president, but the "pearl of the Caribbean" requires help to fulfill its promise. Cubanacán handles its own marketing, publicity, supplies, and sales, is expected to turn a profit, and does.

More surprising than Cubanacán's profits, perhaps, has been the involvement of Cuba's military in tourism. Gaviota, SA, responsible to the Armed Forces Ministry (MINFAR) since 1988, operates hotels, resorts, marinas, weight reduction camps, and game preserves. Its workers are members of the armed forces, and its profits upgrade tourist facilities, not weaponry.[4]

Many hotels with familiar names from earlier tourist eras—Nacional, Hilton (Havana Libre), Riviera, Caprí, Sevilla (Biltmore), Inglaterra, Plaza, Presidente, Comodoro, Varadero Internacional—have been brought up to acceptable standards. Spanish companies are pouring hundreds of millions of dollars into Cuba, and the French Accor group plans to build and manage several hotels. A Spanish hotel firm spent forty million dollars on renovations to the reopened Havana Libre–Guitart. The five-star, twenty-two-story Hotel Melia Cohiba occupies a seaside space adjacent to the Havana Riviera. Lavish jointly owned and foreign-operated resort facilities enliven Varadero Beach and tourist enclaves located on small, exclusive offshore keys. The Melia Las Américas, next to the old DuPont estate in Varadero, will have an eighteen-hole golf course. Jamaica's SuperClub built a luxury resort at Varadero also, and Club Med will enter the competition in the late 1990s. Canadian companies are prepared to build resort facilities and already manage seven government-owned properties. Meanwhile, willing U.S. firms remain sidelined.[5]

Havana is not yet the bright jewel that awed visitors in the 1920s and 1950s, but the stone is being polished. For example, the Tropicana features long-legged showgirls in skimpy costumes with elaborate headdresses. The music pulsates, and rum and cola fill the glasses. But the style is dated, and at times, the show has the feel of a nostalgic museum piece or a time warp. On the other hand, on Camagüey province's northern coast, far east of Havana, the Santa Lucía resort boasts sand, sea, and sunshine—and three- and four-star hotels, tennis courts, swimming pools, open-air theater, and snorkeling and scuba facilities. "Santa Lucía is a temptation," croons the inviting brochure, a place for "happiness and pleasure." It sounds familiar. Tiny Cayo Largo ("isolated, unspoiled, yours") permits topless bathing.

Plans for eleven major tourist enclaves include ecological preserves, beach resorts, yacht harbors, and several golf courses. *Sol y Son*, the colorful magazine given to Cubana Airlines passengers, and *Sol de Cuba*, a tourist industry publication, recommend backpacking in the Sierra Maestra, visits to a variety of unique museums and historic cities, and health cures. Tourists can combine treatment for skin problems and hair loss, or ophthalmic and plastic surgery, with recuperative relaxation on the beach.

The current tourist bureaucracy exploits Cuban culture for profit, as did its predecessors. After two decades in which the government downplayed ethnic distinctions for ideological reasons, it once again emphasizes Cuba's African and Indian heritage and, like other tourist destinations, capitalizes on folklore—authentic or manufactured—as entertainment. Afro-Cuban shows and the shadowy, mysterious religious rituals of African-based *santería* amuse the tourists. A beach resort outside Havana offers "direct contact" with rituals and magic during its Noche Afrocubana. A typical itinerary for visitors includes a rumba show performed by a national folkloric group and visits to the Havana suburb of Guanabacoa to see a folk history museum devoted to Afro-Cuban religion and to the village of Taina to see a replica of a Cuban aboriginal community. Galleries featuring the work of local artists and sellers of antique and rare books proliferate along with street fairs that showcase domestic arts and crafts.

Ernest Hemingway met Fidel Castro for the first and only time at the tenth annual Hemingway fishing tournament in 1960. Now Hemingway's and Cuba's years-long mutual affection anchors part of Castro's tourist effort. The author's house in San Francisco de Paula is on the circuit. Visitors walk around the outside of the house under the watchful eyes of museum guards and view Hemingway memorabilia through open windows. The Hemingway Marina is a departure point for deep-sea fishing, playing on the association with *The Old Man and the Sea* and memories of the yearly competitions. Hangouts in Havana, such as the Bodeguita del Medio and restored Floridita restaurants, are always noted as places where the author drank rum-laced *mojitos* and *daiquirís*. Travel writers frequently mention the Ambos Mundos hotel in downtown Havana, where Hemingway wrote *For*

Whom the Bell Tolls. They like to stay in his room, which the government has preserved, and commune with his ghost.

Revolutionary Cuba also exploits the appeal of event tourism and sports spectaculars. For example, the government announced the 1991 Pan American games, to be held in Havana, with great fanfare. Participation in the games by athletes from the United States ensured media attention in that desirable market. North Americans saw Cuba on television, and Castro no doubt hoped that they would pressure their leaders to let them see the real thing.

Not by accident, either, a sophisticated promotional campaign timed a thirty-page spread in the August 1991 *National Geographic* to coincide with the games. For more than a century, the magazine has made its readers feel at home in foreign countries and has invited them to travel. The underlying message always has been that the natives are friendly. An estimated thirty-seven million people worldwide see each issue, and the National Geographic Society has recently gone into the package-tour business. The *Geographic* piece begins familiarly enough: "Midnight in Santiago de Cuba, carnival is in the air. Trumpeters, drummers, costumed revelers by the score." Below a photo of a young woman dressed in white, her hands flung above her head, the caption reads, "Slow, fast, and then faster, sacred *bata* drum rhythms seize a dancer in Santiago de Cuba seeking communion with the Afro-Cuban divinity Babalú Aye." Uncannily similar descriptions tempted tourists in the 1920s and 1950s. Cuba also reaffirmed the tourist appeal of beautiful women when a 1991 *Playboy* article featured voluptuous, seminude Cuban women.[6] Some readers no doubt wondered whether the more things changed in Cuba, the more some habits stayed the same.

Tourism industry employment has become both reward and risk during Cuba's "special period" of economic travail. Drastic retrenchment in other state-supported industries has decreased the total number of available positions, while tourism produces jobs. Moreover, access to dollars (as tips) imparts additional value to these jobs. Potential employees undergo rigorous screening, and they can be dismissed without recourse for any shortcomings in performance. The industry's continued expansion offers hope of future opportunities to currently unemployed workers and to those who expect to enter the work force in the near future.

On the other hand, the influx of foreigners whose own standard of living and convertible currency permit them to travel abroad and enjoy Cuba's hotels and beaches, transportation, and food takes its toll on the morale of Cubans who experience scarcity and hardships. Many taxis are reserved for tourists, while Cubans rely on bicycles and overcrowded, infrequent buses. Electricity runs hotel elevators when factory machinery is idled. Whispers about favoritism sometimes turn into shouts. Cubans have complained of a "tourist apartheid," because tourist police have turned them away from hotel lobbies and beach resorts where foreign guests enter freely. Hard-pressed Cubans understandably envy well-fed visitors and also might like to share the scarce soap and toilet paper that hotels furnish to guests.

Complaints are endless and justified. Even Castro loyalists who accept tourism as necessary for Cuba's survival bristle at the inequities. Party members with years of service devoted to social ideals may enjoy positions of power or nonmaterial satisfactions, but many peso-earning professionals cannot afford items purchased by taxi drivers and waiters who are tipped in dollars.

HISTORY LESSONS

A tourist industry necessarily changes work patterns, relationships, and expectations. It also often brings unintended consequences. When Machado and Batista encouraged tourism and involved foreigners in the development process, antigovernment forces connected tourism to political and social corruption and used the connection as a weapon. For a more apropos example, consider the former Soviet Union. A decade before *glasnost* and *perestroika*, Turner and Ash concluded in *The Golden Hordes*, in a chapter titled "The Marketing of Moscow," that tourism would be a major destabilizing force in Eastern Europe. Prefiguring Cuba's dilemma, the need for hard currency had pushed communist states toward tourism after a Soviet study had calculated the profits from tourism in equivalencies of traditional exports such as coal, oil, and grain. Westerners had hardly begun to visit the Soviet Union in large numbers on package tours, however, when the strains began to show. They wanted to venture beyond Intourist's tightly controlled venues, and their presence threatened to arouse dangerous expectations among the Soviet peoples.[7]

Recent Cuban debates over tourism policy have disclosed intriguingly similar evidence of tourism-induced threats and adjustments. Tourists needed to change their money for pesos. Cuban citizens were willing to defy the law. Currency black markets became common-place and forced Castro to end restrictions on the possession of U.S. dollars. The government also extended the availability of consumer goods to more people and permitted a measure of self-employment. For example, government-authorized, privately owned household res-taurants now serve both visitors and residents. Most new entrepreneurs expect payment in dollars; some will accommodate their peso-earning compatriots.

The potential for individualism evident in self-employment has be-come an issue of great concern for the Communist Party. In March 1996 the Central Committee examined the impact of the new policies on revolutionary ideology in a closed-door session, then expressed its apprehensions publicly and warned against profiteering and corrup-tion. The committee criticized the "humiliating" reality of prostitution and the changed values brought about by access to dollars, specifically citing the case of Cubans leaving important jobs to take up less skilled work in the tourist industry.[8]

Another galling fact of life is increased prostitution, mostly ama-teurs who trade sexual favors for a restaurant meal, an evening in a nightclub, a shopping spree, or a weekend at a beach resort. Although foreign men arrive every day to be with Cuban women, the practice has little in common with Cuba's prerevolutionary institutionalized sex shows and brothels. Nor does the market begin to compare in scope or intent with the chartered flights of men who buy their tick-ets for "sex without guilt" in Asia and Africa. Nevertheless, purchased sex is troublesome for a government that has spent decades inculcat-ing the values of nonexploitation of fellow humans and gender parity. After the government legalized the possession of dollars, prostitution acquired a structure, that is, networks among those selling sex and pro-curers (taxi drivers, bartenders). In June 1996 the authorities moved to clean up the scandalous situation in Varadero Beach and Havana.

Clearly, Castro confronts a conflict. His country needs hard cur-rency. Tourism is flourishing and is more profitable than sugar. Travelers from capitalist countries do generate expectations among Cubans, but the government cannot risk the internal upheavals that unavoidably diminish the number of visitors. It must be flexible to avoid negative publicity and disaffection but strict to sustain socialist ideals.

In the meantime, Cuba moves ahead with plans for cruise ship terminals and airport expansion, restaurants and entertainment facilities.

The phoenix may not reach spectacular heights until the United States ends its travel restrictions. U.S. policy, in fact, affords Cuba time to control the evolution and impact of mass tourism and to learn from the experience of its Caribbean neighbors, as well as its own. If and when the ban against spending money in Cuba is reversed, the revolution itself most likely will attract curious visitors from the United States who grew up with anticommunism, a repeat of the opening of China in the 1970s. Enforced isolation has enhanced the island's mystique. Many U.S. tourists no doubt also would like to see the places where Americans fought during Cuba's independence war, or where they or their parents romped (or lived) in the 1950s. Or they might be motivated by the opening scene of the film *Godfather II* to want to explore Meyer Lansky's gambling empire. If a gangster tour attracts customers, will Cuba's socialist promoters, like their capitalist predecessors, package it to tempt a new generation of curious pleasure seekers? Given the nature of tourism, they probably will not pass up a unique opportunity.

Introduction

1. Cockburn, *Corruptions of Empire*, 96.

2. *Los Angeles Times*, 24 August 1993.

3. *Los Angeles Times*, 22 August 1993.

4. Morrison, "The Second Life of Jim Thorpe," n.p.; *Los Angeles Times*, 13 January 1991.

5. *New York Times*, 31 October 1991, 27 November 1993.

6. See Leed, *The Mind of the Traveler*.

7. Swinglehurst, *Cook's Tours*, 7–12, 34–35; Urry, *The Tourist Gaze*, 141.

8. Boorstin, *The Image*, 79; Sutton, *Travelers*, 134.

9. Mark Twain, *The Innocents Abroad, or The New Pilgrim's Progress* (Hartford CT: American, 1888), 15.

10. Dulles, *America Learns to Play*, 85–86; Harris, *Cultural Excursions*, 174; Ewen and Ewen, *Channels of Desire*, 81–86.

11. Harris, *Excursions*, 175–83; Norris, *Advertising*, 82.

12. Verrill, *Cuba, Past and Present*, unpaginated introduction and p. 11.

1. Act 1: The Road to Cuba

1. *Havana Post*, 13 December 1925; *Cuba Review*, August 1926, 18, and May 1927, 18–19.

2. *Havana Post*, 14 December 1925; *La lucha* (Havana), 12 December 1925.

3. Carpenter, *Lands of the Caribbean*, 183, 189; *Havana Post*, 26 October 1925.

4. *Havana Post*, 23 October and 31 October 1925.

5. *Diario de la Marina* article, "Impressions," reprinted in *Havana Post*, 29 December 1926; *La lucha*, 31 December 1925; Pan American Union, *Bulletin*, May 1924, 506, August 1924, 824, December 1924, 1254.

6. Fox and Lears, *The Culture of Consumption*, xiii–xv, 3–10; Lears, *No Place of Grace*, xiii, 47–53.

7. Galbraith, *The Age of Uncertainty*, 67–70; *Condé Nast Traveler*, May 1995, 138.

8. Derr, *Some Kind of Paradise*, 37–54; Edward N. Akin, "Castles in the Sand: The Hotels of Henry Flagler," *Florida History Newsletter* 7 (August 1981), 1–6; *Cuba Bulletin*, March 1904, 7.

9. Horowitz, *The Morality of Spending*, 31.

10. Dulles, *America Learns to Play*, 98, 101, 117–18.

11. Kasson, *Amusing the Millions*, 3–5, 34–36.

12. Erenberg, *Steppin' Out*, 67.

13. Albert McLean Jr., *American Vaudeville as Ritual*, quoted in May, *Screening Out the Past*, 33.

14. Galbraith, *Age of Uncertainty*, 70; Turner and Ash, *The Golden Hordes*, 60–61.

15. Feifer, *Tourism in History*, Woon, *From Deauville to Monte Carlo*, foreword.

16. Erenberg, *Steppin' Out*, 75–85, 140–51.

17. Sutton, *Travelers*, 133.

18. *New York Times*, 6 January 1921. Stead, *Film and the Working Class*, and Sklar, *Movie-Made America*, trace patronage from storefronts to movie palaces.

19. Ewen and Ewen, *Channels of Desire*, 81, 86–87, 95–100; May, *Screening*, 207.

20. May, *Screening*, 205–11.

2. Public Works, Politics, Property

1. *Havana Post*, 31 December 1926.

2. Enoch H. Crowder, to Chief, Latin American Division, Department of State, 20 April 1925, Enoch H. Crowder papers, folder 408.

3. Norton, *Norton's Complete Hand-Book of Havana and Cuba*, 82–83.

4. Clark, *Cuba and the Fight for Freedom*, 92–93.

5. Dirección general del censo, *Census*, 1919, 209.

6. Beals, *The Crime of Cuba*, 364–65; Strode, *The Pageant of Cuba*, 277, 302.

7. Beals, *Crime*, 364–67; Pérez, *Intervention, Revolution, and Politics in Cuba, 1913–21*, 5.

8. Norton, *Hand-Book*, 162.

9. *Cuba Review*, January 1904, 8, February 1904, 12, January 1907, 11.

10. *Cuba Review*, December 1908, 21.

11. Photograph Number 624A/219-17, Photograph Collection, Archivo General de la Nación, Havana (hereafter cited as AGN).

12. Photograph Number 620C/212-28, AGN.

13. Norton, *Hand-Book*, 35.

14. *Cuba Review*, April 1928, 14.

15. Inclan Lavastida, *Historia de Marianao*, 128–30.

16. John Jackson to Secretary of State, 16 June 1910, 837.40671, General Records of the Department of State, Record Group 59, National Archives, Washington, DC (Hereafter cited as RG 59, DS/NA).

17. Willard F. Mallalieu to President Taft, 20 June 1910, 837.406; William Mallaliese to Secretary of State, 20 June 1910, 837.40671, RG 59, DS/NA.

18. Telegram, Department of State to American Legation, Havana, 4 November 1910, 837.40671/7; Jackson to Secretary of State, 12 November 1910, 837.406/20, RG 59, DS/NA.

19. Copy of bill submitted to Cuban Congress, enclosure with Jackson to Secretary of State, 8 August 1911, 837.406/20; Jackson to Secretary of State,

13 January 1911, 837.406/16; note, Department of State Bureau of Latin American Affairs, 6 June 1911, 837.406/19, RG 59, DS/NA.

20. *Cleveland Press*, 27 January 1911, included in Memo, Department, Bureau of Latin American Affairs, 6 June 1911, 837.406/19, RG 59, DS/NA.

21. J. E. Barlow, *La Gran Vía de la Habana*. Baron Georges-Eugène Haussmann directed the nineteenth-century beautification of Paris during the reign of Napoleon III.

22. *New York Times*, 28 August and 3 September 1929, 11 February 1930; Senate Subcommittee of the Committee on Foreign Relations, *Property in the Island of Cuba Owned by Certain American Citizens*, 70th Cong., 1st sess., hearings, 7, 10, and 14 May, 1928 (Washington DC: GPO, 1928).

23. House Committee on Foreign Affairs, *Claim of Charles J. Harrah against the Government of Cuba*, 71st Cong., 2nd sess., hearings, March 26, 1930 (Washington DC: GPO, 1930).

24. Compiled from advertisements in the *Havana Post*, January–February 1917.

25. "Informe de la compañía 'Sindicato Territorial de la Habana, SA,' referente a una controversia sobre los derechos que amparon la operación de los propiedades del hipódromo 'Oriental Park,' el Casino Nacional, y el balneario 'La Concha'," undated (c. October 1947), legajo 38, número 12, Fondo Secretaria de la Presidencia, Archivo General de la Nación (Hereafter cited as Secretaria, AGN).

26. Cámara de Representantes, *Diario de Sesiones, 1919–21* (Havana: Congreso, 1919) 31, 6 August 1919, 55–62; for Tijuana's tourist attractions, see Thomas, *The Wanderer in Tijuana, Baja California, Mexico*.

27. *Havana Post*, 31 December 1926; Walter F. Smith to Carl F. G. Meyer, 20 February 1926, E. H. Crowder papers, folder 461; *New York Times*, 31 December 1926.

28. "Expediente sobre el Fomento del Turismo, 8 August 1919–11 May 1934," legajo 72, número 70, Secretaria, AGN; Boaz W. Long to Secretary of State, 30 November 1920, 837.40622/2, RG 59, DS/NA.

29. Chapman, *A History of the Cuban Republic*, 391–92; "Cubans Going into Breeding," *Thoroughbred Record*, January 1920, 5; "Winning Owners at Havana," *Thoroughbred Record*, April 1920, 260.

30. Strode, *Pageant*, 245; Leander J. deBekker, "Cuba and Her President," *Nation*, 21 February 1920, 230–33, cited in Chapman, *History*, 397; *New York Times*, 22 February 1920.

31. *Guía comercial de la isla de Cuba*, 516; Department of Overseas Trade, *Report on the Economic Conditions of Cuba*, 8; Frank L. Coombs, Trade Commissioner, Havana, "Questionnaire Number 110," 7 June 1924, .022 Construction Work, 1919–25, Records of the Department of Commerce, Record Group 151, U.S. National Archives (Hereafter cited as RG 151, DC/NA).

32. Dirección del Censo, *Census 1919*, 186.

33. Coombs, "Questionnaire," 7 June 1924, RG 151, DC/NA.

3. Tempests and Tourists

1. Derr, *Some Kind of Paradise*, 176–78.

2. Colsky, *History of the Miami Biltmore Hotel and Country Club*, 6.

3. Jahoda, *Florida*, 126.

4. Woon, *When It's Cocktail Time in Cuba*, 75–80; *New York Times*, 28 October 1931.

5. *New York Times*, 30 October 1919.

6. Woon, *When It's Cocktail Time*, 76–77.

7. *Cuba Review*, March 1924, 15; *La lucha*, 12 December 1925; Comisión Nacional para el Fomento del Turismo, *Memoria Anual*, 1928–29, 11–12.

8. *New York Times*, 10 December 1928; *Cuba Review*, March 1907, 12; Beals, *Crime*, 208–9.

9. Woon, *When It's Cocktail Time*, 167–70; Terry, *Terry's Guide to Cuba*, unnumbered advertising section.

10. Comité del Cincuentenario de la Independencia, 1902–1952, *Libro de Cuba*, 733; Country Club de la Habana, *Boletín*, November 1922, 5.

11. Country Club Park Investment Company, *Prospectus*, FC Album 312, Biblioteca Nacional José Martí (Havana); Terry, *Guide*, 310–12.

12. Country Club, *Boletín*, 1926, membership list, unnumbered pages; *Havana Post*, 7 August 1927.

13. Country Club, *Boletín*, February 1923, February 1924, February 1927.

14. *Havana Post*, 24 February 1929.

15. H. Thomas, *Cuba*, 569–70; R. F. Smith, *United States and Cuba*, 113.

16. *Diario de la Marina*, 31 October 1925; National City Bank, *Number Eight*, March 1922, 1. *Number Eight* was a monthly publication of New York's National City Bank.

17. H. Thomas, *Cuba*, 581; Jenks, *Our Cuban Colony*, 273.

18. Fitzgibbon, *Cuba and the United States*, 1900–1935, 236–39; Carlos Lazo, "Memorandum: Cuban Public Works Law," *Havana Post*, 20 September 1925, included in Coombs, "Questionnaire," RG 151, DC/NA.

4. Tourism Triumphant

1. New Year's eve accounts compiled from *Havana Post*, 26, 27, 29, 31 December 1926, 2 January 1927; *Cuba Review*, January 1927, 13.

2. *New York Times*, 20, 27 September 1926.

3. *Havana Post*, 7 March 1927.

4. *Havana Post*, 29, 30, 31 January 1927.

5. *La noche*, 1 February 1927, FC Album 319, clippings file, Biblioteca Nacional José Martí (Havana).

6. "Dixie–Cuba Golf Pilgrimage," pamphlet, no author or publisher, Special Collections, University of Miami.

7. *New York Times*, 1 February, 8 August 1927; *Heraldo de Cuba*, 7 August 1927.

8. *Havana Post,* 7 February 1927, 13 January 1928.

9. *Havana Post,* 3 March 1927.

10. *New York Times,* 15 August, 4, 27 November 1927; *Havana Post,* 10 January, 5 February 1928. The Cuban National Syndicate incorporated in Delaware in November 1927 and offered shares to raise $3.75 million to finance the Havana-Biltmore casino and residence construction.

11. Federación de la Prensa Latina de América, ed., *Libro de Cuba,* 90; H. Thomas, *Cuba,* 628.

12. *Havana Post,* 29 April 1927.

13. *Labor,* 12, 25, 26 March 1927.

14. Richter, *Politics of Tourism in Asia,* connects international tourism and the enhanced stature and power of leaders in the Philippines, China, Thailand, and India in the 1960s and 1970s.

15. *Havana Post,* 5 March 1928.

16. *Havana Post,* 1, 2, 3 January 1928.

17. *Havana Post,* 4–20 January 1928.

18. *New York Times,* 22 January 1928.

19. *Havana Post,* 17, 28 January 1928.

20. *Havana Post,* 7, 10 March 1928.

21. *Havana Post,* 8, 10 January, 27 February 1929.

22. Terry, *Guide,* 344–45.

23. *Havana Post,* 3 January, 10 March 1929, 4 July 1926.

24. *Havana Post,* 6 January 1928, 9 January, 26 February 1929.

25. The restaurant Ramón and Rebbe advertised its kosher, Jewish American cuisine in the *Havana Post,* various days during March 1928; Federación, *Libro,* 205–7.

26. *Havana Post,* 25 March 1930.

27. *Havana Post,* 1, 5 March 1928, 2, 3 January, 20 February 1929, 28 March 1930.

28. *Havana Post,* 19 January 1930, 1 March 1929.

29. *Havana Post,* 30 March 1929, 5 January 1930.

30. *Havana Post,* 3 January 1930, 8 March 1927.

31. *Havana Post,* 6 March 1927, 6 March 1928, 15 February 1930.

32. *Havana Post,* 20 March 1929.

5. Manufactured Traditions

1. *Havana Post,* 9, 10 March 1930.

2. Armando R. Maribona, "Cuba como país del turismo," in *Número centenario* (Havana: Diario de la Marina, 1932), 94–95.

3. "Expediente en relación con la causa 1091 de 1926 por el asesinato del asiático Andrés Chiu Lión, 9 abril hasta 13 diciembre de 1926," legajo 25, número 52, Secretaria, AGN.

4. See discussions of cultural commodification in V. L. Smith, ed., *Hosts*

and Guests, 2d ed., and various issues of *Annals of Tourism Research* and *Cultural Survival Quarterly*.

5. *Cannibal Tours*, Direct Cinema, Ltd., Los Angeles, California, reviewed in *New York Times*, 23 August 1989. My colleague Paul Vanderwood contributed personal experiences from his trip to Papua New Guinea.

6. Philip Backmann, "The Maasai: Choice of East African Tourists, Admired and Ridiculed," in Rossel, ed., *Tourism*, 47–63; *New York Times*, 17 May 1996.

7. Annemarie Seiler-Baldinger, "Tourism in the Upper Amazon and Its Effects on the Indigenous Population," in Rossel, *Tourism*, 184–86; Kathleen M. Adams, "Cultural Commoditization in Tana Toraja, Indonesia," *Cultural Survival Quarterly* 14 (1990): 31–34.

8. U.S. Department of Commerce, *The Future of Tourism in the Pacific and Far East*, 95–108, 109–16, 137–46, 147–57.

9. Basil Thompson, "The Paris of the Caribbean," *Travel*, December 1923, 4–9.

10. H. Williams, "The Emerald Isle of Cuba," *Travel*, November 1925, 7–9, 46.

11. Waldo Frank, "Habana of the Cubans," *New Republic*, June 1926, 140.

12. Maribona, *Cooperación al turismo*, a collection of Maribona's 1920s newspaper articles and comments on tourism.

13. Félix Soloni, quoted in Roberts, *Havana*, 220–21; Maribona, *Cooperación*. Translation of cartoon caption is mine.

14. Bruce Bliven, "And Cuba for the Winter," *New Republic*, February 1928, 61–64.

15. Wright, *Cuba*, 79.

16. Wright, *Cuba*, 81; Ewart, *Cuba y las costumbres cubanas*, 27.

17. *Cuba Review*, May 1926, 9.

18. Compiled from various accounts in the *Havana Post*, February 1928, and *Cuba Review*, March 1928.

19. *Havana Post*, 17 March 1930.

20. *Havana Post*, 7, 8 February 1930.

21. *Havana Post*, 1, 4 January, 7 February, 13 March 1930.

22. Every issue of *Havana Post* carried nightclub advertisements during the season, when ships unloaded passengers daily.

23. Bliven, "Winter," 61–62.

24. Terry, *Guide*, 200–201. Aspasia was a Greek courtesan, mistress of Pericles; Aphrodite, the Greek goddess of love and beauty.

25. Rosalie Schwartz, "The Displaced and the Disappointed: Cultural Nationalists and Black Activists in Cuba in the 1920s," (Ph.D. thesis, University of California, San Diego, 1977), 104–24.

6. Culture and Casinos

1. Frederick Todd, Commercial Attaché, memo, 15 January 1931, RG 151, DC/NA; Film number 178.2, Film Collection, U.S. National Archives; Pan American Union, *Bulletin*, 1931, 17–22.

2. *Heraldo de Cuba*, 5 November 1931; *Havana Post*, 26 April 1931.

3. *Philadelphia Record*, 8 December 1929; *Havana Post*, 6 January 1929, 1, 4 January 1930.

4. Fabio Grobart, "The Cuban Working Class Movement from 1925 to 1933," *Science and Society* 39 (September 1975): 79–80, 86–90.

5. *Havana Post*, 15 February 1930, 13, 18, 19, 20 March 1930.

6. *Cuba Review*, May 1929, 17; August 1929, 40.

7. *Cuba Review*, April 1929, 13–14; *Havana Post*, 29 March 1930.

8. *Cuba Review*, January 1931, 13.

9. *New York Times*, 27 April, 27 September, 28, 29 October, 5 November 1931.

10. "Actas manifestando que lucharán hasta que la Playa de Marianao sea propiedad del pueblo sin indemnización a Viriato Gutiérrez, usurpador de la misma," 26 March 1946, legajo 120, número 175, Secretaria, AGN; Inclan Lavastida, *Historia de Marianao*, 195.

11. Frederick Todd to J. P. Seeburg Corporation, 15 July 1931, RG 151, DC/NA.

12. Ellis O. Briggs to Secretary of State, despatch 3866, 22 August 1935, 837.111/97, and Tomás S. Mederos, Banco Comercial de Cuba, to Benjamin Sumner Welles, 23 July 1935, 837.516/294, RG 59, DS/NA; Santamarina, *El turismo*; Maribona, *Turismo en Cuba*, 21.

13. "Expediente sobre . . . turismo," legajo 72, número 70, Secretaria, AGN.

14. Federación, *Libro de Cuba*, 245.

15. Corporación Nacional del Turismo, *Boletín*, July 1935, January, April, May, August 1936.

16. F. Freeman Matthews to Secretary of State, despatch 4906, 837.111/100, 20 December 1935, no. 4926, 837.111/101, 23 December 1935, and no. 4934, 837.111/102, 26 December 1935, RG 59, DS/NA.

17. Charles H. Ducote, report no. 210, 13 October 1936, RG 151, DC/NA.

18. Corporación, *Boletín*, April 1936.

19. Municipio de la Habana, *Las comparsas populares del carnaval habanero*, 7–10, 21–28.

20. "Expediente y recortes de periódicos referentes a la Bosque de la Habana, 10 julio–18 agosto 1937," legajo 4, número 2 and legajo 1, números 33, 38, 62, Secretaria, AGN.

21. Matthews to Secretary of State, despatch no. 6051, 24 April 1936, 837.40622/5, RG 59, DS/NA; "Expediente relativo a la fiscalización del Municipio de Marianao de las utilidades en los juegos de azar obtenidos por el Casino Nacional, 24 diciembre 1937 a 20 diciembre 1938," legajo 85, número 10, Secretaria, AGN.

22. Lacey, *Little Man*, 108–9; Messick, *Lansky*, 67–68.

23. Leaf, *Isles of Rhythm*, 40–43.

24. Maribona, *Turismo*, 223; José Barón to Sumner Welles, 7 January 1939, 837.4063/3; G. W. Elder to Secretary of State, 17 December 1941, 837.40636/1, RG 59, DS/NA.

7. Intermission in Cuba

1. *Week-end in Havana* screenplay, box FX-Prs-964, Collection 101, Twentieth Century–Fox papers, University of California, Los Angeles; film reviews appeared in the *New Yorker*, 15 November 1941, and *Washington Post*, 1 November 1941.

2. *New York Times*, 14, 21 January 1940.

3. Morris, *Nelson Rockefeller*, 134–84, passim. In my investigation of the links between wartime Washington and Hollywood musical features that either were set in Latin America or included musical production numbers with Latin American themes, it is evident that film producers accepted a degree of censorship in developing characterizations of Latinos.

4. Coordinator of Inter-American Affairs, *History of the Office of the Coordinator of Inter-American Affairs*, 67–82.

5. Nelson A. Rockefeller, "Memorandum on Post-War Planning for the Hemisphere," Nelson A. Rockefeller, Personal, series O, Washington DC Files, box 8, folder 36, and "Final Act," Conference of Commissions of Inter-American Development, 9–18 May 1944, box 23, folder 161, Record Group 4, Rockefeller Family Archive, Rockefeller Archive Center.

6. "Girdling the World," *Time*, 25 September 1950, 92–93; "Hotel Chain with Wings," *Business Week*, 28 March 1953, 167–69; "Hilton the Host," *Life*, 28 November 1949, 85.

7. *Fortune*, July 1948, 110; *Business Week*, 22 April 1950, 110–11; Newman, "Joint International Business Ventures in Cuba," 86.

8. *Washington Post*, 1 November 1941; average annual earnings in the United States—in real wages—increased 30 percent between 1940 and 1950.

9. Primera Convención de Turismo de Cuba, *Memoria* (Havana: Corporación Nacional del Turismo, 1942), 3; Segunda Convención de Comités o Asociaciones Locales de Turismo de Cuba, *Memoria* (Havana: Corporación Nacional del Turismo, 1944), 31. In fact, the number of carriers flying Latin American routes expanded from nine in 1945 to sixty in 1958. Fierce competition led to cut-rate fares and increased passenger traffic. See "Cut Rate Boom," *Business Week*, 30 March 1957, 82, and "Dogfight over Latin Air Trade," *Business Week*, 8 November 1958, 130.

10. Julián Alienes Urosa, *Los problemas de la economía de la paz y las soluciones que se apuntan* (Havana: Molina, 1945), 20–38; see also Junta de Economía de Guerra, *Mesa redonda sobre propuestas del gobierno de los Estados Unidos para la expansión del comercio y del empleo*.

11. Spruille Braden to Secretary of State, confidential report, 22 February

1944, no. 6065, 811.593137/23; American Embassy, Havana to Secretary of State, 26 May 1948, 811.503137/5-2648, RG 59, DS/NA.

12. *New York Times,* 29 October 1950; "Readaptación turística," *Cuba econó- mica y financiera,* July 1944; "Plan de Acción Turística Invernal," *Cuba económica y financiera,* October 1946.

13. *New York Times,* 13 April, 6 July, 7 December 1947.

14. U.S. Embassy, Havana, to State Department, 811.503137/5-2648, quoting *Miami Herald, Diario de la Marina,* and *Prensa libre* (Havana), RG 59, DS/NA.

15. *New York Times,* 19 January 1947.

16. Spruille Braden, U.S. Ambassador, to Secretary of State, no. 5682, 13 January 1944, 837.114/237, RG 59, US/NA; Lacey, *Little Man,* 172; Conte Agüero, *Eduardo Chibás,* 490; Messick, *Lansky,* 135.

17. Messick, *Lansky,* 135–37.

18. U.S. Embassy, Havana, to Secretary of State, "Investments in Cuba," no. 452, 23 May 1948, 811.503137/5-2348, RG 59, DS/NA.

19. *New York Times,* 1, 9, 12 December 1948.

20. *New York Times,* 5 December 1948, 9 January, 6 March, 8 May 1949.

21. *New York Times,* 29 October 1950.

8. Blue Water, Green Money

1. "They Were Doin' the Mambo," by Sonny Burke and Don Raye, copyright 1954 by Mayfair Music Corporation; "Mambomania," *Newsweek,* 16 August 1954, 54.

2. "A Working Girl's Debut in Shipboard Society," *New York Times,* 16 December 1951.

3. Eric F. Goldman, "The Eisenhower Equilibrium," in Davis R. B. Ross, Alden T. Vaughan, and John B. Duff, eds., *Recent America: 1933 to the Present* (New York: Crowell, 1971), 183.

4. *Havana Post,* 11 December 1955.

5. "Los arcos de cristal," *El nuevo herald* (Miami), 17 June 1989.

6. Roberts, *Havana,* 224–29.

7. Hamilton Basso, "Havana," *Holiday,* December 1952, 138–40.

8. "Thrifty Havana," *Holiday,* December 1951, 14; Roberts, *Havana,* 221, 249; Leigh White, "Havana," *Saturday Evening Post,* 31 March 1951, 24.

9. A. J. Liebling, "Discovering Havana," *Holiday,* February 1949, 96–97; White, "Havana," 24.

10. White, "Havana," p. 24.

11. *New York Times,* 23 October 1949; Budd Schulberg, "Varadero Beach," *Holiday,* February 1953, 73; "Construction Boom in Varadero," Automobile Club of Cuba, *Bulletin,* June 1958, 35.

12. R. M. Connel, American Embassy, Havana, to Department of State, 11 January 1950, 837.451/1-1150, RG 59, DS/NA.

13. Maribona, *Turismo*, p. 154.
14. *Times of Havana*, 4 March 1957.
15. Basso, "Havana," 138–40.
16. Interviews, Ina Habif, Isaac and Ida Szuchman, Frank and Tony García, Miami, Florida, June 1992.
17. Roberts, *Havana*, 242–43.

9. Shady Business in the Tropical Sun

1. *New York Times*, 4 January 1959.
2. *New York Times*, 5 December 1993, 10 January 1994.
3. Ernest Havemann, "Mobsters Move In on Troubled Havana," *Life*, 10 March 1958, 34.
4. Havemann, "Mobsters," 34–35.
5. Bonachea and San Martín, *Cuban Insurrection*, 31.
6. Pérez, *Cuba*, 284; Szulc, *Fidel*, 136–37, 142, 188–91.
7. Senate Special Committee to Investigate Organized Crime in Interstate Commerce, *The Kefauver Committee Report*, 11, 15. Florida's illegal gambling was one of Senator Estes Kefauver's major focal points.
8. Lacey, *Little Man*, 183–85.
9. Kefauver, *Crime in America*, 11, 15, 24–25, 169; Senate, *Kefauver Report*, 178–83.
10. *New York Times*, 30 July, 6, 25 August 1950; Senate Special Committee to Investigate Organized Crime in Interstate Commerce, *Final Report*, 73, 75; Philip Chapman, "Gambling in Cuba," *American Weekly*, 9 November 1952, 9.
11. *New York Times*, 12 March 1952.
12. American Embassy, Havana, to Department of State, operations memorandum, 19 September 1952, 837.4535/9-1952, RG 59, DS/NA; *Miami Herald*, 25 September 1952; *Havana Herald*, 10 February 1953; Lester Velie, "Suckers in Paradise," *Saturday Evening Post*, March 1953, 33, 181, 183.
13. *New York Times*, 26 October, 14 December 1952, 7, 11 January 1953; *El mundo*, 1, 4 January 1953; P. Chapman, "Gambling," 9.
14. Lacey, *Little Man*, 85–86.
15. Messick, *Lansky*, 197; Lacey, *Little Man*, 247; interviews with Julio Luís, Agustín Menéndez, Otto Mérida, Tony Gálvez, Alberto Ardura, Luís Barranca, and Eddie Millán, Las Vegas, Nevada, December 1991.
16. Velie, "Suckers," 181; Scott McLeod to Senator Charles Tobey, 27 May 1953, 837.455-2753, RG 59, DS/NA.
17. Lacey, *Little Man*, 226–28; Havemann, "Mobsters," 32–36.

10. Batista Stages a Tourist Boom

1. Maribona, *Turismo*, 23, 73, 86; Banco Nacional de Cuba, *La economía cubana en 1955–56*, 17; *Newsweek*, 20 July 1953, 69; Instituto Cubano del Turismo, *Doctrina*, 9–10.

2. C. Y. Thomas, *The Poor and the Powerless*, 144–45.

3. Lacey, *Little Man*, 175.

4. *New York Times*, 10 March 1954.

5. *Havana Post*, 27, 29 January, 18 February 1955.

6. *Havana Post*, 25 February 1955.

7. *Havana Post*, 1, 6 December 1955; Phillips, *Cuba*, 280–81.

8. *New York Times*, 1 January 1953; Phillips, *Cuba*, 271; Eric N. Baklanoff, "International Economic Relations," in Carmelo Mesa-Lago, ed., *Revolutionary Change in Cuba* (Pittsburgh: University of Pittsburgh Press, 1971), 254–58.

9. Carla Kirkeby, letter to author, 15 September 1989; William Zeckendorf, *The Autobiography of William Zeckendorf* (New York: Holt, Rinehart & Winston), 255.

10. *New York Times*, 6 November 1954; Lacey, *Little Man*, 228–30.

11. Cuba counted fifty-two retirement funds in the middle of the 1950s, with revenues of about fifty-three million dollars.

12. *Havana Post*, 5, 9 January 1952.

13. Newman, "Business Ventures," 86.

14. Joaquín Martínez Sáenz to Fulgencio Batista, 31 May 1955, legajo 587, número 16, Fondo Banco Nacional de Cuba, Archivo General de la Nación (Hereafter cited as Banco, AGN); "Expediente referente a solicitud de Préstamo de la Caja de Retiro y Asistencia Social de los Trabajadores Gastronómicos para la construcción del Hotel Habana Hilton, 1955–58," legajo 589, número 16, Banco, AGN; Memo, Acosta, Director, Banco Cubano del Comercio Exterior, to Martínez Sáenz, 24 September 1956, legajo 587, número 16, Banco, AGN.

15. Newman, "Joint Venture," 112–14.

16. Lacey, *Little Man*, 155, 158, 309–10; Messick, *Lansky*, 32, 73, 113, 132; *Havana Post*, 30 November 1955.

17. "Expediente relativo al préstamo solicitado por la Cía. de Hoteles La Riviera de Cuba, S.A., 1956–61," legajo 519, números 7 and 8, Banco, AGN.

18. Banco de Desarrollo Económico y Social (Bandes), *Memoria* (Havana: Bandes, 1955–56/1956–57).

19. "Expediente relativo al . . . Riviera," legajo 519, número 5, Banco, AGN.

20. *Times of Havana*, 4 April 1957; "Expediente relativo al . . . Riviera," legajo 519, número 5, Banco, AGN.

21. "Expediente relativo al . . . Riviera," legajo 519, número 5, Banco, AGN.

22. "Expediente referente a solicitud de financiamiento hecha por la Cía.

Hotelera Shepard, S.A. (Hotel Caprí), 1958–61," legajo 483, número 16, Banco, AGN.

23. Edward J. Bash to Department of State, despatch no. 1084, 25 June 1958, 837.181/6-2558, RG 59, DS/NA; Miller, *Ninety Miles from Home*, 242. Miller interviewed a Cuban exile whose brother-in-law claimed to have made a million dollars arranging the sale of a public park to American gamblers who wanted to build a hotel on it. The brother-in-law fled to the Dominican Republic after the revolution; "Expediente referente al préstamo a Montañas Occidentales, SA, para la construcción de un centro turística en Santa Ana de Soroa, Pinar del Río," legajo 571, número 12, Banco, AGN.

24. *Times of Havana*, 25 November, 2, 10 December 1957; *New York Times*, 6 November 1954.

25. *Times of Havana*, 5, 25 December 1957, 16 January 1958.

26. *Time*, 20 January 1958, 32; *Life*, 10 March 1958, 28–29.

27. *New York Times*, 26 April 1958; *Times of Havana*, 28 April, 2 May 1958.

28. *Times of Havana*, 2 May 1958; "Expediente referente a . . . Hotelera Shepard," legajo 483, número 16, Banco, AGN.

29. "Expediente referente al . . . Santa Ana de Soroa, Pinar del Río," legajo 571, número 12, Banco, AGN.

30. "Proyecto para la construcción del Hotel Miramar, 1958," legajo 492, número 12, Banco, AGN.

11. The Tourist Stage as Rebel Battleground

1. Ryan, *Tourism, Terrorism, and Violence*, 5–6.

2. Ryan, *Tourism*, 1–4.

3. *New York Times*, 8 January 1995.

4. Ryan, *Tourism*, 6; *Los Angeles Times*, 2 January 1994.

5. Ryan, *Tourism*, 10.

6. *New York Times*, 5 December 1948.

7. *New York Times*, 16 March 1952.

8. Interviews with Julio Luís, Agustín Menéndez, Otto Merida, Tony Gálvez, Alberto Ardura, Luís Barranca, and Eddie Millán, Las Vegas, Nevada, December 1991.

9. Harnecker, *Fidel Castro's Political Strategy*, 31, 47.

10. Phillips, *Cuba*, 283–84; Bonachea and San Martín, *Insurrection*, 72–73.

11. *Times of Havana*, 21, 28 February 1957.

12. Phillips, *Cuba*, 303–6; *Times of Havana*, 14 March 1957.

13. Phillips, *Cuba*, 306–7.

14. *Times of Havana*, 28 March 1957, citing *New York Times*.

15. *Times of Havana*, 11 March, 13 May 1957.

16. *Times of Havana*, 8 April, 2, 3 May 1957.

17. *Times of Havana*, 8 April 1957.

18. Phillips, *Cuba*, 312.

19. Phillips, *Cuba*, 316; *Times of Havana*, 25, 29 April 1957.

20. *Times of Havana*, 2 May 1957; Congressman John W. Heselton, First District, Maine, to Secretary of State, 30 September 1957, and State Department to Heselton, 7 October 1957, 837.181/9-3057, RG 59, DS/NA.

21. Phillips, *Cuba*, 335.

22. Lacey, *Little Man*, 234–36; *Times of Havana*, 21 November 1957.

23. *Times of Havana*, 10 December 1957.

24. *Times of Havana*, 20 January, 3 February 1958.

25. Harnecker, *Political Strategy*, 55; Szulc, *Fidel*, 436–37.

26. J. M. Álvarez Acevedo, "Juego, turismo y tahurismo," *Cuba económica y financiera*, October 1956, quoted in Roig de Leuchsenring, *Males y vicios de Cuba republicana*, 249–54.

12. No Peace, No Pleasure, No Tourists

1. Cummings and Volkman, *Goombata*, 42–45.

2. Lacey, *Little Man*, 238–39.

3. *New York Times*, 9 January 1958.

4. *Times of Havana*, 9 January 1958.

5. Lacey, *Little Man*, 244–45.

6. *Time*, 20 January 1958, 32.

7. Ernest Havemann, "Mobsters Move In on Troubled Havana," *Life*, 10 March 1958, 32.

8. *New York Times*, 17 January 1958; *Times of Havana*, 20 January 1958.

9. Schwartz, *Lawless Liberators*, 248–49.

10. *Times of Havana*, 20, 27, 30 January 1958.

11. *Times of Havana*, 13, 17 February 1958.

12. *New York Times*, 16 February 1958; *Look*, 4 February 1958, 24–29.

13. *New York Times*, 24 February 1958; *Times of Havana*, 24 February 1958; Juan Manuel Fangio and Roberto Carozzo, *Fangio: Cuando el hombre es mas que el mito* (Buenos Aires: Sudamericana/Planeta, 1986), 250–51.

14. Fangio, *Fangio*, 249. Translation is mine.

15. *Times of Havana*, 10 March 1958.

16. *Life*, 10 March 1958, 28–29.

17. *New York Times*, 27 February 1958.

18. *Times of Havana*, 10 March 1958; Jules DuBois, *Fidel Castro*, 215–25.

19. Horace Sutton, "Not So Far from the Crowding Mob," *Saturday Review of Literature*, 19 April 1958, 31ff.

20. *Times of Havana*, 10, 14 April 1958.

21. *Times of Havana*, 2, 8, 15, 22 May 1958; Leonard H. Price, Commercial Attaché, American Embassy, Havana, to Department of State, no. 923, 5 May 1958, 837.181/5-958, and no. 612, 12 December 1958, 837.181/12-1258, RG 59, DS/NA.

22. *New York Times*, 29 December 1958.

23. *New York Times*, 2 January 1959.

24. *New York Times*, 4 January 1959; *Times of Havana*, 4, 8 January 1959.

25. *New York Times*, 4 January 1959; *Times of Havana*, 5, 8, 10 January 1959.

26. *New York Times*, 4 January 1959; *Times of Havana*, 12, 17 January 1959.

27. Szulc, *Fidel*, 477; *New York Times*, 3 January 1959.

28. *Times of Havana*, 12, 17 January 1959.

29. *Times of Havana*, 5, 17 January 1959.

30. "Expediente relativo al . . . Riviera," legajo 519, número 5, Banco, AGN.

31. *Times of Havana*, 28 February, 2 March 1959.

32. E. A. Gilmore Jr., American Embassy, Havana, to Department of State, 25 June 1959, 837.181/6-2559; Leonard H. Price to Department of State, 29 June 1959, 837.181/6-2959, and 12 August 1959, 837.181/8-1259, RG 59, DS/NA.

33. Horace Sutton, "That Week in Havana II," *Saturday Review of Literature*, 13 December 1959.

34. *Times of Havana*, 17–19 October 1959; Convention Files, American Society of Travel Agents Headquarters, Alexandria, Virginia.

35. Travel Agents, Convention Files.

36. *Times of Havana*, 31 December 1959, 4 January 1960.

37. "Expediente relativo al . . . Riviera," legajo 519, números 5, 6, 7, Banco, AGN; Lacey, *Little Man*, 312.

38. Interviews with Ina Habif, Ida and Isaac Szuchman, and Valerie Stallings, 1992; Miller, *Ninety Miles*, passim.

13. Act 3: The Phoenix Rises

1. Comité Estatal de Estadísticas, *Estadísticas de migraciones externas y turismo*, 94–95.

2. *New York Times*, 28 July, 13 August 1989; Henry W. Goethals, "Competing for the Tourist $$," *North-South*, August/September 1993, 31.

3. Miguel Brugueras, Vice Minister of Tourism, *Cuba Update*, February/March 1995, 19.

4. "Tourism: The Front Runner," *Cuba Update*, Summer 1994, 13, 16; "Gaviota: When the Military Turns to Play," *Cuba News*, June 1994, 9.

5. G. V. Dryansky, "Carving up post-Castro Cuba," *Traveler*, July 1995, 44, 46.

6. "Cuba at a Crossroads," *National Geographic*, August 1991, 94–95; "Cuba Libre," *Playboy*, March 1991, 68–78.

7. Turner and Ash, *Golden Hordes*, 224–28.

8. *New York Times*, 31 March 1996; "Dateline Havana," *Cuba Update*, March/April 1996, 19.

SELECTED BIBLIOGRAPHY

Books, Articles, and Papers

Aguilar, Luís E. *Cuba, 1933: Prologue to Revolution*. New York: Norton, 1972.

Alienes Urosa, Julián. *Los problemas de la economía de la paz y las soluciones que se apuntan*. Havana: Molina, 1945.

Banco Nacional de Cuba, *La economía cubana en 1955–56*. Havana: Cenit, 1957.

Barlow, Joseph E. *La Gran Vía de la Habana*. Havana: Joseph E. Barlow, 1923.

Beals, Carleton. *The Crime of Cuba*. Philadelphia: Lippincott, 1933.

Blutstein, Howard I., et al. *Area Handbook for Cuba*. Washington DC: U.S. Government Printing Office, 1971.

Bonachea, Ramón L., and Marta San Martín. *The Cuban Insurrection, 1952–1959*. New Brunswick NJ: Transaction, 1974.

Boorstin, Daniel J. *The Image: A Guide to Pseudo-Events in America*. New York: Atheneum, 1985.

Brightbill, Charles K. *Man and Leisure: A Philosophy of Recreation*. Englewood Cliffs NJ: Prentice-Hall, 1961.

Bronner, Simon J., ed. *Consuming Visions: Accumulation and Display of Goods in America, 1880–1920*. New York: Norton, 1989.

Carpenter, Frank J. *Lands of the Caribbean*. Garden City NY: Doubleday, Page, 1925.

Chapman, Charles E. *A History of the Cuban Republic*. New York: Macmillan, 1927.

Clark, James Hyde. *Cuba and the Fight for Freedom*. Philadelphia: Globe, 1896.

Clark, Sydney A. *Cuban Tapestry*. New York: McBride, 1936.

———. *All the Best in Cuba*. New York: Dodd, Mead, 1956.

Cockburn, Alexander. *Corruptions of Empire: Life Studies and the Reagan Era*. New York: Verso, 1987.

Collazo Pérez, Enrique. *Cuba, banca y crédito, 1950–1958*. Havana: Editorial de Ciencias Sociales, 1989.

Colsky, Andrew E. *The History of the Miami Biltmore Hotel and Country Club*. Miami: n.p., 1987.

Comisión Nacional para el Fomento del Turismo. *Memoria anual, 1928–29*. Havana: n.p., 1929.

Comité del Cincuentenario de la Independencia, 1902–1952. *Libro de Cuba*. Havana: n.p., 1952.

Comité Estatal de Estadísticas, Dirección de Demografía. *Estadísticas de migraciones externas y turismo*. Havana: ORBE, 1982.

Conte Agüero, Luís. *Eduardo Chibás, el Adalid de Cuba.* Miami: La
Moderna Poesía, 1978.

Coordinator of Inter-American Affairs. *History of the Office of the
Coordinator of Inter-American Affairs.* Washington DC: GPO, 1947.

Corporación Nacional del Turismo. *Boletín.* Havana: n.p., 1935.

——. *Memoria.* Havana: n.p., 1944.

Country Club de la Habana. *Boletín.* Havana, n.p., 1922–24.

Country Club Park Investment Company. *Prospectus.* Havana, n.p., c. 1923.

Cummings, John, and Ernest Volkman. *Goombata: The Improbable Rise
and Fall of John Gotti and His Gang.* New York: Avon, 1992.

Department of Overseas Trade, Great Britain. *Report on the Economic
Conditions of Cuba.* London: His Majesty's Stationery Office, 1923.

Derr, Mark. *Some Kind of Paradise.* New York: Morrow, 1989.

Dirección general del censo. *Census, 1919.* Havana: Maza, Arroyo & Caso,
1920.

DuBois, Jules. *Fidel Castro.* New York: Bobbs Merrill, 1959.

Dulles, Foster Rhea. *America Learns to Play: A History of Popular
Recreation, 1607–1940.* New York: Appleton-Century, 1940.

Erenberg, Lewis A. *Steppin' Out: New York Nightlife and the
Transformation of American Culture, 1890–1920.* Westport CT:
Greenwood, 1981.

Ewart, Frank C. *Cuba y las costumbres cubanas.* New York: Ginn, 1919.

Ewen, Stuart, and Elizabeth Ewen. *Channels of Desire: Mass Images and
the Shaping of American Consciousness.* New York: McGraw-Hill,
1982.

Federación de la Prensa Latina de América, ed. *Libro del Cuba.* Havana:
Federación de la Prensa Latina de América, 1930.

Feifer, Maxine. *Tourism in History from Imperial Rome to the Present.* New
York: Stein & Day, 1985.

Fitzgibbon, Russell H. *Cuba and the United States, 1900–1935.* New York:
Russell & Russell, 1964.

Fox, Richard Wightman, and T. J. Jackson Lears, eds. *The Culture of
Consumption: Critical Essays in American History, 1880–1980.* New
York: Pantheon, 1983.

Galbraith, John Kenneth. *The Age of Uncertainty.* Boston: Houghton
Mifflin, 1977.

Gámez, Tana de, and Arthur R. Pastore. *Mexico and Cuba on Your Own.*
New York: Cortina, 1956.

García Álvarez, Alejandro. *La gran burguesía comercial en Cuba,
1899–1920.* Havana: Editorial de Ciencias Sociales, 1990.

Ginger, Ray. *Age of Excess: The United States from 1877 to 1914.* New York:
Macmillan, 1975.

Glasser, Ralph. *Leisure: Penalty or Prize.* New York: Macmillan, 1970.

Graburn, Nelson H. *Ethnic and Tourist Arts.* Berkeley and Los Angeles:
University of California Press, 1976.

Grossack, Martin M. *Understanding Consumer Behavior*. Boston: Christopher, 1964.

Guía comercial de la isla de Cuba. Madrid: Bailly-Bailliere, 1924.

Harnecker, Marta. *Fidel Castro's Political Strategy from Moncada to Victory*. Translated by Margarita Zimmerman. New York: Pathfinder, 1987.

Harris, Neil. *Cultural Excursions*. Chicago: University of Chicago Press, 1990.

Horne, Donald. *The Great Museum*. London: Pluto, 1984.

———. *The Public Culture*. London: Pluto, 1986.

Horowitz, Daniel. *The Morality of Spending: Attitudes toward the Consumer Society in America, 1875–1940*. Baltimore: Johns Hopkins University Press, 1985.

Inclan Lavastida, Fernando. *Historia de Marianao*. Marianao, Cuba: Editorial "El Sol," 1943.

Instituto Cubano del Turismo. *Doctrina, proyecciones y actividades, 20 febrero 1953–20 febrero 1954*. Havana: Instituto Cubano del Turismo, 1954.

Jahoda, Gloria. *Florida: A Bicentennial History*. New York: Norton, 1976.

Jenks, Leland H. *Our Cuban Colony*. New York: Vanguard, 1928.

Jules-Rosette, Bennetta. *The Messages of Tourist Art*. New York: Plenum, 1984.

Junta de Economía de Guerra. *Mesa redonda sobre propuestas del gobierno de los Estados Unidos para la expansión del comercio y del empleo*. Havana: Junta de Economía de Guerra, 1946.

Kaplan, Max. *Leisure in America: A Social Inquiry*. New York: Wiley, 1960.

Kasson, John F. *Amusing the Millions: Coney Island at the Turn of the Century*. New York: Hill & Wang, 1978.

Kefauver, Estes. *Crime in America*. Garden City NY: Doubleday, 1951.

Lacey, Robert. *Little Man: Meyer Lansky and the Gangster Life*. Boston: Little, Brown, 1991.

Leaf, Earl. *Isles of Rhythm*. New York: Barnes, 1948.

Lears, T. J. Jackson. *No Place of Grace: Antimodernism and the Transformation of American Culture, 1880–1920*. New York: Pantheon, 1981.

Leed, Eric J. *The Mind of the Traveler from Gilgamesh to Global Tourism*. New York: Basic, 1991.

Leuchtenberg, William E. *The Perils of Prosperity, 1914–32*. Chicago: University of Chicago Press, 1958.

Lew, Alan A., and Lawrence Yu. *Tourism in China*. Boulder CO: Westview, 1995.

MacCannell, Dean. *The Tourist: A New Theory of the Leisure Class*. New York: Schocken, 1974.

McCracken, Grant. *Culture and Consumption: New Approaches to the Symbolic Character of Consumer Goods and Activities*. Bloomington: Indiana University Press, 1990.

Maribona, Armando R. "Cuba como país del turismo." In *Número Centenario*. Havana: Diario de la Marina, 1932.

———. *Cooperación al turismo*. Marianao, Cuba: Imprente Marianao Alegre, 1931.

———. *Turismo en Cuba*. Havana: Lex, 1959.

Martin, Lawrence, and Sylvia Martin. *The Standard Guide to Mexico and the Caribbean*. New York: Funk & Wagnalls, 1957.

May, Lary. *Screening Out the Past*. New York: Oxford University Press, 1980.

Messick, Hank. *Lansky*. New York: Berkley Medallion, 1971.

Miller, Warren. *Ninety Miles from Home*. New York: Avon, 1961.

Morris, Joe Alex. *Nelson Rockefeller: A Biography*. New York: Harper, 1960.

Morrison, Jim. "The Second Life of Jim Thorpe." *American Way* (onboard magazine of American Airlines), December 1991.

Municipio de la Habana. *Las comparsas populares del carnaval habanero: Cuestión resuelta*. Havana: Municipio de la Habana, 1937.

Newman, Philip C. "Joint International Business Ventures in Cuba." Unpublished research study, Columbia University, 1958.

Norris, James D. *Advertising and the Transformation of American Society, 1865–1920*. New York: Greenwood, 1990.

Norton, Albert J. *Norton's Complete Hand-book of Havana and Cuba*. Chicago: Rand, McNally, 1900.

Pérez, Louis A., Jr. *Cuba between Reform and Revolution*. New York: Oxford University Press, 1988.

———. *Intervention, Revolution, and Politics in Cuba, 1913–21*. Pittsburgh: University of Pittsburgh Press, 1978.

Phillips, Ruby Hart. *Cuba: Island of Paradox*. New York: McDowell, Obolensky, 1960.

Richter, Linda K. *The Politics of Tourism in Asia*. Honolulu: University of Hawaii Press, 1989.

Roberts, W. Adolphe. *Havana: A Portrait of a City*. New York, 1953.

Roemer, William F., Jr. *War of the Godfathers*. New York: Ivy, 1990.

Roig de Leuchsenring, Emilio. *Males y vicios de Cuba republicana: Sus causas y sus remedios*. Havana: Oficina del Historiador de la Habana, 1959.

Rossel, Pierre, ed. *Tourism: Manufacturing the Exotic*. Copenhagen: International Work Group for Indigenous Affairs, 1988.

Ryan, Chris. *Tourism, Terrorism, and Violence*. London: Research Institute for the Study of Conflict and Terrorism, 1991.

Santamarina, Victor. *El turismo: Industria nacional*. Havana: Patronato del Balneario de San Diego de los Baños, 1944.

Schwartz, Rosalie. *Lawless Liberators: Political Banditry and Cuban Independence*. Durham NC: Duke University Press, 1989.

Senate Special Committee to Investigate Organized Crime in Interstate Commerce. *The Kefauver Committee Report*. New York: Didier, 1951.

———. *Final Report*. Washington DC: GPO, 1951.

Sklar, Robert. *Movie-Made America*. New York: Vintage, 1975.

Smith, Robert F. *The United States and Cuba: Business and Diplomacy, 1917–1960*. New York: Bookman, 1960.

Smith, Valene L., ed. *Hosts and Guests: The Anthropology of Tourism*. Philadelphia: University of Pennsylvania Press, 1989.

Stead, Peter. *Film and the Working Class*. London: Routledge, 1989.

Strode, Hudson. *The Pageant of Cuba*. New York: Smith & Haas, 1934.

Sutton, Horace. *Travelers: The American Tourist from Stagecoach to Space Shuttle*. New York: Morrow, 1980.

Swinglehurst, Edmund. *Cook's Tours: The Story of Popular Travel*. Poole, Dorset: Blandford, 1982.

Szulc, Tad. *Fidel: A Critical Portrait*. New York: Morrow, 1986.

Terry, T. Philip. *Terry's Guide to Cuba*. Boston: Houghton, Mifflin, 1926, 1928.

Thomas, Clive Y. *The Poor and the Powerless: Economic Policy and Change in the Caribbean*. New York: Monthly Review, 1988.

Thomas, Edward C. *The Wanderer in Tijuana, Baja California, Mexico*. Los Angeles: Wanderer, 1922.

Thomas, Hugh. *Cuba: The Pursuit of Freedom*. New York: Harper & Row, 1971.

Turner, Louis, and John Ash. *The Golden Hordes: International Tourism and the Pleasure Periphery*. London: Constable, 1975.

Urry, John. *The Tourist Gaze: Leisure and Travel in Contemporary Societies*. London: Sage, 1990.

U.S. Department of Commerce. *The Future of Tourism in the Pacific and Far East*. Washington DC: GPO, 1961.

Verrill, A. Hyatt. *Cuba Past and Present*. New York: Dodd, Mead, 1920.

Woon, Basil. *From Deauville to Monte Carlo*. New York: Liveright, 1929.

———. *When It's Cocktail Time in Cuba*. New York: Liveright, 1928.

Wright, Irene A. *Cuba*. New York: Macmillan, 1910.

Archival Sources

Cuba, Fondo Secretaria de la Presidencia, Archivo General de la Nación, Havana.

Cuba, Fondo Banco Nacional de Cuba, Archivo General de la Nación, Havana.

Enoch H. Crowder papers, University of Missouri, Columbia MO.

Rockefeller Family Archive, Rockefeller Archive Center, New York.

U.S. Department of State, Record Group 59, U.S. National Archives.

U.S. Department of Commerce, Record Group 151, U.S. National Archives.